THE BUSINESS OF MULTIMEDIA

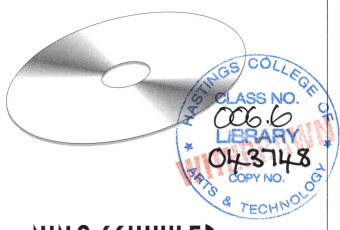

NINA SCHUYLER

ALLWORTH PRESS, NEW YORK

TO PO

Published by Allworth Press, an imprint of Allworth Communications, Inc.
10 East 23rd Street, New York, NY 10010

Cover design by Douglas Design Associates, New York, NY

Book design by Sharp Designs, Holt, MI

ISBN: 1-880559-31-5

Library of Congress Catalog Card Number: 95-76689

TABLE OF CONTENTS

ACKNOWLEDGEMENTS

Many CD-ROM developers, publishers, consultants, financiers, distributors and venture capitalists contributed to the information presented in this book. In particular, I would like to thank the following people who took time out of their busy schedules to help clarify concepts or retell an anecdote about a player in the multimedia industry.

Michael Scott, author of *Multimedia: Law & Practice*, founder of Wildwood Interactive, Inc., and counsel to the San Francisco law firm Steinhart & Falconer; Robert Derber, general counsel at Maxis; Mark Stevens, multimedia lawyer at Fenwich & West in Palo Alto, California; Andrew Nelson, co-founder of CyberFlix in Knoxville, Tennessee; Don Daglow, president of Stormfront Studios; Daniel Kaufman, with DreamWorks Interactive; Caroline Mead, multimedia lawyer with Graham & James; Timothy McNally, chief financial officer for Mechadeus in San Francisco; and Rick Giolito, vice president of business development at Vortex Media Arts in Burbank, California. Thank you, again, for your insights.

INTRODUCTION

This book is the result of over one hundred interviews with the top CD-ROM developers, publishers, distributors, venture capitalists, lawyers, agents, and artists who comprise the multimedia industry. While the general media continues to beat the multimedia hype drum, the real players in the industry are concerned about the day-to-day issues of financing, licensing, and retaining talented employees.

Behind the hype, there is, after all, a business to run.

A developer can no longer survive by attending only to technology issues. Nor can she rely exclusively on her understanding of the software industry. With the convergence, or some say collision, of Silicon Valley and Hollywood, an amalgamation of different business practices, cultures, and principles has formed. While the multimedia industry was once solely dominated by the software industry model, now developers have to tackle the more complicated and financially draining entertainment model of doing business.

New practices, different from both the software and entertainment worlds, have also evolved. A developer needs to know a little about everything to survive. There are distribution agreements to consider, nondisclosure forms to sign, and budgets to create.

The purpose of this book is to give new developers, as well as publishers, writers, artists, computer scientists, content providers, financiers of all types, and lawyers, an understanding of the business of multimedia. Through the stories of those companies in the industry, you will learn: how much it costs to create shrink-wrapped consumer-oriented multimedia titles; the sales channels in which multimedia is selling; and the royalty rate earned on each title sold; the criteria to consider before signing with a publisher or distributor. For the creator of multimedia, armed with this information, the hope is that you will avoid some of the perils of the path from concept to gold master disk.

In this book, Rand and Robyn Miller who created *Myst* talk about what they would have done differently and what rights they had to give up to produce their popular title. The founders of the publishing company CyberFlix reveal which guerrilla marketing techniques helped push their products to the top of the best selling Macintosh titles. Arnowitz Studios explains how the company made the transition from developer to publisher, only to downsize again to developer after the Christmas 1994 season. Rick Giolito at Vortex Media Arts highlights the way he crafts development agreements with publishers so that his company can survive until the multimedia market matures.

The developers and publishers interviewed for this book are impassioned by the new media. If they could, they would only think about story line, plots, and interactive game play and turn the business issues over to someone else. But as with all small businesses, the founders of these multimedia companies do everything from culling through resumes and negotiating licensing agreements to writing code and creating interfaces. Until these companies become financially strong enough, the founders of multimedia companies are spending as much time on business and legal issues as they are on technology problems. And that's the way it should be if these companies want to be around when the next platform arrives, according to Ann Winblad at Hummer Winblad Venture Partners, who explains here how she determines which multimedia companies her fund should invest in.

"So many people think they can launch a full-fledged company without realizing how difficult it can be," says Winblad. "You need to be aware of so much more than development issues. There's the distribution channel issue, for instance, but some people never think that far along and their business suffers for it."

This book will help you understand those difficulties through examples and anecdotes. Through practical advice from those who have gone through the hard times, the hope is you will avoid pitfalls and thrive in this rapidly growing industry.

CHAPTER ONE

THE MARKET FOR MULTIMEDIA

YOU ARE TEX MURPHY, private investigator extraordinaire, zooming through the city in your "speeder," on a mission to find a stolen statue. You travel city roads, searching for clues, interviewing suspects, doing your P.I. job until you see it, the statue, right there. You reach for it and as your hands wrap around the cool form, you are knocked out from behind. You never saw it coming. When you awaken, the statue is gone and the search begins again, leading you to an evil cult that is involved in an Earth "purification" conspiracy. Your goal is to save humanity from global annihilation. Be a hero, destroy the space station, and get out before it blows.

The CD-ROM title *Under a Killing Moon*, a whopping four disk product by Access Software in Salt Lake City, Utah, is a movie-like production designed to satisfy the hyped consumer expectations for multimedia. The product includes 3½ hours of live video, an interactive plot line, and actors—Brian Keith, Margot Kidder, and James Earl Jones.

Technologically, financially, and content-wise, *Under a Killing Moon* is touted by developers as a significant benchmark in the evolution of entertainment multimedia. Chris Jones, the developer, co-writer, director, and lead character of this adventure title, spent $2.5 million and two years in production. That cost figure does not include the CD-ROM product's movie-like marketing budget, which could run as high as the development budget.

As the consumer-oriented multimedia market has matured, it has acquired all the characteristics that lead to hit-driven, big budget titles. Like other capital intensive media businesses, multimedia companies face a limited amount of shelf space—at least until electronic distribution becomes a viable option—and retail prices that are still much greater than the cost of goods sold, thereby creating large gross margins. In addition, variable costs—the expense associated with making an individual CD-ROM unit—are close to zero.

"The economics of a hit title are phenomenally better than a product that sells o.k.," says Dean Frost, senior managing director at Frost Capital Partners in San Francisco, an investment banking firm that specializes in entertainment and education software deals. "The sales channels [retail outlets] have figured this out and only want hits. They can't justify the shelf space for 'B' titles. Like the book publishing industry, however, there will be niches where developers can be small and survive. But what drives the industry are the big hits."

In 1994, the contours of this market first appeared. The Software Publishers Association, a trade association for the personal computer software industry in Washington D.C., reported that U.S. sales of computer software programs on CD-ROM reached $648 million in 1994, triple the previous year's figure. In units, 22.8 million units were sold, an increase of 199 percent from 1993. In the fourth quarter of 1994 alone, the fifty-two companies reporting in the SPA's program had sales of $298 million on 10.2 millon CD-ROMs.

For the first time in the seven quarters the Software Publishers Association has been tracking CD-ROM software sales, "content products"—such as encyclopedias, guide books, and reference works—were not the largest selling category. The top sellers of all CD-ROMs in 1994 included game products at $169 million, reference products with total sales of $156 million, home education products at $107 million, and language/tools products with total sales of $103 million.

The SPA also found that consumers are increasingly purchasing CD-ROM titles rather than using only the products that are already loaded on their computer, called "bundled" software. In 1993, non-bundling channels accounted for 49 percent of units sold and 74 percent of CD-ROM software revenues. For 1994, non-bundling channels grew to account for 61 percent of units and 89 percent of revenues.

While bundling revenue has also increased—by 37 percent compared to 1993—this source of revenue has not increased as rapidly as other sales channels, which grew 296 percent.

Market experts speculate that the CD-ROM market will continue to expand, eventually generating the amount of revenue necessary to fund the ever larger development budgets. By the year 2000, Dataquest, a San Jose market research firm, predicts that the worldwide interactive multimedia market could grow to $10 billion, which would be nearly as big as the current home video market (at $12 billion in 1994) and twice as large as the current motion picture industry.

These figures are attracting companies from all different industries—cable, telephone, book publishing, magazine publishing, utilities—to the

CD-ROM market. As a result, competition has intensified and resulted in market consolidation, with thirty CD-ROM publishers in 1994 accounting for almost 75 percent of all CD-ROMs sold, according to PC Data, a Reston, Virginia based market consulting firm. That number should remain steady in 1995, say market analysts, and eventually even fewer publishers will control the market.

To prepare for this competitive market, developers are becoming much more business savvy. They are doing upfront homework about the industry and their competition. They are designing marketing plans, long before the product hits the retail shelves, negotiating better terms with publishers, and finding creative ways to make money. Each possible revenue source—third party catalogs, bundling deals, direct mail, retail, and on-line—is being carefully studied, and when it makes sense for the particular titles, used by developers.

In this chapter, a macro view of the markets is presented, including the educational and the international markets. A micro view is also provided, based on developers' experiences of how much money a developer can expect to bill, on average, from different revenue sources.

DIFFERENT TYPES OF CONSUMERS

As with any market for a new consumer product, there is a process of consumer acceptance and finally adoption. Technology-based products follow a particular pattern of acceptance-adoption, which seems to apply to multimedia software products. Multimedia developers who track the pattern can determine where the multimedia market is in terms of size and, more importantly, the type of consumer that the developer needs to attract to sell her products.

A market for a technology-based product forms when the first consumers snap up the product. These consumers are the "innovators." The innovators want all the new technological gadgets and do not pay particularly close attention to quality. While other consumers might buy CyberFlix's title *Lunicus* because they want to play the lead character whose mission is to free Earth from alien drones, the innovators purchase the title because the CyberFlix team has created an original authoring system that moves the user quickly through a 3-D environment. The innovators are technologically savvy and are fascinated with technology for technology's sake. The majority are male, under forty, single and make up anywhere from .05 percent to 1 percent. To appeal to this consumer, it would be enough to emphasize the advancement in technology that your product introduces to the market.

Next in the consumer foodchain are the "early adopters" of technology. The early adopters are also among the first to embrace a new technology and, similar to the innovators, are fascinated by the progress of technology—the amazing way a character in a game can walk fluidly down a corridor—than by the product itself. They are influenced by the purchases of the innovators, but tend to wait a longer period of time before buying a product, after the first price decrease. This group makes up about 5 percent of the market.

"I think in all markets, in all cases, in all of history, it always starts out with early adopters," says Trip Hawkins, founder of Electronic Arts in San Mateo and the 3DO Company. "Initially, you have to get the customer who is the most enthusiastic user of the predecessor technology—who understands it best—because you can't go out and spend a zillion dollars trying to beat people over the head. You really have to count on the early adopter to be a part of your initial marketing effort."

The next segment of the market is made up of the "early majority"— about 35 percent of the market. The early majority consumers purchase a technology-based product in part because of the technology. More importantly, they want the product to work without any problems and to be interesting, engaging, or fun. When the average price of computers decreased 50 percent in 1994 from 1991, computers reached a price point that drew these consumers into the market to buy their first IBM/PC or Mac. These are the consumers who in 1994 rushed to the stores before Christmas and purchased two-hundred thousand copies of Walt Disney's CD-ROM *The Lion King* in a six week period and MGM's CD-ROM *Blown Away*, based on the movie (developed by Imagination Pilots and published by IVI Publishing Inc. in Minneapolis). The "early majority" may occasionally read a computer magazine, but only out of curiosity. They are not techno phobes, but neither are they locked into the techno lingo. Prices need to decrease substantially to attract the early majority. The way to appeal to this consumer is to emphasize the uniqueness of your product's content.

The "late majority" consumers follow the early majority. The late majority makes up 40 to 50 percent of the market. They need easy-to-read instruction manuals and software programs that are priced cheaply, comparable to a book or home videotape. Computers, fax machines, and voice mail are viewed suspiciously—as possible contributing factors to the downfall of society. For this group, the multimedia product is one of many entertainment options that include movies, books, or plays. They will not purchase a consumer game because of the brilliant blue background in an otherwise slow-moving shoot-em-up product.

Finally, the "laggers" make up 12–13 percent of the market, and they are the true techno phobes. It is questionable whether members of this group will ever buy a CD-ROM disk, use on-line services, or, for that matter, a computer.

For the first time in 1994, the multimedia industry saw the early majority consumers enter the market. According to a survey completed by the Multimedia/PC Marketing Council in Washington D.C., the typical purchaser of software for the home in 1994 was a thirty-six year old male, and 52 percent of purchasers reported that they knew the title they wanted to buy before purchasing it.

CHOICES OF PLATFORMS

Despite the explosion in PC and Mac computer sales, the multimedia industry as a whole will struggle to reach its potential until the industry does three things. First, the industry must agree upon uniform technical standards. Second, the industry must create and make available to consumers quality products that meet customer expectations, reducing the return rate and converting first-time buyers into repeat customers. Third, it must create products at a relatively low price to attract the mass market consumer.

In many ways, the multimedia industry finds itself at a crossroads, not unlike the video rental industry in the 1980s. It was only when the rental industry settled on VHS, instead of Betamax, that the market exploded.

In the multimedia industry, the new early majority consumers who are not well versed in computer technology are frustrated when they purchase a product that requires a 32 bit microprocessor and find out only after the purchase that they only have a 16 bit computer. Publishers and developers have seen their costs increase dramatically because they have had to hire more customer support staff to answer calls from angry customers. After Walt Disney Company's *The Lion King* CD-ROM hit the market in 1994, the studio was inundated with calls, and the company's support staff leaped from eight to fifty.

Developers are also financially affected another way. Because of the variety of incompatible platforms—from computer-based systems, such as the Multimedia Personal Computer, or MPC, and Apple Macintosh, to television-based systems, such as the 3DO's CD-ROM based Multiplayer, Sony's 32-bit CD-ROM based Playstation, Sega's 32-bit CD-ROM based Saturn, Atari's cartridge driven Jaguar, and Philips CD-i—a developer has to make an initial gamble and choose a potential "winner" from among the many platforms, developing for that medium. That decision is partly governed by the audience the developer is trying to reach: if the developer is creating a shoot-em-up game or twitch game, she is aiming for the 30 million owners of home videogame players whose preferred platform is the cartridge. The gamers, who are used to playing products using a console hooked to the TV, are the most likely to convert to a TV set top, box-based system (as soon as the systems reach a reasonable price point) to play CD-ROM-based shoot-em-ups. Still, the developer faces many unknowns, such as which system, such as Sega Saturn, 3DO, or the Sony Playstation, she should choose.

If the developer bet wrong, she may have to spend money and create different versions of the product, also called "porting," sometimes at $100,000 or more for each new platform if the product has to be completely redesigned and rewritten. Developers are increasingly releasing simultaneous versions of their products, but at a substantial cost.

Companies such as IBM and Apple Computers are trying to ease the technology problem, at least for personal computer-based products. The IBM/Apple joint venture, Kaleida Labs, Inc., a company designed to establish a single communications standard, started selling two products in December 1994. Kaleida's language software, ScriptX, allows multimedia software developers to write one program that runs on both IBM and Apple computers; the Kaleida Media Player, resides as a program in both computers and recognizes the ScriptX language. These products, however, do not solve the problem caused by the variety of other available platforms.

Despite the many different platforms available in the marketplace, most small developers start by creating for the Macintosh—which has roughly 25 to 30 percent of the multimedia market—and convert it or "port" the product to the Multimedia Personal Computer or "MPC."

Part of the reason most small developers have settled on the Macintosh and MPC is because the cost of developing for other platforms is high. The physical cartridge and licensing fee for a proprietary videogame product costs anywhere from $12 to $20. The manufacturing cost of the CD-ROM disk, however, ranges from less than $1 to $1.80, depending on quantity and turn-around time, and neither Apple, IBM, or IBM clones charge licensing platform fees. The cost of storage is extremely low and so is shipping, roughly fifty to sixty cents for first class mail in the United States.

San Francisco-based Substance Interactive decided to create its electronic magazine *substance.digizine*, geared for Generation X readers, initially for the MPC because the founders felt that most other developers were creating for the Macintosh. If they created for the MPC, they might interest MPC-related hardware companies to donate equipment.

"We had originally approached Apple about donations, but they didn't seem interested," says Alex Ragland, one of the founders. "But when we talked to MPC-based hardware companies, we found a lot of companies willing to help us out." Only later did the company introduce its product for the Mac.

On the other hand, Knoxville, Tennessee-based CyberFlix, a publisher whose titles include the twitch games *Lunicus* and *Jump Raven* developed its titles originally for the Mac, in part because the expertise of well-known computer guru Bill Appleton resided with this computer system.

Developers have also turned to the CD-ROM because of its storage capacity, which significantly reduces the cost of goods sold. The CD-ROM, "compact disk read only memory," can hold 600 megabytes of information, enough space to hold a sixty minute MPEG-1 quality video or six hundred five-by-seven inch color photos of famous paintings on one disk, the equivalent of seven hundred floppy discs.

The choice of Mac or MPC seems to be a good one because the number of MPC and Macintosh systems in the home is exploding. In the world of consumer electronics, an installed base of 10 million units is the beginning of a mass market. The video rental industry for the VCR, for instance, did not take off until the installed base of machines reached 10 million.[1] The multimedia industry crossed that threshold for Mac and MPC CD-ROM in 1994.[2]

The nascent mass market means that in the future, developers should be able to generate more revenues. This prediction seems particularly likely because many consumers who are purchasing PCs are doing so for the stated purpose of using the computer to run multimedia titles.[3] In addition, for the first time in December 1994 more computer games were sold on CD-ROM than on floppy disk. "We've been seeing CD-ROMs take the lead over floppies for the past six months," says Ann Stevens of PC Data. "CD-ROMs have been outselling floppies 60 percent to 40 percent."

More established publishers are retooling for the transition. Sanctuary Woods has reduced the number of floppy-based titles and increased the number of its CD-ROM based titles, for both the PC and Mac. Electronic Arts has also increased its CD-ROM-based products: half of the one hundred new titles it plans to release during the 1995 fiscal year will be made for CD-ROM, with CD-based games expected to account for 15 to 20 percent of sales compared to 5 percent in 1994. By 1996, the company predicts that CD-ROM titles will make up nearly half of its sales.[4]

CHOICE OF GENRE

Of the many genres of multimedia titles, a significant part of the CD-ROM sales are originating from reference, business, and text-based works. Despite the hype and media attention, the game and entertainment products account for only 20 percent of all title revenue.[5] But the predictions of a huge multimedia market are primarily based on the latter types of products.[6]

"In the nineties, the sheer volumes of the consumer marketplace mean the biggest events will happen there first," says Paul Saffo, director of emerging information technologies at the Menlo Park-based Institute for the Future.

The consumer CD-ROM entertainment games, (as opposed to "edutainment" or education), particularly the twitch and shoot-em-ups, have tremendous financial upside for a small developer. These genres tap into the existing consumer base for cartridge-based video games, which generated most of the $4 billion in sales of video game systems, games and accessories in 1994. For instance, the intense motorcycle racing and no-holds-bar fighting of *Road Rash* for the Sega Genesis (by Electronic Arts) has been revamped for 3DO and Sega CD-ROM 32-bit Saturn to tap into the new markets.

To create a successful title in the game genre, the developer does not have to spend months or years trying to license preexisting content or a well-known trademark. The CD-ROM titles that have done extremely well—*Myst* with its eerie, mesmerizing pictures, *Doom* and *Doom II* with their action-packed, addictive-playing sequences, *7th Guest*, or *Jump Raven*—were all created by using original material. The added kicker is that these types of products also command the highest retail prices, an important consideration in an environment in which prices are falling.

The home education and edutainment software market also show promise in 1995, partly because 42 percent of American households with children own computers, well above the 37 percent average of all households with computers.[7] Sixty percent of the seven million computers sold in 1994 went to households with children.

Parents, anxious about their children's education, are buying titles like *Word Stuff*, published by Sanctuary Woods, an interactive program that teaches kids new words through animation and *Bill Cosby's Picture Pages: Numbers and Shapes*, published by Take 2 Interactive, in which Cosby leads kids through matching and counting exercises.

A study by the Software Publishers Association supports the growth potential of the edutainment and education market. The study found that third quarter 1994 sales for educational software for the home was $113 million; in 1993, that figure was $66 million. The combined three quarters for 1994 amounted to $281 million, versus $144 million in 1993. Of those numbers, CD-ROM sales accounted for $50.2 million for the first three quarters of 1994, a 270 percent increase over 1993.

"There's never been a better year for kids' software," says Robin Raskin, the editor of *PC* magazine. "Because of [advances in] the technology, the frustrations involved in the early versions are gone."

THE SIZE OF THE CD-ROM MARKET

From 1992 to 1993, only the innovators and early adopters were purchasing CD-ROM products. These groups of consumers were the ones in 1992 who owned the nine-hundred thousand PCs and Macs with CD-ROM players in the U.S. They were sophisticated purchasers of technology, tuned into the computer magazine and culture, and did not need mass marketing to capture their attention to purchase multimedia hardware or software. Plugged in, the innovators and early adopters bought the latest technology because of their fascination with technology itself. The multimedia industry as a whole was more aligned with the software industry than any other.

But in 1994, the market, through exaggerated reports by the media, attracted a new type of customer: the "early majority." Computer manufacturers reported a fourfold increase in sales of computers capable of playing CD-ROMs. At the start of 1995, 13.4 million PCs and Macs were in U.S. homes, with the largest new group of computer owners the "early majority." (Dataquest, a market research firm in San Jose, pegs that number slightly lower, with 10.3 million multimedia PCs shipped in 1994, up from the 2.5 million units shipped in 1993, a 312 percent growth.) This new consumer purchased her computer primarily to use multimedia products, which she includes among her array of entertainment options. For the first time, multimedia companies started to compete with the movie and book publishing industry for consumers' entertainment dollars. The multimedia industry, which before had turned to the software industry for its models of success, now had to look to the entertainment model. Since then, the financial stakes have been raised.

Based on a continued pattern of unprecedented growth in 1995 of the sale of hardware necessary to run multimedia software, the entertainment model for multimedia is now a permanent fixture.

The dramatic growth of the multimedia computer market should continue, especially with the announcements by IBM and Compaq that they will be replacing the 5½ inch floppy disk drives in their computers with CD-ROM drives. Developers should watch these sales numbers closely to track where the multimedia market is in terms of new types of consumers. Knowing who has been added to the target audience will help developers and publishers further refine their marketing plans.

With the explosion in MPC and Mac computer sales, the multimedia software market became more competitive. In 1994, about one thousand new CD-ROM titles were available. At this market size, developers still had a good chance of making it into the retail channel and onto the shelves.

By Christmas 1994, two thousand new titles had been introduced, changing the dynamics of sales and marketing. By the end of 1995, at least another two thousand are expected to be introduced to the marketplace.

With most retailers placing on average only three hundred to four hundred titles on their shelves, developers now have to create products with a clear understanding of the marketplace—the products that sell, the competition, a profile of the customer that includes where that person shops and the price she is willing to pay for multimedia software—and establish a significant marketing budget to gain access to retail shelf space and attract consumers.

One of the common misunderstandings among multimedia developers who come out of the software industry is that the software model still applies to multimedia. Under the software model, a programmer might raise some money from friends and others, create a software application program, and maintain a market by issuing upgrades to the original title.

But the multimedia industry is now following an entertainment paradigm, in which the titles are "hit" driven, similar to books, films, or video games.

With a multimedia entertainment game, for instance, retailers give a new title twelve to sixteen weeks to move. In that window of time, there are two ordering periods in which the retailer can place an order to the distributor and receive the product. After that period, if the product has not sold well, the retailer returns it to the developer.

Similar to the book publishing industry, there are also "evergreen" products, in which titles attract a following and sell year after year. For instance, Orinda, California based Maxis' line of *Sim* titles have sold over six million copies since 1989. Ideally, a developer will have a mix of both hits and evergreens, with the latter titles helping the company to survive during the difficult years.

PRICES ARE DROPPING

Consumer-oriented software prices have been decreasing, as much as 10 to 20 percent a year. In 1992, for instance, the average retail price for a multimedia product was $129. For the first few months in 1995, the suggested retail price, or SRP, was $35 and the sticker price—the amount charged by the retailer, which is typically 15 to 20 percent below the suggested retail price—was around $29–30, according to InfoTech, a research firm in Woodstock, Vermont.

For instance, Packard Bell jumped into the software market in 1995 with eight children's interactive storybooks on CD-ROM at a suggested retail price of $19.95. The products are slower, not as elegant as the products made by its competitor, Living Books, but they cost half as much at retail and have the potential to be impulse items. Even the state-of-the-art *Under a Killing Moon*, which might be expected to retail at $100 or more (and might have a year ago), can be purchased for under $50 at Sam's Club, a computer retail store.

According to market consultants, few software publishers and developers are building this price slide into their business models.

"There's an assumption that the industry will increase the volume and at the same time maintain the current retail price level," says Nick Donatiello, CEO of the San Francisco research firm Odyssey. "History would indicate that this is not the way it works."[8]

Market researchers have found that the price for multimedia products has consistently fallen twice a year: once in February, right after Christmas, and then again in August, right before the industry gears up for holiday sales.

Except for the slick shoot-em-up games, a developer who is creating edutainment titles for the mass market should plan for this continued price decrease in his business plan. She should also figure out the maximum amount of development dollars that she can spend and still break even.

Part of the price drop is because of competition. The number of CD-ROM titles published this year will nearly double to 4,000 over last year's 2,400, according to PC Data. Other industry observers are even more bullish, saying the figure may be as high as 7,000. More than 1,000 children's programs were available last year, and in 1994 alone, developers and publishers introduced roughly 330 programs for young children. So many titles are flooding the market that shelf space has become a rare commodity and it is a buyers market. Large publishers, like the Learning Company in Fremont, California, are pushing retailers to display their entire line of products together. That way, customers will buy multiple titles, says John Stacey, vice president of sales and marketing at the Learning Company. In the face of competitive pressure from industry leaders, smaller publishers and developers are lucky to get any shelf space.

Almost every day, Sanctuary Woods receives a call from a developer who has used his own resources to finance a CD-ROM title and has tried to introduce his product to the retail channel, only to face rejection. The small developer finds out that retailers prefer to review a catalog of many titles, priced to attract the mass market, rather than meet with hundreds of small developers, who have one or two titles that are priced to help the company make it another year.

Another reason for the price decrease is that, as noted earlier, the multimedia industry has chosen the entertainment industry model, rather than the software model, to reach the mass market. To attract this market, prices must drop to compete with books, movies, and videos rather than be priced like word processing software.

---

1. *Folio: the Magazine for Magazine Management,* March 15, 1994.
2. *Wall Street Journal,* Dec. 27, 1994.
3. *Wall Street Journal,* Dec. 27, 1994.
4. Electronic Arts financial report and interview with investor relations.
5. Digital Information Group's CD-ROM *Factbook.*
6. *Fortune,* September 18, 1994.
7. Marvin Zauderer, manager of educational products group at Apple.
8. *Fortune,* October, 1994.

CHAPTER TWO

FROM CONCEPT TO GOLD MASTER DISK

After quitting his job at Paracomp (which merged with Macromind and became Macromedia in San Francisco) and working as an independent contractor for the TV network CNN, Drew Huffman formed his own company, Drew Pictures, to create multimedia products. He had heard about the CD-ROM platform, tested it out, and concluded it was a promising medium. He and three other programmers started brainstorming and slowly developed the script for *Iron Helix*, in which an interstellar warship, armed with a planet-busting bomb, experiences an accident during a war-game simulation that kills the crew, but the ship's computer finds a new target for the bomb: an inhabited world. In the game, you are flying nearby, on the only ship in the area and are the only one who can disable the doomsday machine and save the world.

For thirteen months, beginning in 1992, the four programmers worked nonstop in Huffman's living room to create their first title using $60,000 worth of equipment that Huffman had accumulated while working for CNN. They were driven by the need to make a quality title, with high production value and a compelling interactive design, all of which costs money. The team self-financed the title by doing production service work for other companies ($70,000 worth) and tapping into private investment money. As they approached the final stretch, they made some calls to potential distributors. Spectrum HoloByte made a proposal and in 48 hours, a deal was closed between the two companies.

As is common among many developers, Huffman ignored budgetary constraints and was driven by his passion to make a cool product. "Some companies are trying to make a lot of product," says Huffman. "We've taken the opposite approach, making a few products, but making them as good as we can. It means that some people will make more money than us in the next few years. But if the industry is really going to succeed, if we are going to succeed, it's going to be based on quality products. And that requires talented people."

Three main entities exist in the multimedia industry. The first entity, the developer, is responsible for creating the product and turning over to the publisher a finished product, called a gold master. The second entity, the publisher, assumes most of the risk for the undertaking—financing the in-house or third party production of the multimedia product; the manufacturing, including the stamping of the CD-ROM, the packaging, the reproduction of the CD-ROM; and providing the marketing and sales support. The third entity, the distributor, stores and ships products and sends invoices to retailers. The lines separating the main parties are not ironclad, however: a developer may fund some of his own titles and thus become a publisher in some instances; and a publisher may also provide distribution. The focus in this chapter is primarily upon the costs assumed by the developer.

The cost categories encountered in moving from an idea for a title to a *gold master* disk are fairly well defined, with the specific amount of money dependent upon on how many steps in the production process your company assumes. Cost is also highly dependent upon the type of product you want to produce, with budgets for entertainment titles, as opposed to edutainment products, steadily climbing into the stratosphere.

The largest cost component of preproduction, production, and postproduction of a multimedia title is labor, and the job titles and responsibilities used throughout the industry are a combination of the software business and film and video production. There are producers, who oversee the creative process, writers, programmers, and engineers who convert analog content to digital form.

"The industry has become very specialized," says Steven Rappaport, founder of Digital Trivia, Inc. in San Francisco and developer of the title *Radio Active: The Music Trivia Game Show*, a CD-ROM title that allows users to appear on a computer game show, not unlike the TV program, "Name That Tune." "There's multimedia programmers, artistic designers, 3D artists, and everyone gets about $75 to $100 an hour, except the developer who founded the company who probably isn't paying himself anything."

As the industry becomes more competitive, developers are pressured to offer work environments and compensation packages to attract the most talented people to create the best titles in a particular genre. Potential employees who come from a software background, for instance, are used to stock options and generous benefits to offset lower salaries offered by a start-up company.

"Software developers like us are constantly trying to prove ourselves and that takes talented employees," says Rick Giolito, vice president of business development at Vortex Media Arts in Burbank, California, a developer that creates titles—*Buzz Aldrin's Race into Space* and *Madeline and the Magnificent Puppet Show*—for several publishers, including Time-Warner Interactive, Electronic Arts, EA/ABC Home Software, and Hasbro. Vortex employs and contracts with thirty-five to forty employees and independent contractors, some of whom earn more money than the original founders of the company.

According to Giolito, the pressure of the industry never subsides. As a result, work environments need to consistently attract quality employees. "You are only as good as your last title. It's a hit driven industry," says Giolito. "We are constantly asked by publishers who are considering our company as a producer of titles, 'how many units did your last title sell?' Every time we deliver a title and it does well, the value of our company goes up. If it does poorly, it might be due to marketing or to development. It's difficult to know who's to blame, but we all know that shit rolls down hill."

Because the software technology used to create multimedia products seems to change every eighteen months and new platforms are introduced every three or four years, developers also have to hire employees familiar with the latest technology or train existing employees to use it. If the developer or publisher is creating entertainment products, there is also pressure to incorporate Hollywood-type production, techniques, and corporate structure.

"The disciplines of filmmaking need to be brought over to the game industry," says Scott Walchek, president of San Mateo, California based Sanctuary Woods Multimedia Corporation. Walchek says that developers and publishers need to thoroughly understand the narrative challenges and technology required to create quality products and to accurately predict development budget. "You have to look early at risk, since these are million-dollar budgets we're having to commit to," Walchek says.[1]

The bottom line is: there must be enough upfront planning, financing, and in-house talent to create compelling titles.

"To succeed in this business, the most important thing a developer can do is make a quality product," says Huffman. "That requires a quality work environment because you need to keep people motivated and you have to attract good people. For our first title, a tiny team willed *Iron Helix* into being. I couldn't do it again. After we finished the title, I was exhausted and walked around in a daze for six months. Now we have ten people creating our second title. We pay realistic, competitive salaries, and although no one works a forty hour work week, we know we can't have everyone suffering."

Not only do the creative people want a quality work environment, they want to create more and do more with the latest technology, which increases costs. The market reinforces the desire to create quality products by demanding titles with high production value.

Not far from Huffman are two of his former Paracomp colleagues, Joe and Maura Sparks, who together with Kent Carmical formed in December 1991 the publishing company Pop Rocket. The Pop Rocket lean team of three immediately started work on their title *Total Distortion*, with Joe Sparks as the main designer, Kent Carmical as the musician, and Maura as the video producer. The Sparks worked out of their San Francisco flat and Carmical used his audio studio that was located underneath his apartment.

"We've been working on it [*Total Distortion*] ever since," says Maura Sparks, whose background includes marketing, video production, and writing. After four years of intensive labor, *Total Distortion* was finished in 1995.

In *Total Distortion*, you have inherited a lot of money from an uncle and head for the Distortion Dimensions in search of fresh material to make music videos and hopefully to earn lots of money. To win, you must gain fame, fortune, or both, and to accomplish that, you need to travel to the Halls of Distortion to find and videotape new talent and media treasures.

The total cost of the title exceeded $500,000, which does not include payment of salaries to the original founders.

"We've survived by the help of family, friends, credit cards and advances through our distributors," says Sparks.

In 1993, another employee joined the team to provide marketing. The company has received tremendous publicity, with the marketplace anxiously awaiting Pop Rocket's genre bending title. The prepublicity also attracted the venture capital firm Hummer Winblad Venture Partners in Emeryville, California which invested over one half million dollars in Pop Rocket in May 1994. With this money, the company hired an employee to port the product from Mac to Windows, allowing *Total Distortion* to be simultaneously released on two platforms. It also permitted the original owners to pay themselves for the first time and, after working three years out of their apartments, the team moved into an office space.

OVERALL DEVELOPMENT BUDGET

For a consumer-oriented CD-ROM game title, the average development costs in 1993 ranged from $100,000 to $400,000. In 1994, that range jumped to $250,000 to $750,000. Gistics, a Larkspur, California based market research firm specializing in interactive telemedia, pegged average development costs in 1994 at $383,000. In 1996, a $1 million budget is expected to be a minimum for a hit consumer game title.

A 1994 survey of Bay Area based multimedia companies completed by the San Francisco based Multimedia Developer's Group, a trade organization for the multimedia industry, found slightly lower ranges: $150,000 to $300,000 for consumer CD-ROM titles and $150,000 as the median cost for educational projects (kindergarten through twelve and higher education). The survey also found, however, that more than 10 percent of the developers were involved in consumer titles that cost more than $500,000.

Because the market for edutainment titles, or "nonfiction" type products lags behind the entertainment market in terms of sales, consultants say the developer should plan his development budget carefully so it does not exceed $300,000. Otherwise the company will not reach its break-even point. Developers recommend creating a concept for an edutainment title that lends itself to a series of products: if the first title does well, you can make a more accurate prediction of the company's budget and cash flow for the next titles in the series. It is also easier to attract funding from publishers or private investors because the revenue stream is more certain.

Maxis in Orinda, California, which went public in 1995, successfully followed this philosophy with its *Sim* product line. So has Stormfront Studios in San Rafael, California with its line of *Tony La Russa* baseball products. The edutainment genre most closely follows the book publishing industry model, in which "perennial" books are created that sell year after year with little or no marketing. For edutainment multimedia, the same selling pattern can occur, as long as the product is enhanced or revamped to include the latest updates in technology.

Whether you produce products for the edutainment or entertainment market, developers have a hard time keeping costs down because of the nature of software development.

"It's easy to have products delayed which drives up costs," said Dean Frost, senior managing director at Frost Capital Partners in San Francisco, an investment bank that specializes in entertainment and education software industry. "You fix the amount of time you are going to take to develop a title or the money you need to spend, and that number is obsolete almost as soon as you fix it because software development is not a mature business practice. People know when the product is finished, but they don't know exactly how long it will take."

Though the development budgets for both edutainment and entertainment titles seem three years ahead of a market that can support such costs, one way developers are keeping costs down is by producing for the CD-ROM platform rather than the cartridge: unlike the proprietary cartridge-based platforms, there are no license fees associated with the CD-ROM for the Macintosh or IBM/PC clone, and the physical manufacturing of a CD-ROM itself costs less than $1 compared to a cartridge, which costs $12–

$20. In addition, developers are eliminating overhead by working out of their homes and paying themselves little or nothing at all to stretch their limited dollars.

Minoo Saboori and Matthew London, founders of Eden Interactive, a small San Francisco development company that creates edutainment titles, have been logging in the hours in their live/work space, where they created their first title *Greg LeMond's Bicycle Adventure*, which cost $150,000 in "soft" and "hard" dollars. The figure is an aggregate of the amortization of equipment, the value of the bargains that the two founders were able to strike with vendors, the amount of frequent flier miles used to conduct business, and their time, which went unpaid.

The developers have been as innovative funding their titles as creating them. For Eden Interactive's *Greg LeMond* title, the company hired photographers at a reduced rate because Saboori agreed to include the photographers' names on the screens when their photos appeared.

"We now do that for all our titles," says Saboori. "That allows us to decrease our costs. It's a bargaining tool that has worked."

Eden Interactive used the same creative bargaining skills to acquire the video footage of LeMond's bicycle riding. They agreed to exchange copies of the finished product for the rights to video footage, which were owned by a company that produces the mail order catalog, Famous Cycling Video. For their third title, *American Visions: 20th Century Art from the Roy R. Neuberger Collection*, an interactive CD-ROM tour of 20th century American art, Eden Interactive received funding and photos from a museum in exchange for creating a kiosk for the museum. That arrangement paid for roughly one-half of the $350,000 title. Eden also agreed to pay the museum a royalty based on wholesale price.

Modern Media Ventures, a small San Francisco developer of interactive educational game titles—the *Gus Goes to Cybertown, Gus Goes to Cyberopolis* series—keeps its development budgets around $100,000. They started storyboarding their first title concept in the first quarter of 1993. During the rest of the year, relying on three computers, two of which they already owned, the three founders hired independent contractors to develop the title.

"We hired a couple programmers to write the code," says Bruce Goedde, one of the co-founders. "Our first employee was an illustrator/ animator, who was familiar with working on a computer." Goedde attributes his low development budget to several things.

"We haven't hired expensive people, just good inexpensive people. We don't have big offices so we don't have a lot of overhead, and we got in at a time when a lot of people were wanting to learn about the industry and therefore were willing to be paid less than what they could earn in other industries."

Once the development company starts to grow, however, it needs capital in amounts that are far beyond the barter and "student living" mode. The artists' and producer's goals start to require more time, money, and effort to achieve. The core team grows weary of the hundred hour work week. At this point, and hopefully sooner, a developer has put into place the traditional business techniques and tools, such as financial accounting methods, the management team, and the product development schedule, to make the transition to a functioning company. Only then will the company be able to attract the kind of private investment or the corporate partner who can provide the influx of capital to finance the next spurt of growth.

The crew at Drew Pictures, for instance, is creating its second title, which costs 75 percent more than their first title, or over $700,000.

"Development costs are increasing tremendously," says Huffman. "To a large extent what is driving this increase is that we as a company are more ambitious. Our goal is to leapfrog ourselves and our products with every new product. If you look at our first game, *Iron Helix*, it's pretty simple. We would never do a game like *Iron Helix* again. We want to make the last product we did look bad."

To make *Iron Helix*, one programmer designed it and three others worked on it every minute they could stay awake. For the second title, the size of the staff has exploded: the company has three sophisticated C programmers and ten additional artists, designers, and producers.

"When we first started, I was balancing the checkbook in my head," says Huffman. "We were not businesslike in the beginning, just passionate about the game. We used to have a drawer full of receipts. That was our accounting system. Now we have a director of operations and finance who works with our outside accountants, Cooper & Lybrand. We needed all this to raise $1.3 million in March 1994 from an investment banking firm and venture capitalists. Now, one hour after we get sales reports, we can generate our quarterly numbers. It's great."

INCORPORATION

Most developers incorporate their companies in the first six months of setting up shop. The most compelling reason to incorporate is that it reduces or eliminates personal liability. If your corporation is sued, it is the corporation's assets and not your personal assets that are at risk.

Incorporation also provides a better vehicle for soliciting investors. Investors can be given a share of ownership, while limiting their liability. If your company has employees, incorporation also allows you to fully deduct medical insurance and expenses. Even if you are the only employee, if you incorporate, you can give yourself health insurance, deducting 100 percent of the cost.

It will cost you something to incorporate, both in time and money. General start-up legal fees run around $500-$1,000, state registration fees from $50 to $1,000, and annual fees from $15 to $50. The company must also maintain a corporate record book. Taxes play a significant role in deciding what form of corporate structure to adopt.

1. Sole Proprietorship

If you do not incorporate, you are a sole proprietorship. The advantages of a sole proprietorship are that your tax, legal, and bookkeeping problems are simpler. You can file one income tax return and operate in any state free from regulations imposed on corporations. Business losses can be used to offset personal income.

The sole proprietorship structure, however, exposes you to unlimited liability. You are personally responsible for all its debts, even if they exceed your investment. If you are sued, you will be personally liable for any judgment rendered.

2. Partnership

Though few developers use this form, another alternative to incorporation is a partnership structure. Partnerships do not pay federal or state income taxes, and, instead, profits or losses pass through to the individual partners, who pay the taxes on their personal returns.

In a partnership, two or more people pool resources and operate a joint profit-making business. The Uniform Partnership Act (UPA), which is legally enforceable in all states, has established rules that guide partners' actions and you will need to check with an attorney to make sure you comply.

Under the UPA every partner is an agent of the partnership. If your partner does something illegal, you are liable too. You also may not know about business debts incurred by your partner, but you will be personally responsible for paying them.

Unlike a sole proprietorship, under a partnership agreement, the partners must jointly make decisions. Unless your partnership agreement says otherwise, each partner has an equal vote in management.

3. The C Corporation

Most developers and publishers operate under a "C" corporate structure. The disadvantage to such a structure is that profits are taxed twice. First, you pay corporate taxes on money earned by the company. When dividends are paid, the dividends are taxed at the recipient's personal income tax rate.

Because of the double taxation, accountants advise against a C corporate structure if you know the company will be sold soon.

The reason so many developers choose this structure is that few, if any, developers pay out dividends to their investors and instead, plow profits back into the company. For most business owners, the first $75,000 of profits are taxed at a lower rate than the personal income tax return and so a C corporation makes financial sense. (Corporate tax rates are 15 percent for the first $50,000 in profits; 25 percent for the next $25,000, 34 percent over $75,000, 35 percent over $10 million (and a surcharge of 5 percent between $100,000 and $335,000).

The C structure is even more attractive because of tax changes in 1993 that increased the top tax rate on an "S" corporation's income to 39.6 percent, six points higher than the top tax rate on a C corporation's earnings. Growing companies, desperate for cash, are increasingly turning to the C structure to capture some of this tax savings.

4. The S Corporation

With an S corporation, all gains and losses are treated as an owner's personal income, like a partnership. As a start-up company, that works well if the company is likely to lose money its first couple years in operation. You can reduce your personal taxes by this loss, and at the same time gain the liability protection that comes with incorporation.

If you know the company will be sold soon, an S corporation is a preferred structure. The sale would be taxed once—at the individual tax rate.

The disadvantage of this type of structure is that S corporations cannot have more than thirty-five investors, none of which can be corporate or foreign investors. (This feature, however, may be changed by federal legislation proposed in 1995). In addition, if any shareholder-owner is in the highest federal tax bracket (now 39.6 percent on taxable income over $256,500), the pass-through feature means that some corporate profit will be taxed at that high rate. Even profits never removed from the corporation's coffers will be taxable to the owners.

S corporations are also more limited in fringe benefits than C corporations. An S corporation can deduct the costs of health insurance, medical reimbursements, and group term life insurance for employees, but those owning more than 2 percent of the stock must count the benefits as taxable income.

5. Limited Liability Company (LLC)

In forty-six states, you also have the choice of a limited liability company, or LLC structure. Similar to an S corporation, income earned by a LLC is taxed when it is distributed to the members, not at the corporate level. But unlike S corporations, there is no limit on the number of shareholders and shareholders can be foreign persons or companies.

Unlike C corporations, which require corporate bylaws and articles of incorporation, an LLC functions according to an "operating agreement," which can be customized in many states to fit the entity's needs.

The disadvantage of an LLC is that the structure is relatively new and there is a lack of court decisions that flesh out the ramifications of this form of corporation.

CyberFlix in Knoxville, Tennessee incorporated as a C corporation, with co-founder Bill Appleton holding most of the equity in the company because of his $100,000 start-up capital contribution. Since the four other owners were working for less wages than they would be earning in an established company, they also received equity. But because Appleton contributed the initial funding, he held a "reverse buy back"—an option to buy back the stock after a set period of time. In addition the four other founders were given stock options that could be exercised if the individual stayed with the company more than two years. "Even if the individual exercised the options, Bill is by far the largest owner of the company," says Erik S. Quist, one of CyberFlix's co-founders.

Substance Interactive in San Francisco also incorporated as a C corporation, but they made a grave error. They did not build in a time specification that required the five original owners to stay with the company before their equity vested. Thus, when one of the original founders left after a year, he walked away with 20 percent of the company.

After you have incorporated, you can always change your structure. Cyan, Inc., the developers of *Myst*, incorporated as a C corporation, but they are in the process or reorganizing into three separate corporations, two of which will operate as an S corporation and one as a limited liability partnership.

"We're changing our structure because there are better tax benefits this way," says Rand Miller. "It's also a logical breakdown of what is happening here." One company will focus on the development of entertainment software. Another entity will focus on the creation of books, movies, and other derivative products from the computer games. The third company will house a design group, which will supply ideas to the other two companies.

PREPRODUCTION

Experienced developers say that the more time spent in the preproduction stage—thinking through the issues, storyboarding ideas, inquiring into the cost of preexisting content and weighing alternatives to that content—the more money and time a developer will save in the production phase.

"Because we are actually shooting stuff on film and video, we don't have the luxury of fixing it very much after it's shot and filming your own original work is expensive," explained Garry Hare, president of Fathom Pictures, which has created a number of CD-ROM titles, including *Return to CyberCity*, *The Riddle of the Maze*, and *Escape from CyberCity*. "As a result, we storyboard almost everything and sometimes to extremes. The boards become a production path. They are not artwork, but a guide to what we are trying to create. We make notations for coding and audio. The boards become a visual reference point for all the various production technologies that go into a product."

For Fathom's product *CD Coach*, a personal trainer on CD-ROM, the creative team storyboarded for five months. Based on the user's age, sex, height, weight, level of condition, and physical activity, the program tracks each workout and automatically adjusts the level of difficulty based on the user's progress. "It took forever to do, but we think it saved money in the long run by doing so much of the work upfront," says Hare.

Robyn and Rand Miller spent two months working out the concept for *Myst*, which was based on the Jules Verne classic, *Mysterious Island*. Before setting anything down on a computer, they had worked out the story line for the product, including the Ages of Myst, the Mechanical Age, the Stoneship Age, Channelwood, and Dunny.

"It's quite a challenge because it's not the kind of thing where we're all sitting around throwing out ideas that just start to develop into more ideas," says Robyn Miller. "It's more like we're all sitting around racking our brains for ideas. It's like we sit around for twenty minutes throwing out one dumb idea after another. At the end of that you might have one good idea."

Maura Sparks, who is responsible for most of the video production at Pop Rocket, plans most of her shoots before she enters the studio. She has determined the appropriate lighting, camera angles, and colors that work best for the computer screen.

Despite the upfront preproduction planning, if your company's strategy is to be the "best" in your category of product, the production time frame can stretch out over years. Pop Rocket's title *Total Distortion* required over three years of development.

"It's a very ambitious product and very rich in content," says Maura Sparks. "Sometimes people look at it and say it could be a couple of products. It's easy to underestimate how much time a title takes to develop. There's no track record to look at. People tend to look at the model for floppy games and say it should take eighteen months to create a title, but that's a little floppy disk and this is a CD with six hundred times the space."

The preproduction phase of development was partly responsible for driving up the cost of Humongous Entertainment's title *Freddi Fish and the Case of the Missing Kelp Seeds*. At the Woodinville, Washington based company, fifteen artists hired by the company sketched twenty thousand animation cells for the CD-ROM. The designs created by hand took more than twice the time it would have with digital production techniques. For co-founder and creative director Ron Gilbert, the extra cost was worth it.

"There is just nothing more powerful than an animator, a pencil, and a piece of paper," says Gilbert. "And I don't really know why that is."[2]

In general, developers break the preproduction phase into four broad steps:

1. The idea or concept for the product;
2. The plan to produce the product, including budget, staff, schedule, and design document. This document often includes the script, storyboards (visual drawings), flowcharts, interface designs, screen layouts;
3. The licenses or clearances required for all third party materials that will be used in the title; and sometimes
4. The creation of a prototype.

In addition to the benefits already discussed, the more preproduction steps that are completed by the developer, the better the deal the developer will strike with an established software entertainment publisher.

For instance, Steven Rappaport, founder of Digital Trivia, Inc. obtained a license for the multimedia rights—which includes both the synchronization rights and the mechanical rights—to 240 hit songs before approaching Sanctuary Woods about becoming the publisher and providing the funding for the project. (See chapter 11 about how Rappaport licensed the multimedia music rights.) Rappaport also created a working prototype, an outline of how the game played, and had two previous products to his name. These elements created a unique situation: he negotiated and retained the copyright to the final product *Radio Active*. This allowed Rappaport to keep the rights for all platforms not licensed to Sanctuary Woods, as well as all follow-up products in the series.

Licensing Preexisting Material

For most small developers, the option of purchasing preexisting content is almost nonexistent because the prices are too high, relationships with key decision makers have not been formed, and the bureaucracy of the content holders is too time consuming, quickly adding to an already tight budget.

Maura Sparks at Pop Rocket lists the creation of original content as one of the primary ways the company has saved money.

"We have a small, lean team working with off-the-shelf products to create every pixel, sound effect, graphic, and animation," says Sparks. "We have saved money by using these products to create our own content."

Developers point to another significant reason why at least some developers want to create their own intellectual property: whatever the company creates will be its own.

For example, a developer muddles her way through the bureaucracy at the Walt Disney Company and is able to obtain a license to the Disney character, Goofy, in exchange for an advance plus royalties to the studio. The developer builds a game around Goofy and the title does well. From the revenue stream, the developer will pay a certain percentage to the studio to satisfy the royalty requirement. In this case, the developer received one of the company's treasured properties and is most likely paying a high royalty rate of its use.

Disney might even require the developer to enter into a "co-publishing" arrangement with the studio and give up some of its rights. For instance, the studio may agree to license Goofy and supply other assets in exchange for the copyright to the final product. The developer pays an advance against royalties to the studio for the license, and the studio charges the developer a fee for the production assets supplied by the studio.

If someone comes along and wants to make a movie, cartoon show, or consumer product based on the title, some of the money from this ancillary deal will go back to Disney.

"If you've got the talent to create content, there is no incentive to license someone else's content," says Dan Kaufman, part of the management team at DreamWorks Interactive in Los Angeles.

For this very reason, Sanctuary Woods, which used to be heavily involved in licensing preexisting material, has decided to cut back dramatically.

"We want to create our own characters and stories," says Michael Scott, formerly with Sanctuary Woods and now founder of Wildwood Interactive, a California based financing company for multimedia. "We may license a song now and then, but we are looking for opportunities to create and then use our intellectual property in other mediums—like Saturday morning cartoons or movies. This approach creates long term value in our products which we can then exploit in other media."

For those developers who intend to license content, the most common mistake is timing, says Jill Alofs, founder of the Mill Valley, California-based company, Total Clearance.

"Some developers get so focused on the creative side that they let the clearance issues go until later," says Alofs. "The ramifications are that the developer has less flexibility and therefore less negotiating room to strike a favorable deal." (See chapter 10, How to Determine Your Licensing Needs.)

PRODUCTION

The production budget varies widely depending on the type of product and also the platform, with the highest costs associated with the entertainment titles for next generation platforms. For instance, Electronic Arts producer Randy Breen spent $1.5 million and eighteen months to create *Road Rash* for the 3DO system. His core team of eight programmers and designers created the game's interactive play sequences and menuing screens. At some point during production, another forty-two people were involved in putting the product together. The gameplay sequences are derived from independent photographs that are edited and composited together to give the illusion of a three dimensional image.

Breen hired an outside industrial video director who shot twenty-two minutes of live action video using Electronic Arts employees as extras and stunt men on motorcycles. The linear video served as introductory screens and also appeared after each race. Breen also licensed fourteen songs from six alternative rock bands, including Soundgarden, for an undisclosed amount of money, and synched the music to the video sequences.

"We needed to take the 3DO version to the next level," says Breen. "I think we've done that."

During production, the "project manager" or producer is considered by most developers to be the key employee, monitoring the production, ensuring the staff meets deadlines and stays within the budget. The project manager monitors the work of the programming staff, provides direction and technical support. As one developer put it, this person "let's you know when you are in trouble."

The project manager does not come cheap. In a Coopers & Lybrand survey of twenty-four software companies that had less than ten employees, the project manager earned $52,000 a year. For forty-one companies with ten to twenty-four employees, the project manager was paid, on average, $64,000. New developers often avoid this cost because a publisher typically appoints an in-house production manager to the developer's project to ensure that it meets production milestones.

The senior engineer is another key hire for a developer. The software engineer develops software programs, designs, codes, tests, and debugs the product, earns, on average $41,000, according to fifty-three software companies with less than ten employees that responded to a survey conducted by Coopers & Lybrand. An entry level engineer at the same size company earns, on average, $29,000.

Throughout the production period, developers continually test the product to make certain that it meets specifications. The development agreement between the developer and publisher specifies that the developer is obligated to turn over a "bug-free," or error-free, product to the publisher. At different stages of development, the publisher might also reserve the right to present the prototype or a partly completed product to a focus group to gather initial reaction to the concept and provide feedback to the developer. Some publishers, such as Spectrum HoloByte or Electronic Arts, use their testers who debug the final product to also test if the product concept is "fun."

Increasingly, publishers are asking for prototypes from developers to pretest the software, using a focus group before funding the entire product. Developers, however, have trouble hiring programmers to produce a prototype because the majority of programmers are looking for secure, full-time jobs.

"We end up shoe-horning in prototypes using the people we already have," says Rick Giolito, vice president of business development at Vortex Media Arts.

Live Action Video and the Use of Actors

Like Breen at Electronic Arts, some developers of CD-ROM based games are hiring live actors and actresses to create video footage to include in their titles. While the use of live action can heighten the quality of the product, it most likely will take time to find the right actor or actress who wants to work in interactive media.

"When you get involved in celebrity negotiations, there's a tremendous range of personality types and attitudes toward being involved in multimedia," says Don Daglow, president of Stormfront Studios Inc. in San Rafael, which created the well-known series of *Tony La Russa* baseball CD-ROM titles.

Daglow describes his experience as follows: if you talk to five celebrities and their agents, one out of five times, the agent kills the deal before the celebrity even finds out about it. The agent unilaterally decides that the project is not worth the time or money to bother the celebrity.

One out of five times, the agent tells the client, but advises his client not to do it because it is too small of a deal. One out of five time, you will deal with very genuine agents and celebrities who are sincerely interested, spend time negotiating a deal, and then decide that though they want to be involved in the industry, they want to hold out for more money. You hit one out of five who negotiate a tough deal, but recognize multimedia as a new medium and an emerging opportunity. The celebrity signs because not a lot of time is involved, he or she is intrigued by the project, and it represents incremental revenue. Another 20 percent of the time, a developer is negotiating a deal with a celebrity who is not a central personality, who wants to do the project, and the deal is closed almost overnight.

The developer Mechadeus in San Francisco found the right celebrity and agent when it successfully negotiated and hired Tia Carrere from

Wayne's World to appear in *The Daedalus Encounter*, as one of three survivors of a twenty-second century intergalactic war. Her companion is Zack, soap opera star Christian Bocher.

"We are combining feature film production values, name talent, advanced computer technology, an interesting storyline, and interactivity," explained John Evershed, co-founder and executive producer at Mechadeus. "[We think] using name talent will enrich the game and its consumer appeal. Tia and her co-star get the player involved in a compelling, movie-like experience."

Using talent also enriches the budget. The development budget for *The Daedalus Encounter* is more than $1 million, and a significant factor driving up that cost is the use of live action. Mechadeus received its development funding from its publisher, Media Vision Technology Inc. in Fremont, California (which later went bankrupt.)

"You have the cost of doing the video shoot, which includes a substantial amount of equipment and a large number of people," says Timothy McNally, CFO of Mechadeus. "Then you've got the cost of talent and the facilities. In your development budget, there will be one period—anywhere from one to four weeks or longer—where your costs skyrocket."

It is possible to keep the cost of the product somewhat in line with the multimedia market. The developer's first title, *Critical Path*, was produced for roughly $400,000. In *Critical Path* a live actress plays the role of a young female helicopter pilot named Kat. Kat meets up with thugs, also played by live actors.

Using Union Talent

If you use union talent, you must negotiate with the performing arts guilds, American Federation of Television and Radio Artists, or AFTRA, and the Screen Actors Guild, or SAG.

While there is some blurring of representation between the two unions, SAG is the bargaining unit for performers in the movie and television industries. AFTRA is the union for television and recording artists. Both unions, interested in being part of multimedia, have created an "interactive media agreement" and two types of contracts: one for one-time use of talent, or a "one production only," OPO agreement; the other contract states that for present and future projects, you agree to abide by the contract.

Under SAG's and AFTRA's rules, you can use the OPO three times, then you must sign a contract that lasts three years. You cannot skirt the rule by using an OPO three times with SAG and then an OPO three times with AFTRA before signing a three year contract.

The minimum wage rate for an AFTRA or SAG on-camera performer is $504 for an eight hour day. Extras' rates are $103 per eight hour day. (These rates are set to expire in 1995, but mostly will be extended until

1996). The rates charged are on a half day or per day basis, regardless of how many lines are recorded or scenes acted. Under the interactive media contract, a producer has the right to distribute the original content on all existing platforms or platforms that come into existence, excluding remote delivery or video servers or video on demand. To distribute the content via on-line or through video servers, the contracts require the producer to make an additional payment. If you want to "integrate" the original content into a second title in a series, says Marie Salerno, associate executive director of AFTRA, you must purchase this supplemental right.

The developer must also contribute to AFTRA and SAG's retirement and health plans, an amount equal to 12.65 percent of the gross compensation due each performer.

Developers typically misunderstand two implications of hiring union talent. First, if you sign the interactive media agreement with SAG or AFTRA, are you only allowed to hire union talent for present or future productions?

No, according to Salerno. Under the federal labor union laws, if a producer signs an interactive media contract with one of the unions, she can still hire nonunion talent. However, if the contract specifies a certain wage that would have been earned if a union talent was hired, the producer must abide by the contract terms and pay that amount to the nonunion worker. "If you sign a union contract, you are agreeing to treat everyone equally," says Salerno.

The other major area of misunderstanding is the employment status of union talent. When you sign a union agreement, which gives you permission to use union talent, that talent is considered an employee, not an independent contractor of the developer. That means the producer will have to pay all the state and federal taxes associated with hiring employees, including Social Security and other employment taxes, state disability, and workers' compensation.

Union Rates

On Camera Performers

For the day	$ 504
For three days	$1,227
For a week	$1,685

Off Camera Performers

Voice Over Performer	$ 504
Sound Effects Performer	$ 334
Singers	$ 504
Extras	$ 103

Special Ability Extras .... $ 127
Silent Bit Extras .... $ 185
Swimmers, Skaters.................. $ 310

Other Unions

Most of the other unions are negotiating with multimedia developers on a case by case basis. These unions include:

1. The Directors Guild of America
2. Writers Guild of America
3. American Federation of Musicians
4. Songwriters Guild of America
5. Producers Guild of America

POST PRODUCTION

At the post production stage, more testing is done, both alpha testing, to make sure the product functions properly, and beta testing, to ensure the product works under normal playing conditions.

If live action video was used, edits are finalized during this period. Breen at Electronic Arts also finished synching the music to the video, added special effects, and colorized parts of the video to make it look similar to other parts of *Road Rash*.

OVERHEAD

Most small developers start out by reducing their overhead as much as possible by working out of their homes, garages, or warehouses. They do not pay themselves, and they ask others to take a reduced wage. They rely as little as possible on legal services and avoid hiring a high profile management team.

"I was at a used furniture place today, buying a $75 desk for my top programmer," says Rick Giolito of Vortex Media Arts. "You almost have to be an Arab rug merchant in dealing with your suppliers. You need skills in hard bargaining."

Giolito, like other business development managers at small multimedia companies, has found many ways to reduce overhead. For a long time, the company did not insure its equipment. The company operates twenty-four hours each day, with artists working double shifts, sharing computers, desks and phone lines. And, except for some used desks and chairs, there is little office furniture.

While most publishers refuse to include in the advance paid to the developer the financing to purchase equipment, Vortex has found some ways around that rule.

"We've negotiated what's called "publisher's assistance," in which the equipment is essentially borrowed from the publisher," says Giolito. The assistance is included in the advance amount given to the developer, but the publisher has the right to repurchase the equipment at a depreciated value after the project is completed.

Giolito also asks publishers for as much software assistance as possible. "The big publishers get the stuff gratis or at reduced prices," says Giolito. "They are usually happy to help their developer get the project done."

Eventually, the company will begin to allocate funds to overhead, which includes financing for the corporate infrastructure, the accounting function, human resources, legal services, rent, and any management information systems personnel. Typically the general and administrative overhead will amount to 5–15 percent of revenues less a reserve for returns. Overhead is higher if the company is new and has recently hired an experienced president, chief financial officer, or other executives to form a management team. It will also increase when the company is involved in a financing deal, a private placement, or initial public offering, in which lawyers and investment banking fees must be paid.

LIST OF DEVELOPERS' COSTS FROM CONCEPT TO GOLD MASTER DISK

DEVELOPER	TITLE	COST	TYPE*
Luminaria	*Wrath of the Gods*	$700,000	A
Cyan, Inc.	*Myst*	$700,000	A
Eden Interactive	*Greg LeMond*	$150,000	B
Eden Interactive	*American Vision*	$350,000	B
Drew Pictures	*Iron Helix*	$400,000	A
Mechadeus	*The Daedalus Encounter*	$1.5 million	A
Modern Media Ventures	*Cybergus*	$100,000	B
Electronic Arts	*Road Rash-3DO*	$1.5 million	A
Eden Interactive	*Golf*	$150,000	B
CyberFlix	*Lunicus*	$400,000	A
Substance Interactive	*substance.digizine*	$50,000/issue	C
Pop Rocket	*Total Distortion*	$500,000	A
Imagination Pilots	*Blown Away*	$900,000	A
Humongous Entertainment	*Freddi Fish*	$300,000	B
Activision	*Return to Zork*	$1.5 million	A

* A = Entertainment, B = Edutainment, C = Magazine

FLOW CHART OF DEVELOPER'S COSTS
FROM CONCEPT TO SHRINK-WRAPPED BOX

$40	Retail price that the consumer pays
$12	Retailer's cut
$7–8	Distribution fee
$4–7	Development costs (mostly labor, also licenses)
$3–4	Manufacturing
	— $1.25 disk and jewel case
	— $1.00 cardboard box
	— $1.00 manual
	— $ .25 other
$.50	Package Design
$.00	Platform license fee
$4–7	Marketing
$7–8	Distribution
$3–5	Tech support, product enhancement, localization Overhead
———	
$1–4	Profit before taxes

1. *Digital Media*, November 17, 1994.
2. *Seattle Post Intelligencer*, August 13, 1994.

CHAPTER THREE

GOLD MASTER DISK
TO THE HOME COMPUTER

The founders of the publishing company CyberFlix in Knoxville, Tennessee spent months putting together the award winning twitch game *Jump Raven* in which the user becomes Raven, who flies his hovercraft down New York streets, engaging enemies in real time dog fights. The user chooses a copilot, musical scores, and a weapon system.

Impassioned about their second title (the first one was *Lunicus*), the CyberFlix turned their creativity toward designing the right packaging and box for the product. They considered the profile of the likely purchaser—what this consumer watches, does, and reads—and the tone of the product and developed a graphic, eye-catching box cover. On the left hand side in the foreground stood a decrepit Statute of Liberty, with her face blown off. A hover jet is flying directly toward you with a blonde, buxom woman staring straight ahead, machine gun smoking in her right hand, ready to fire.

"The design was based on what we thought were the tastes of our target audience," says Andrew Nelson, one of the co-founders of CyberFlix. But Paramount Interactive, CyberFlix's distributor, had hesitations and wanted a redesign. CyberFlix protested and after much debate, Paramount compromised, and put together a focus group to test their reaction to the box.

"They loved it," says Nelson. CyberFlix's design made it to the retail stores because the founders knew their customers extremely well. They had spent time looking at other products that were geared to the same audience and that had sold well.

You have taken the product from concept to the gold master disk stage. At this step, most developers move on to their next title, turning over the rest of the responsibilities to a publisher. In many ways, however, this is just the beginning. In this chapter, developers and publishers explain why it is critical for the developer to be involved in the next phases, particularly when it comes to the packaging, marketing, and selling of the title.

PACKAGE DESIGN

The package design, the physical cardboard box that holds the CD-ROM, jewel case, and manual, has become so important to the selling of CD-ROM titles that it deserves a separate cost consideration. Retailers admit that packaging is often what determines whether they find shelf space for the product.

"I put a lot of importance on packaging," says Chuck Whitakker, the Division Merchandise manager for Software Etc. "It's 80 percent of whether or not we carry the product."

As the multimedia market has expanded to include the "early majority" consumer, packaging has become a developer's most important marketing tools. With the entry of this type of consumer and as price points decrease, the multimedia market gravitates toward the browse and impulse-buy type of product, away from the read-the-reviews type of product.

As a result, developers and publishers are spending more creative time and money designing the packaging for their products. For guidance, some publishers are following the model created by the videotape rental and sale industry, which spends enormous amounts of money designing the perfect package to convince the consumer to rent it.

For multimedia products in 1995, to successfully design a package for a box, developers and publishers say that it takes on average $12,000 to $15,000. It can go higher. The packaging for *Blown Away* developed by Imagination Pilots in Chicago was over $30,000. Although this expense is high, part of this time and money can be allocated toward the creation of point-of-purchase materials, such as store displays, demos, and racks, which can be placed in the retail outlet to draw attention to the product. If you have someone in-house with design and marketing experience, the cost of package design can be reduced.

But developers caution not to skimp on design.

"The product depth and design will give the retailer the confidence that you will be around for awhile," says one developer. "If your packaging is well done, you give the message to the retailer that you are going to work with him to build a product line and generate sales. You aren't just a fly-by-night, here today, gone tomorrow operation."

Part of the reason for the emphasis on packaging is the lack of preview mechanisms available for consumers to review the title before parting with $30 to $120 dollars. Books have book review sections in newspapers and magazines. Television shows have trailers announcing the show before it airs. Movies have reviews and trailers.

Some preview mechanisms for multimedia are emerging, such as the new magazines—*CD-ROM Today*, *Mac Home* (strictly for Macintosh users), and *PC Gamer*—some of which include disc samplers. Already new forms of preview mechanisms are developing, like the "iStation," created by Intouch Group, a San Francisco-based music-sampling kiosk pioneer. iStation is an in-store kiosk that allows consumers to sample 250 different CD-ROM titles. Using a touch screen, consumers can view a thirty second clip of a title and sample five different levels of gameplay. Similar to its book club, Columbia House has instituted the "CD-ROM Direct."

Eventually, say industry experts, CD-ROM titles will have a plethora of preview mechanisms, including their own newspaper review sections. Until then, packaging is the best way to catch the eye of retailers and consumers.

The designs for packaging can take up to six months to create and should be completed long in advance of the scheduled ship date to distributors' warehouses. Publishers say that preliminary package design should be shown to the distributor's sales force to solicit their input before going to final printing. A developer can also solicit feedback from local retailers.

Every segment of the retail market has different packaging requirements. You need to research the different sales channels, talk to retailers, and find out what packaging does well in that particular channel.

For instance, several CD-ROM magazines, such as *Stream* and *Medio*, are packaged to resemble conventional magazines. In their 8½ by 11 inch glossy cardboard cover, they are being sold at many newsstands, next to traditional magazines.

Bookstores, on the other hand, prefer slimmer boxes that are comparable to the size and shape of books. Mass merchant retailers, on the other hand, report more success selling multimedia titles that are packaged in larger boxes.

If the publisher has yet to land an affiliate label arrangement or a relationship with a national distributor, the publisher should spend only enough to create a conceptual packaging design. The distributor or publisher providing the affiliate label program will require that he sign off on the packaging, arguing that he knows what sells in the channel. While sometimes true, garage-type developers and publishers, like CyberFlix, have found that they are the ones most in tune with their consumers.

MANUFACTURING AND TESTING

After a developer finishes the gold master disk and the packaging designs have been created, the publisher either manufactures copies using in-house facilities, or more likely, turns to an outside manufacturer. Most publishers have their CD-ROMs manufactured in the U.S. rather than by offshore facilities because the amount of product being produced does not justify offshore shipping costs.

If the estimated release date for the product is Christmas (when 30 to 40 percent of all sales occur), the publisher must ship the finished product to the distribution warehouses by September. Working backwards then, the gold master must be sent to the manufacturer at the beginning of August, so that it can be pressed, packaged, shrink-wrapped, and ready to ship to distribution warehouses.

The manufacturing process involves three steps. The first step, called "premastering," involves taking the work that is on disc or tape to a disk manufacturing company, which inserts coding information, such as error correction and detection bytes. Premastering ranges from $1,000 to $1,800. Then, a master disk is created, which is used to develop a stamper. The stamper "stamps" or places the specific data pattern on each CD-ROM disk.

Manufacturing costs are relatively nominal, and the process is well known because third party manufacturers have gained experience from stamping audio CDs. Disc Manufacturing, Inc. in Wilmington, Delaware says that for a quantity of ten thousand or more disks, the cost of manufacturing a stamped CD-ROM disk, a two color label, and the plastic jewel box is a little under $1. It could be higher, depending on the turn around time. The cost of the cardboard box that holds the CD-ROM in its jewel box ranges from 75¢ to $1, depending on the quantity ordered: the developer will pay a lower rate as the amount of requested boxes increases. Some companies, like Disc Manufacturing, Inc., are now offering one-stop manufacturing, in which they will manufacture the CD-ROM, the jewel box, the cardboard box, and the manual.

The average packaging specifications in 1995 were 9 to 10 inches high, 1½ to 2 inches on the spine and 8 to 9 inches across. Developers who have created smaller boxes have found that their products tend to be turned spine out, rather than face forward, thereby receiving less exposure in retail stores.

The cost of the paperback manual ranges from 30¢ to $1 and very rarely should it exceed $1. The cost of the manual depends on a number of things, including whether it is spiral bound, the thickness of the covers, the number of colors used on the cover, the quality of paper, and the page length. When contemplating this cost in your budget, remember that consumers do not usually spend much time with manuals, referring to them only when they need to troubleshoot.

Most developers also include in their box, at a minimum, a registration, system, and order form card for other titles. These cards cost from two cents to twenty-five cents each.

The total cost for a shrink-wrapped software entertainment product that can be purchased at Egghead Software amounts to $3 to $4.

The cost is higher for products targeted for the educational/school market, because the consumer expects a detailed teacher's manual and a supplement for children.

Throughout the development of the product, and after the product is completed, or nearly done, it must be tested to ensure it does not have errors, or bugs. Typically the developer will run tests, including alpha testing—the initial testing of a computer program by non programmers under actual usage conditions—and beta testing, which is the final phase of testing. The developer delivers the final product, or gold or golden master disk, to her publisher who runs more tests. One industry expert pegged the testing cost for the developer at "in the $10,000 range." The more complicated the product, however, the more testing that must be done before it can be shipped to consumers.

PLATFORM FEES (PROPRIETARY)

For products designed for Sega Genesis, Sony and Nintendo platforms, the developer must not only pay for the actual cartridge but also a license fee for each unit produced. In 1994, the license fee for a Sega cartridge-based product was $7–$8. For Sony, the platform license fee was rumored to be $7. In addition, companies such as Sega and Nintendo use restrictive licensing agreements to maintain quality control. If a developer creates a game, it could be subject to veto by these companies.

The cost of goods sold for cartridge-based games is high, anywhere from $12 to $20, not including the license fee.

"Twenty dollars is a lot of capital for a young developer to come up with," says Ruth Kennedy, at Electronic Arts. "For most developers, this cost makes the cartridge market prohibitive."

For next generation systems, companies such as 3DO also require licensing fees. In 1994, the licensing cost was $3 for each copy of a game sold that was designed for the 3DO playstation and another $3 for a "market development fund" to boost advertising and marketing efforts of the Redwood City based company, 3DO Co.

In contrast, no license fees are required for products designed for the Mac or MPC.

MARKETING

The battle for limited retail shelf space intensified in 1994 and 1995 and many quality products never made it out of distributors' warehouses.

The traditional retail outlets that have carried multimedia titles, the software stores—Egghead, CompUSA—typically stock a maximum of three hundred CD-ROM titles. While mass retailers, such as WalMart,

Sears, and Target, are starting to carry multimedia titles, they are only carrying the top thirty or forty titles.

Because of the competition, the head of marketing has become a key hire in the multimedia industry. According to a 1994 Coopers & Lybrand survey of compensation of thirty-nine companies in the software industry, the head of marketing and sales for a company with less than ten employees was paid roughly $50,000 a year. If the company's revenues ranged from $250,000 to $1 million, the salary edged closer to $60,000. Public relations agencies, which can be placed on retainer, typically cost anywhere from $1,500 to $3,000 a month, but those PR firms with experience in the multimedia market are still fairly rare.

The head of marketing and sales needs to bring creativity to the position. Advertising in computer magazines is no longer sufficient. Instead, those companies on the cutting edge of entertainment-type titles have adopted hit driven models that are used by the movie industry.

The movie model dictates a one-to-one ratio between the cost of making a product and the cost of launching it. Marketing consultants argue that the ratio should be even higher, one-to-one and a half or two. Few multimedia publishers who come out of the software industry, however, have allocated this much money to marketing and most prefer not to. But the entry of Hollywood studios into interactive multimedia entertainment means that the multimedia industry as a whole will be moving toward an entertainment model approach to marketing.

There is more bad news: these dollars must be spent upfront, before any product is sold, to generate interest in the product among consumers.

CompUSA, for instance, gives a multimedia product approximately sixty days on its retail shelves, and if it has not sold well, it returns the unsold units. Therefore, the publisher and developer must have spent marketing dollars to create a buzz among consumers to buy the product during that sixty day window.

Market researchers recommend feeding tidbits to the press about the product about eight months before ship date. Sixty days before the launch date, promotional pieces and "comps," or examples of the packaging, should be sent to reviewers and retailers.

Pop Rocket, for instance, included a demo version of its title *Total Distortion* in the April issue of *Electronic Entertainment* magazine to help prime the market for the release of the product.

But Fritz Bronner, president at Vortex Media Arts, cautions against too much hype, unless the company can deliver.

"Hype is good for attracting money," says Bronner. "But it can also work in reverse by heightening expectations. My advice is to lay low, do good work, and let the product speak for itself. If it's really good, then you can blow your own horn!"

Most companies, however, cannot afford to lay low, especially because the videogame companies are continuing to allocate more money to their marketing budgets.

Acclaim Entertainment based in Oyster Bay, New York adopted the movie premiere approach and spent $10 million to launch *Mortal Kombat II*. The campaign featured print and television advertising and a forty-five second commercial that played nationwide in two movie theater chains. In return, the company received advance orders for 250,000 games at a wholesale price of $40. In its first week of release, *Mortal Kombat II* racked up over $50 million in retail sales,[1] and the company expects at least 2.5 million units will be sold. At an average retail price of $60, the game may gross $150 million or more. The original version sold more than 6 million since its introduction in September 1993.[2]

"What this is about is creating an event," says Robert Holmes, Acclaim's president and chief operating officer.[3]

Before launching *Donkey Kong Country* for Christmas 1994, Nintendo put together an unprecedented $17 million marketing campaign that included extensive TV advertising, a mailing of two million videotapes that showed a thirteen minute teaser for the product, and an on-line chat. During the first week on the retail shelves, the titles sold five hundred thousand units.

GT Interactive Software, a unit of Good Times Entertainment, ran a $3 to $5 million campaign for *Doom II*, turning to game magazines and the popular press, like *People* magazine, to run advertisements. The marketing plan also included TV ads on MTV. GT Interactive, which licensed *Doom II*, has received orders to ship 420,000 units worldwide at an average wholesale price of $39. The company expects to sell at least one million, at a retail price of $55, which should generate $55 million in gross revenue.

Walter Miao, who follows the industry as vice president of technology at Link Resources, a marketing research firm, says the way that *Doom II* was sold is a recognition of the maturation of the multimedia industry and the type of consumer who is now purchasing CD-ROM titles. It is a move away from "preaching to the converted," says Miao. "This marks the first mass-market directed advertising campaign [for PC games] aimed at the average TV viewer, unlike past ads, which tended to be in very specialized media."

Doom II's campaign is on the other end of the marketing spectrum from the original *Doom*, in which Mesquite, Texas-based Id Software, the makers of the game *Doom*, lacked a marketing budget and decided to go directly to the consumer. It chose to put its product on-line. Millions of copies of *Doom* were downloaded, and one-hundred thousand full game versions at $45 a unit were ordered—enough to build word of mouth for its next product, *Doom II*.

Mortal Kombat and the original version of *Doom* represent two extremes. Both models will continue to be used, but most other companies will rely on traditional types of advertising methods—direct mail catalogs, software magazines, trade shows, product reviews—to create "pull marketing," or the kind of buzz that causes consumers to buy or "pull" the product off the shelf.

As an affiliate label, responsible for its own marketing, Drew Pictures, for instance, spent $40,000 on direct mail order catalog advertisements in October to create consumer awareness.

"When we first shipped *Iron Helix*, we talked with anyone and everyone to explain why our product was cool," says Huffman. "It launched well, but as we've started working on our second product, we didn't do as many interviews, and sales slowed down. But at the same time, the market [of CD-ROM players] has doubled this year. There's 100 percent more people with CD-ROM players out there now compared to a year ago. These are brand new people who weren't listening when we were telling them how cool we were. The moral here is you've got to have a sustained marketing effort."

Guerrilla Marketing Techniques

Even developers who do not have the official responsibility for marketing in their agreement with their publisher are devoting resources to promoting their products because of the highly competitive market. Though their marketing budgets are small, developers often find their efforts effective, sometimes more potent than their publishers, because they know their consumers.

"It is important for a developer to have an in-house marketing and public relations team to position the company and provide more detailed insight into its products than would otherwise be provided by a publisher's marketing campaign," says Timothy McNally, chief financial officer of Mechadeus, developer of *Critical Path* and *The Daedalus Encounter*. "Even if the publisher is providing a strong marketing campaign, there are a number of interesting marketing and PR angles for the developer. For instance, the story of how the developer started 'from the garage' is interesting. You also want to make sure that your company name is heard by the industry, and a marketing person can make that happen. You know your titles better than anyone else, and for marketing purposes, you need to provide the public and the publisher with the best views of the title."

Mechadeus also has their PR person review the publisher's materials on the development company's titles to make certain that the publisher highlights the products' unique features. It has created a sales kit for the sales force of its publisher/distributor, Virgin Interactive, which includes product descriptions, screen shots from the title, and unique features about the product. At the request of its publisher, the company regularly provides its publisher with updated demo versions of the product. Nearly every month of production, Mechadeus created a new demo version of its title, *The Daedalus Encounter*, to show the press and retailers.

"You need to plan for the 'down time' associated with creating demo versions that occurs regularly throughout the production process," says McNally. "In the early stages of development, you have a great deal of independent pieces of art and animation. As you get further along in the production process, the changes are even more rapid, and the need for updated demo versions increases, as well as the need for versions for testing. The title starts to take shape and the programming is developed to link the images together. You have a lot of playable sections and the publisher is anxious to show this new stuff to create excitement in the marketplace."

Pop Rocket, which has had several major mainstream publications write about the company and its product *Total Distortion* long before the title hit the shelves, hired a marketing person in 1993, two years after founding the company, and a vice president of sales in late 1994. The founders, active and visible in the industry, with Pop Rocket's sales vice president and marketing manager, have attracted attention to the product. In addition, the company showed demo versions of its product at most of the major trade shows, which helped to generate interest long before the product hit retail shelves.

Because of their small size, Pop Rocket plans to generate word of mouth about its title when it appears in retail outlets by having an active online presence.

"We will keep our forums lively and updated," says Maura Sparks, cofounder of Pop Rocket in San Francisco. "We will respond quickly to questions." The small publisher also intends to create a derivative product from its fifty original songs, manufacturing an audio CD of the game that will be sent out to radio stations, members of the press, and possibly sold directly to the public.

CyberFlix took the position that they knew their market better than anyone else. While they did not have a lot of money to devote to marketing, they did what they could, adopting guerrilla marketing tactics to spread the word about their titles.

One of the co-founders, Andrew Nelson, was a former journalist and understood the media and how to attract press attention. He hired an intern who compiled a database of magazine and media sources, including telephone numbers, fax numbers, addresses, and, in a move that proved particularly savvy, e-mail addresses.

"We communicate via e-mail to journalists on our list," says Nelson. "It's easy, cheap, and efficient. It's also given us an international presence because we are corresponding with so many journalists abroad."

CyberFlix also lurks on-line, listening to on-line chats about its titles, which provide feedback about the publisher's products and a way to instantly respond to technical problems. In a discussion about a CyberFlix product, if someone defends one of its titles, CyberFlix sends the fan a T-shirt to show the publisher's appreciation for the support.

Instead of mailing mass quantities of review copies of its titles, Nelson reduces costs by sending out product information; if the media contact is interested in a review copy, he or she sends a fax to CyberFlix and requests a copy. This information is also added to the database.

CyberFlix also created their own professional press kit. The company purchased black glossy folders and printed stickers that had the product's title and the company's logo. They pasted the stickers on the black folders to create customized press kits for a low price.

Cheap, easy, and effective were Nelson's guiding criteria when he also ordered bumper stickers with the company's name. When anyone in the company or a friend travels somewhere, Nelson packs a load of stickers for the traveler, who puts them on sign posts, walls, billboards, anywhere.

"I just shipped forty to a friend of mine working for AP [Associated Press] in Hanoi," says Nelson. The reporter called and said she'd located a scooter company that planned on stickering their scooters with CyberFlix bumper stickers.

"These things become little cyber moments," says Nelson. CyberFlix has stickered London, Tokyo, Prague, and the East Village in New York.

CyberFlix also turned to the media to help reward underpaid employees.

"We had an intern whose job was to get a feature of each of our employees in the home town paper," says Nelson. "She did it. All across Tennessee, except for Memphis, we were able to give our employees some sort of fame, a small town hero story."

A big distributor can do the more resource-intensive things, such as beta mailings and mass mailings (in paper form) of marketing information, while the developer maintains some control over her message through guerrilla marketing techniques.

"If you are doing something radically different with your product, you need to make sure the press sees what you are doing and receives this message," says Nelson. "Often the developer is the one person who truly understands his product and can explain to the media how it is pushing the boundaries of the medium."

DISTRIBUTION

The task of distribution, which includes warehousing, invoicing, and delivering product to retail outlets, usually amounts to 25 percent of the wholesale price. See chapter 7 for a detailed look into distribution.

Marketing Development Fund

On the royalty statement from a publisher or as part of an affiliate label agreement, a developer might see a deduction for the publisher's marketing development fund, or MDF. For instance, in 1994, the 3DO Company announced that it was charging developers an additional $3 for MDF to boost its advertising and marketing efforts.

The MDF money does not go toward a specific product, but to a more generic advertising effort, such as promoting the 3DO platform so that all developers who are creating for the 3DO platform benefit.

In the typical arrangement, the publisher collects $40 from the retailer for the sale of a product, deducts $1 for the MDF and reduces the developer's royalty base to $39, against which the royalty rate is applied. This arrangement should be negotiated in advance with the publisher.

Similar to the MDF, you should consider revenue that is directed toward cooperative, or "coop" advertising: in exchange for 5 percent of the invoice amount, a distributor allows its publishers to share its space at trade shows, advertise in the distributor's catalogue, participate in direct mailings to retailers, and fax announcements to the distributor's best retail accounts.

The retailers will also ask for their cut, too, typically 2.5 percent of the invoice amount. The retailers, such as Egghead Software or CompUSA market to the end user by sending special fliers and running newspaper ads.

ONGOING TECHNICAL SUPPORT

Amuse Interactive Learning Environments in Tiburon, California scheduled to release its first product in 1995, is watching the news stories about the problems many consumers have had with their PCs and is planning its own response.

"Many people don't know how to use these new products or are having problems with their computers," says Roberto von der Heyde with Amuse. "Although the general computer problems might have nothing to do with our product, we recognize that people will be calling us with questions. We know we'll have to hire technical support staff to field these calls. It's just the nature of PCs today."

A developer must plan to set up a 1-800 number to provide technical assistance for CD-ROM users. A Coopers & Lybrand survey of forty-five software companies with ten to twenty-four employees found that the salary for the head of customer support amounted to $43,000. For software companies with twenty-five to forty-nine employees, that figure increases to $60,000.

Some publishers who have created strategic or adventure games earn extra revenue by setting up a 1-900 number for users to dial in and obtain hints on how to play the game. Others, like Luminaria, a San Francisco-based publisher who created the CD-ROM title *Wrath of the Gods*, built the hints into the game to help the consumer save money.

RESERVE FOR RETURNS

When designing a budget, you need to consider that, in most cases, retailers have full return rights with floppy-based and CD-ROM based products. In 1994 and 1995, the average return rate for the industry was 20 percent.[4] That rate might increase in 1995, however, as more than two-thousand new titles flood the retailers, and instead of letting a title languish on the shelf, retailers return products and try out another.

"If the product isn't very interactive and of high quality, the consumer purchases the title, takes it home, unwraps it, puts it on their computer, and looks at it once or twice. They then take it back to the store," says Garry Hare, president of Fathom Pictures in Sausalito, California who says that his company has a 4 percent return rate. "The store gives them credit and the consumer buys another title. This can go on and on."

Because of the return rights, you must determine the appropriate time to realize revenue—not when the product is shipped, but months later.

When Minoo Saboori, co-founder of Eden Interactive, received her first call from a retail store representative who explained that they were returning some of the company's titles, she felt nauseous. Eden Interactive had been receiving a steady stream of registration cards from purchasers of the title, indicating that the product was selling. Yet the retailer insisted upon returning the remaining products.

"Little companies like us are at the mercy of retail stores like Egghead Software who think they have a cash flow problem or believe that they've got too much inventory," says Saboori. "They pick out products and return them with the stipulation that they are not selling through [to customers]. I didn't understand why the store would want to return our products."

Some companies are building into the CD-ROM market a model that is based on the cartridge market. With cartridge-based products, because of the high cost of goods sold, distributors "price protect" the product: the retailer can mark down the price of the product until consumers start to buy it, and the publisher credits the retailers' account.

PRODUCT ENHANCEMENTS

In your budget, you need to set aside enough funding to update and enhance evergreen titles to make them more compelling and more vivid. Most developers recommend an enhancement every eighteen months.

Don Daglow, president of Stormfront Studios, followed this model and developed a series of baseball titles: *Tony La Russa's Ultimate Baseball* in

1991, *Tony La Russa's Baseball II* in 1993, and *Tony La Russa's Baseball III* in 1995.

"In some ways, it's like the word processing market," says Daglow. "Products with legs and a following enhance themselves over time. As a result they tend to build up long feature lists and get into arms-race like situations of steadily escalating features."

For Daglow, the enhancements have been more akin to overhauls of prior products because of changes in technology.

"Every single pixel has been changed and there are no surviving visuals from version two to version three," says Daglow. "The only thing that's enhanced is the mathematical simulations of the baseball games."

LOCALIZATION

The developer should include enough resources to localize the product for foreign markets, which account for 50 percent of all CD-ROM sales. Localization typically involves translating the CD-ROM product into the local language for the particular foreign country's market. It can also require changes to the product to account for cultural and language differences and porting (converting) to the most popular platforms in that market.

The cost of localizing a product can range from $20,000 to $50,000, depending on the title and how much preplanning for localization occurred during the development phase. Either the developer must absorb that cost or the foreign publisher or distributor who carries the product.

It is fairly easy to miscalculate the time and cost of localization. One German publisher agreed to localize and distribute a U.S. developed CD-ROM title. The title seemed straight-forward. It was done in black and white with text and graphics, and the German publisher thought it would take about three weeks to localize it for the German market.

Immediately, the German publisher ran into problems. When the U.S. developer created the title, he forgot that the German language is lengthier than English. It took eight weeks to shorten the text. In addition the U.S. developer refused to give the publisher access to the source code, so the publisher completed the translation and sent it to the developer who did the compilation. Four master copies were created at a total cost of $25,000 before the German publisher had the final copy.

The same German publisher purchased a product from a French developer who created a children's adventure series, using animation and audio. The developer, intent on tapping the international market, produced the product in four languages. However, the German audio was done by a nonprofessional who had a lisp. The product had to be completely redone by the foreign publisher at a cost of $15,000.

COST INCREASES

In addition to development costs, sales and marketing expenses are climbing rapidly and should continue to escalate. The downward pressure on products' prices means decreasing revenues and narrowing gross margin (net revenues minus the cost of goods sold). Publishers can decrease their cost of goods sold only so much. To keep the gross margin at a healthy 65-70 percent, the publisher attempts to earn more net revenues by increasing sales and marketing costs. Increasingly, publishers are using different types of promotional efforts—cooperative advertising, and even TV commercials—to drive up sales. As more publishers conclude that multimedia industry is following an entertainment industry model, these costs should increase further.

---

1. *Variety*, September 26, 1994.
2. *Wall Street Journal*, August 24, 1994, B1.
3. *Wall Street Journal*, August 24, 1994, B2.
4. Garry Hare, president of Fathom Pictures.

CHAPTER FOUR

SALES CHANNELS

Arnowitz Studios' hit title *The San Diego Zoo Presents … The Animals* propelled the small Sausalito, California based developer into the limelight, drawing awards, talented employees, and enough financing to create two titles under their own label, *Coral Reef: The Vanishing Undersea World*, which focuses on the sights, sounds, and struggles of the ocean's ecosystem and *Daring to Fly: From Icarus to the Red Baron*, which explores the fascination with flight from the early visionaries to World War I. The company grew rapidly, from a handful of employees to fifty.

But the production team fell behind schedule and Arnowitz shipped its self-funded titles one month late, in October instead of September, for the 1994 holiday buying season. The lost sales and still nascent edutainment market meant that three months later, in January 1995, Arnowitz found itself hundreds of thousands of dollars in debt and laying off nearly all of its employees.

There are many morals to Arnowitz' story, but one of the principal ones is succinctly captured by CyberFlix co-founder, Erik S. Quist: "You need to be on the shelf."

RETAIL

Market researchers report that, on average, retail sales for consumer-oriented titles in early 1995 accounted for 37 percent of revenue for developers. The Software Publishers Association pegs that number even higher. For all of 1993, channels in which products were not bundled accounted for 49 percent of units sold and 74 percent of CD software revenues. For 1994, channels in which products were not bundled grew to account for 61 percent of units and 89 percent of revenues. This figure is up considerably from previous years in which most revenue was derived from sales of products that were bundled with hardware or software.

"It isn't that OEM [bundling] channels are not growing," said SPA Research Director David Tremblay. "OEM channel revenues grew 37 percent in 1994, but non-OEM channel sales grew 296 percent. For CD software publishers, OEM sales represent an important part of the business. But, as the number of installed CD drives increases, retail, direct and other channels will become an increasingly important part of the distribution mix."

If a developer does not include bundling revenue, approximately 60–70 percent of revenue in early 1995 resulted from retail sales. Eighty to 85 percent of sales in early 1995 occurred through the top ten retailers.[1]

It is a sign of a healthy market when consumers, on their own initiative, go to the retail stores to purchase multimedia titles. It also helps developers and publishers who say that in 1994, based on average development costs, for a CD-ROM game or entertainment title to be successful and turn a profit for a company, fifty-thousand units need to be sold. A "hit" is considered to be a product that sells one-hundred thousand. Many developers report more units sold of their PC-based Windows products compared to others, including the Mac, because most consumers have Windows on their computer.

Regardless if the product is issued for the Mac or PC, if historical patterns continue, most retail sales, 35–40 percent, will take place in the last quarter of the year: in 1993, sales in the fourth quarter equaled sales in the previous three quarters. As Arnowitz discovered, companies are made or destroyed during this critical fourth quarter.

For a nongame product, such as an education or edutainment title, in 1994, sales of fifteen thousand to twenty-five thousand units must be made for the product to be considered successful. This figure assumes development costs of about $200,000 to $300,000.

For both edutainment and entertainment products, there is not much retail shelf time given to the product for it to sell that many units. For CD-ROM games, Electronic Arts has found that the average shelf life of its product is six weeks, unless it becomes a hit. On average, most multimedia game titles have a shelf life of twelve to sixteen weeks. With a flood of new titles hitting the market in 1995, it is a buyers' market and retailers are buying, but they are also quickly removing titles from shelves, reducing shelf life.

"It's a tough business," says Ruth Kennedy of Electronic Arts. "It's been our experience that if the product (consumer oriented software title) hasn't succeeded in the first month, it probably won't."

There is a little more grace period given to educational and informational titles. For instance, Brøderbund's *Print Shop*, with an installed base of over six million users, has been a strong seller for several years and can be found in almost any software retail store. Maxis, a publisher in

Orinda, California, has developed a series based on its successful *SimCity* title, which has been selling well since 1989.

At first glance, it appears that there are many retail outlets that are now carrying multimedia titles. The retail sales channel, after all, is a broad category, encompassing many different facets such as computer stores— Egghead Software, Fry's Electronics, CompUSA—book and record stores, discount and department stores. Despite the breadth of possible retail outlets, roughly 90 percent of all 1994 retail sales were generated in computer retail stores, according to the industry players Microsoft, Virgin Interactive, and Warner Interactive.

Some industry experts estimate that less than 2,500 stores carry CD-ROM titles, and on average, most outlets carry only 250 to 300 titles. What developers are hoping for soon is much more shelf space at the 7,000 bookstores, 15,000 record stores, and 25,000 video stores in the U.S.

"People go to computer stores to spend their productivity and tool oriented dollars," explained Minoo Saboori, co-founder of Eden Interactive and creator of the titles *American Visions, The Great Golf CD,* and *Greg LeMond's Bicycle Adventure.* "Entertainment dollars are spent at Blockbuster Video, record and book stores. That's where we need to be."

The mass market retail outlets that are presently carrying CD-ROM titles, however, typically wait to review the sell-through numbers from traditional software stores and then "cherry-pick" and stock only the top twenty-five titles.

In 1995 and 1996, more channels are expected to open as the price points (the price at which most sales occur for a particular product) for new interactive multimedia decrease. Microsoft expects that consumer electronic stores and mass merchandising stores will make more shelf space available. Warner Interactive predicts that record stores will be big sellers of CD-ROM titles: Warner found that in 1993 only 8 percent of music retailers reported customers inquiring whether they might carry CD-ROM products; in 1994, that number leaped to 50 percent. Toys "R" Us earned $400 million in 1994 from cartridge-based game products. But with this market softening because of the transition to CD-ROM, the retail store is expanding its pilot program for CD-ROM products from 5 stores to 220 in 1995. Video stores, which accounted for only 4 percent of CD-ROM sales in 1994 will also pick up a larger share of the market.[2] As more mainstream channels open and expand, retail figures should steadily increase.

"By December 1996 the technology will have improved, the installed base of computers capable of playing CD-ROMs will have expanded, and consumer acceptance of this new form of education and entertainment will have increased," says Greg Riley, formerly with Arnowitz Studios.

Before all channels are wide open, you should spend time becoming familiar with the different retail outlets. Each retail sales channel has its own buyer, its own marketing habits, different price points, and preferred packaging for its products. For instance, although there are seven thousand bookstores in this country, only nine hundred write large enough orders for books to be worth a publishers' sales representatives' time to physically visit and service the store's needs. Over the years, these representatives have developed personal relations with bookstore staff and buyers. The rest of the bookstores place their orders with wholesalers, relying primarily on the recommendations of wholesalers to make their purchases.

In the music retail business, the average price point is lower than $15, and the smaller the store, the greater the price point sensitivity, according to Eric Paulson, president of Navarre Corporation, a Minneapolis based distributor of music and interactive home entertainment products. For packaging, this industry prefers multimedia CD-ROMs in their jewel cases, without the large, bulky cardboard boxes.

One developer finally got her titles into the bookstores, only to find that the stores ripped open the CD-ROM packaging and placed the CD-ROM disk behind the counter so it would not be stolen. She quickly discovered that bookstores prefer different packaging than computer stores.

Developers who have gotten their titles into the department discount stores, such as Price Club or Costco, say that their products received a six week trial period. Unless one hundred units per stock keeping unit, or SKU, were sold per weekend day—Friday, Saturday, and Sunday—during the last three weeks of the six week period, the store returned the product. In addition, to reach the mass market, the retailers at the large discount stores typically prefer the product marked significantly below its list price (also called suggested retail price, which is the price printed on the box). For instance, during Christmas 1994, K-Mart and Toys "R" Us marked down games like *Gauntlet* and *SolarStriker* from $30 or $40 to $9.99.[3]

To address this medley of different business practices, developers are increasingly signing with several publishers and distributors, rather than only one, because it is rare to find a distributor or publisher who has the necessary experience and relationships with each segment of the retail market.

DIRECT MAIL

Sumeria, a small publisher in San Francisco, has collected names of people who have ordered their products, *OceanLife II, III, IV,* and *Exploring Ancient Cities*, creating their own mailing list of over ten thousand names. When the company produces a new title, they hire a designer, who works as an independent contractor to create a direct mail piece. The mail piece is done on glossy paper and is folded three times, so it resembles an 8½ by 11 inch letter. It includes screen shots of the product, text to describe the title, and a series of options for consumer to purchase the title—via phone call, fax, or mail.

The company takes the mailer to a mail order house, which pastes on the labels, folds, stamps, and sends them out to potential customers.

"While our main form of distribution is through an affiliate label program with IVI Publishing, direct mail really helps us out a lot," says Janine Lee, Sumeria's coordinator of operations.

While pursuing retail sales, most successful developers also implement direct mail campaigns. Developers who bundle their titles with Apple Computer, Inc. are able to negotiate access to Apple's direct mailing list. Developers who sell through Brøderbund, Electronic Arts, or Compton's NewMedia have found that these publishers' direct mailing lists are extremely effective in generating sales.

Direct mail is particularly effective for Mac-based titles. According to Apple representatives, 50 percent of Mac owners buy software and hardware through the mail. Mail order is also fairly popular with all multimedia consumers: over 36 percent of all CD-ROM titles for all platforms was sold through the mail. Columbia House, founders of the book of the month club, recognized the value of mail order and have instituted the "CD-ROM Direct," where members can receive two discounted CD-ROMs after signing an agreement to purchase four more titles over a two year period.

The beauty of this sale is that the developer keeps 100 percent of the revenue after administrative costs. If the business plan calls for a $200,000 to $500,000 in development costs alone, most multimedia consultants advise developers to build in a direct sale mechanism to customers who might have bought a previous title that is similar to the one the developer is creating, or a product that indicates the consumer is interested in purchasing a title like the developer's.

To conduct an effective direct mail campaign, developers say you need a large enough mailing list and the right list. Irving Green, founder of Scanrom Publications in Cedarhurst, New York and creator of the CD-ROM title, *The First Electronic Jewish Bookshelf*, successfully relied on Jewish mail order catalogs and bookstores to sell his title. For niche products with little chance of earning a spot on the retail shelf, direct mail is critical.

Developers purchase mailing lists from CD-ROM manufacturers who collect the names of consumers from their registration cards. The problem with manufacturers' lists, however, is that a developer does not know whether the CD-ROM drive or other periphery product was purchased for home or office use and therefore whether the user is interested in game and entertainment products or business titles.

Developers also create their own lists by including registration cards with their products. Apple Computer allows developers who bundle their products with Apple's hardware to include their own registration card. Customers fill out the cards, providing valuable information, such as the purchase location, the preferred retail outlet for purchasing CD-ROM products, the type of computer used, the name of the title they purchased, their address, birthdates of any children, and primary use of the product—at home, school, or work.

To gather those names, some developers have created a built-in incentive for customers to return the registration card, such as a free piece of software that is tied to the product. One developer used the line drawings from one of her CD-ROM product's sets, put the drawings on a floppy, and created an electronic coloring book. If the customer returned the card, she received a free floppy-based coloring book.

Despite the advantages of this sales channel, developers risk offending retailers. For example, the Miller brothers have decided not to use direct mail and instead rely on Brøderbund to distribute their CD-ROM product for the PC and Macintosh.

"Brøderbund has developed good relations with its resellers," says Rand Miller, creator of the popular title *Myst*. "When you start selling things yourself through a 1-800 number or direct mail catalog, you're cutting these resellers out. After spending so much time developing these relations with retailers, you might be shooting yourself in the foot to go the direct route."

Some developers have tried to go directly to the retailers, eliminating the distributors in order to earn a greater percentage of the revenues. This approach, however, is time consuming and many large retail chains prefer to deal with a direct sales person with a large selection of titles, rather than one developer with a single title.

THIRD PARTY CATALOGS

Many publishers and developers rely on third party catalogs to provide an additional source of revenue. More commonly, the catalog serves as another type of preview mechanism for your product.

Generally, you are required to sell your product to the catalog owner 50 percent below the retail price, with the catalog owner having the right to return products that do not sell. Most owners will also ask you to purchase an advertisement in the catalog and allow you to pay for the ad with cash or with product. Although it is tempting to pay with product, developers recommend that you pay cash. Some developers who paid with product have had catalog owners sell thousands of units of their title. But when it comes time for the developers to receive a check for the sales, they instead receive a box filled with the product given to the owner as payment for the ad.

Other developers have been hurt by catalog owners who also own their own multimedia products. The owner's products are promoted, while the developers' titles are returned without reimbursement for the advertisement. In essence, the developer is in danger of being used by the catalog owner to fill up the pages of a catalog. Developers have also found that when a customer orders the developer's title, the owner may mislead the customer, stating he has run out of that product, or there is a bug in the developer's title and recommend his own similar title as an alternative.

As with every sales channel listed here, a developer cannot rely on only third party catalogs to generate her revenue. CyberFlix's *Lunicus* was originally distributed only by Educorp Computer Services via mail order. Despite great product reviews, the company did not receive as many orders as it thought it should, says CyberFlix's Erik S. Quist.

BUNDLING

Rip off the plastic covering of *CD-ROM Today* magazine and pop in the metallic CD-ROM disk—an extra treat included, or bundled, with the publication. Click on the demo version of *Periodic Table of Elements* by Paradigm Interactive and suddenly, your old high school chemistry class comes alive. An image pops on the screen, a 3-D crystal structure of the gas, Aragon. It also appears in geometrical form and also a brief text based description. Return to the main menu and click on *Jewels of the Oracle* by Discis, *Anyone for Cards?*, or *World Cup Golf*.

Though most developers probably prefer to have their products sold through the retail channel to experience the pleasure of consumers choosing their product, the bundling channel is one that should not be rejected, especially if your development budget is above $200,000. Bundling is still what typically puts developers over the break-even point. The Software Publishers Association estimated that in 1993, two-thirds of all CD-ROM title sales came from bundling. In 1994, consultants estimated that sales earned from bundling had dropped, roughly equaling the amount sold through retail sales, or 39 percent.

Bundling deals typically pay a low rate per unit, anywhere from a $.50 to $20, depending on the volume of the order placed by the purchaser, the quality of the product, and the profit margin associated with the primary piece of hardware, software, or magazines that the bundler is selling. If the developer turns over finished shrink-wrapped product, she will receive a higher unit price, $6 on average. Popular titles also receive more per unit. While the hardware and software companies and magazines that bundle may not, on average, pay much per unit, they order in large volumes. As a result, it is not uncommon to complete a $200,000 bundling deal. For bundling deals with European based companies, developers report that they receive cash upfront. See the section on the International Market in this chapter for further details.

Garry Hare, president of Fathom Pictures, has made several million dollars through bundling deals because of the cutting-edge technology used to create some of his titles.

"You can earn that much from bundling deals if you're where the technology is hot," says Hare. "The companies coming out with the MPEG boards want MPEG titles to show off these boards. We are the only company with three finished MPEG titles, and so we find ourselves in a very advantageous position for the next six months [January to June 1995], until everyone else catches up." In other arrangements, Hare has done bundling deals for $8 to $10 a unit.

Developers and publishers still view bundling as a strong source of revenue, but it may start to fade. When disk drives were selling for $600 or $700 dollars, hardware companies felt the need to give people more perceived value for their dollar and create added value for the consumer by bundling software products. When hardware prices drop, the perceived value of owning a disk drive that costs $200 is roughly equal to the price of the drive. Over time, hardware manufacturers might be less inclined to spend lots of money on bundling. A force counterbalancing this trend, however, is that more hardware companies and traditional software companies, such as Microsoft, are entering the multimedia market and have an interest in promoting the multimedia software industry. In this type of situation, bundling is viewed less as a source of revenue and more as a preview mechanism, attracting new consumers to the product.

Bundling also extends the life of the product and seeds the market for the developer's upcoming titles, enough so that even the developers of popular CD-ROM games like *Myst* are considering a bundling deal.

"*Myst* isn't bundled yet, but it could be in the future," says Rand Miller. "We are looking into exclusive, limited bundling deals right now. We'd do it to try and get overall penetration of the market."

Companies that bundle CD-ROM titles with their products typically have an employee who reviews and selects titles to bundle. The reviewer usually asks the developer to provide a copy of the product, any published product reviews and product descriptions. The developer should also include the system requirements.

Bundlers are looking for games, entertainment, and early learning products for ages three to eight. In 1995, bundlers are also acquiring adult education titles, and the newest genre to be bundled is music titles with CD Plus.

To improve your chances of being selected for a bundle, you need to determine the audience of the underlying bundled product and the type of computer system. For bundles that are sold in computer stores, for instance, bundlers may want a title that requires more memory than an average computer.

The trend has been for developers to hand over watered-down versions of their titles for bundling, such as a demo disk or a partial or "crippled" presentation. Bundlers are increasingly uncomfortable about receiving anything but the full title of a product.

"We want the hottest title for little money," says Vicki Vance, manager of the CD-ROM Initiative at Apple New Media. "The developers want the exposure, distribution, and mailing lists."

If you are Pop Rocket, however, with a demo version of a hot title that fills 50 megabytes, you might get away with bundling the demo rather than the full length product.

Vance recommends waiting to tap the bundling market until you have more than one title, or at least are prepared to introduce to the market your second title relatively soon after the bundled title.

"You shouldn't bundle one title and then not follow through with any more," says Vance. "The real reason to bundle is to sell the rest of the series."

A developer should ask the company that is developing the bundle to include on the opening screen of its program a preview of its other products and a 1-800 number to order the products.

While there are many advantages to bundling, serious problems also arise. Somewhere along the distribution chain, from the warehouse to the retail shelf, CD-ROMs are being taken out of the package, or "unbundled," and sold separately in retail stores or on the street at deep discounts. Instead of increasing incremental sales, unbundling substantially reduces both the developer's and publisher's profit margin. If a consumer sees *Myst* on the shelves for $49 and another copy that has been unbundled for $20, the consumer will opt for the latter and the developer never receives the royalty payment she could have earned by selling the first copy.

The correct legal advice that a private lawyer might give you is—don't bundle. But at the same time, bundling represents enough of an incremental source of revenue that most companies do not want to miss the opportunity. Developers tend to use the more practical advice of investigating how their publisher/distributor is approaching the unbundling problem.

For instance, some publisher/distributors like Mindscape (formerly Software Toolworks), which does a great deal of bundling, are coming up with creative solutions to the problem. They have strengthened their agreements with retailers and, like other publisher who bundles, are placing labels on disks—"this is a bundled product and should not be sold separately"—that are bundled with hardware and software. But a stricter contract and a label will only gets a publisher so far, and then she runs into an enforcement problem of tracing the incidents of the unbundling to the culprit.

Mindscape has responded by placing on its top selling products a special coding that identifies the particular hardware or software company that has agreed to bundle that product.

Another method that some publishers use to discourage unbundling is to place the bundled product in a baggie, rather than its retail box, so that there is a disincentive to take it out and sell it on the retail shelf.

Electronic Arts limits the amount of bundling it does with hardware and software manufacturers. It also imposes a time lag of six months after the product has been introduced to the market before it will enter into a bundling agreement for the particular title. By doing that, Electronic Arts hopes to reduce the amount of replacement revenue that the bundled product might be causing and increase the amount of incremental new revenue. Electronic Arts also limits bundling to companies that it believes will conform their conduct to the contract.

But the time lag solution runs into problems.

"It requires close communication throughout the company because most publishers distribute in a number of different territories and at different times," says Jim Kennedy, general counsel of Mindscape. "Once you start your bundling in one territory, it is going to affect sales everywhere."

In terms of payment, developers try to include in their development agreement with their publishers/distributors a minimum price at which the product can be sold in a bundling deal, a higher royalty rate, or a time frame during which the title can be bundled.

"You have to be extremely careful with bundling arrangements," says Drew Huffman, co-founder of Drew Pictures. "We did a couple bundling deals with Creative Labs and it worked out great. They were awesome and shipped tons of product. When they see violation of terms, they go after the violator. But the second tier players aren't so good about violators and your market ends up really hurt. I pick up *MicroTimes* [a computer magazine] and see six ads that sell *Iron Helix* for $25. And I just think, What the hell is going on here? It's pretty bad."

THE SCHOOL MARKET

The school market is for developers who are interested in creating children's educational CD-ROM based titles. Schools are the primary purchaser of educational products, with the Software Publishers Association reporting the educational software market as the fastest growing software market in 1993–94. The school market also directly affects sales of educational software for the home. According to a survey done by the Multimedia/PC Marketing Council in Washington D.C., home purchasers of educational software gave a school or teacher's recommendation as their number one reason for purchasing a specific title.

The school market, however, is distinctly different from any other market. Critical to successfully selling to this market is the understanding that although the 47 million students in the U.S. are the ultimate users of the products,[4] the buyers of a developer's titles are the teachers, superintendents, and principals at the individual schools and the administrative types at the district level. Because the purchasing power lies in the hands of someone other than the final user, a developer is more likely to succeed if the buyers of the products see that the titles are in some way tied to the class curriculum.

That is not to say that children are excluded from the development process. Knowledge Adventure, one of the most successful developers of children's titles, relies on kids' input throughout the preproduction and production phases.

"We made the mistake with several reference titles of bringing too much adult perspective to the product," says Ruth Otte, president of Knowledge Adventure in La Crescenta, California. "Now we make sure kids are involved in the process. We have a kids lab and kids are constantly going through our office, playing with the products and reacting to them."

Two layers exist in the school structure: the district level, of which there are 115,000 in the U.S.; and the individual school level, of which there are 103,000, according to the Department of Education. Each layer has different purchasing powers. For instance, in California, at the district level, administrative personnel primarily buy productivity-type software programs.

At the school level, however, a budget exists to purchase curriculum-type programs, with 58 percent of all money spent by schools in 1994 allocated to reading or language arts software programs.[5] Teachers who use CD-ROM products expect to receive a thirty day preview period so that they can test the software before purchasing it. In some districts, it is mandatory that a title be previewed before it can be purchased.

In the past, states allocated funding for educational technology separately from other materials and textbooks. Now, if the software product is linked to the curriculum, in at least twenty-three states, textbook money can be used to purchase software products. The three largest markets for textbooks that allow the substitution of software products to consume some of this budget are California, Florida, and Texas.[6]

Characteristics of the School Market

Developers say that several characteristics are critical for designing a successful multimedia product. Because of the wide range of understanding about how to use a computer among the school and district buyers, the simpler a developer can make a program, the better. Mirroring this aspect of the market is the wide spectrum of computer technology that is in the schools, from the early Apples to state-of-the-art computers. Successful developers of educational titles have tamed the impulse to create the ultimate, state-of-the-art software that requires the latest technology. Brøderbund has confronted this problem by writing detailed teacher's guides that take into account all different kinds of computer situations. For instance, Brøderbund gives suggestions that describe how to use its products if there is only one computer with a CD-ROM drive in the classroom and also if there are five.

In the consumer market, a developer can do fairly well with one or two SKUs, or stock keeping units. But in the education market, a developer probably needs at least four: a school edition that includes teacher guides, lesson plans, and other tools to help the teacher integrate the program into the curriculum; lab pacs that have five to ten software programs in a box; a network version in which computers and peripheral devices can be connected; and a retail version. Since most school budgets disappear after June, June tends to be the biggest sales month of the year. If schools do not spend their allotted budget amounts, they risk receiving less funding for the following year.

The schools prefer products with user friendly interfaces so that kids can use the product without supervision and direction from a teacher. For a written manual to be used by students, it also must be user-friendly, so that students can solve software problems without a teacher's assistance. The software that is selling well easily fits into the curriculum in some way, such as helping students with math or reading; science-related software titles; or with a basic task, such as writing or page layout designs.

Some of the best selling titles include Brøderbund's *Print Shop Deluxe* and the *Children's Writing and Publishing Center*. Of the top twenty-five best selling school software products, fourteen are teacher tools or productivity type programs like Brøderbund's original *Print Shop*.

How to Get the School's Attention

Developers have a menu of ways to capture the attention of the educational software buyers. As in any market, word of mouth is probably the most important. Because few preview mechanisms exist for multimedia, successful developers rely heavily on product reviews in one of the many professional magazines that are specifically designed for teachers, such as *Technology & Learning* magazine. Teacher conferences are held throughout the year, and developers can set up booths and demonstrate their products at these events.[7] (See the appendix for some of the teacher's conferences that are held each year.)

Find a Quality Publisher

As a developer creating a children's educational product, it is critical to locate a well-known quality publisher, such as Brøderbund Software Inc. in Novato; Davidson and Associates in Torrance, California; or The Learning Company. In 1994, The Learning Company accounted for nearly 14 percent of education sales, making it the largest educational software publisher. For the CD-ROM platform, Brøderbund was the largest, capturing 9 percent of the market, edging out Microsoft, according to PC Data. Brøderbund's annual report shows that of the 1994 sales of $110 million, $10 million came from the school market, generated by selling lab pacs, school editions, site licenses, and networks. Brøderbund also estimates that 15 percent of its titles sold in the consumer market are also sold to educators who take and use them in the schools.

Davidson & Associates; Maxis in Orinda, California; Electronic Arts; and Compton's NewMedia also have affiliated label programs that sell into the school market.

Publishers can help fund the development of a title or distribute a self-funded product in their affiliate label programs (see chapter 5, under Deals for the Self Funded Titles). Over the years, these multimedia publishers have established a strong market presence, with direct sales forces that exclusively service the school market, which are entirely separate from the sales forces that cater to the retail channel. Teachers have come to know the publishers who provide quality products and consumer support services. Often they purchase new multimedia software based on the name of the quality publisher alone. In addition, Brøderbund has one of the best in-house mailing lists of families with children who have previously purchased multimedia products.

Developers who succeed in the school market reap a valuable benefit. Once a school purchases a title and it is well-received by teachers and students, the school continues to buy the product for many years.

"Schools are very loyal to products," says Diane Rapley, educational technology consultant and former director of educational sales and marketing at Brøderbund. "Once your title sells to a school, it sells for years, long after it's died in the consumer market."

The interconnection between the school market and the home market should also not be missed. As mentioned earlier, a survey completed by the Multimedia/PC Marketing Council found the following factors motivated a family to buy a specific education title. A teacher or school's recommendation ranked number one. Concern with the specific subject matter came next. Third, the purchaser saw a demonstration. Trailing factors were: a friend's recommendation; familiarity with the publisher; the product's receipt of an award for excellence; the product's best seller status; the consumer reading a magazine review; and lastly, the buyer seeing an advertisement.

Other means of distribution to the school market and to children in particular are growing. Egghead Software announced in 1994 that it was setting up a separate direct sales force to market to the schools.

Another company, Club KidSoft in Los Gatos, California, has bypassed the school market altogether and appeals directly to kids. Club KidSoft has created a software club for kids, ages four to twelve—a potential market of approximately 37 million in the United States. Since its inception, Club KidSoft has received membership fees from forty-thousand kids, and in return, these new members receive quarterly issues of *Club KidSoft* magazine and the company's CD-ROM (Mac or Windows). On the CD-ROM are activities and contests for kids, and, of particular interest to new developers, pre-screened software created by outside developers.

"We review it internally, looking for the best quality software that is nonviolent, fun, engaging, and educational in scope," says Maggie Young, Club KidSoft's director of corporate communications. After it passes the corporate tests, the company has kids, teachers, and families review the software. If the developer's program is selected, the developer pays a quarterly fee of $2,000 to be in the *Club KidSoft* magazine and CD-ROM. Like third party catalogs, the company takes a certain percentage of sales.

Well-known titles have been included on Club KidSoft's CD-ROM, including Modern Media Ventures' *Gus Goes to Cybertown*; Humongous Entertainment's *Putt Putt Joins the Parade*; *Treasure MathStorm!* developed by The Learning Company, and *Beginning Reading* from Sierra On-Line.

ADVERTISEMENTS

Electronic magazines, such as *substance.digizine, Launch, Blender, Go Digital*, and *Medio*, have all found another source of revenue by selling advertisements. Unlike traditional ads that are priced based in part on circulation, electronic magazines are charging by the megabyte. *Launch*, published by 2Way Media, a company in Los Angeles, charges advertisers $2,500 a megabyte. The magazine has 650 megabytes, and 180 are allocated to advertisements.[8] It is not clear whether advertising will creep onto consumer oriented multimedia titles like they have onto video rentals and movie screenings, but it is something for developers to watch for.

THE INTERNATIONAL MARKET

Most developers create a long-term business plan to expand into foreign markets, which account for 35 to 50 percent of all interactive product sales, the majority of which is still primarily videogames. The market in Japan is especially attractive, ranking second behind the United States in multimedia software sales, at 22 percent. While the PC is a popular platform, the console market—Sega, Nintendo, and Sony—are significant markets in Japan.

Behind Japan are Germany, France, the United Kingdom, and Canada, each roughly 3–8 percent of the market for multimedia products, both cartridge and CD-ROM based.

Unlike the U.S. market, the international market in 1995 and probably 1996 provides immediate cash flow and a steady stream of revenue. European distributors do not demand the right to return products that do not sell. As a result, they order less units, but the orders they place with a developer represent firm sales, and they pay cash upfront. European hardware and software companies that bundle multimedia products also typically pay cash upfront, rather than a royalty rate, which is more commonly used by U.S. based companies.

Market consultants say that the international market lags two to three years behind the U.S. market, but will quickly catch up as U.S. titles flood their market, inducing European and Asian consumers to buy the necessary hardware. According to Dataquest, the European market for CD-ROM titles is growing at a rate of 36 percent. That number should continue to grow for quite some time: unlike the U.S., the European online market is expected to take off slowly because consumers do not have a flat rate for local calls. Each time a European household picks up the phone, the meter starts ticking. As a result, there will probably be a longer window of opportunity for CD-ROM titles in Europe than in the U.S.

Developers say that the European market is fragmented. Each country has a different multimedia market, with different hardware preferences and title tastes. For instance, the German market tends to favors serious titles, with educational titles selling well. The French market prefers games and cultural titles, a genre that is not found in the U.S. Cultural titles are those that focus on museums, palaces, a specific artist's work, and travel.

This fragmentation means that the selection of a foreign distributor, publisher or republisher is very important. Developers have used several business models to enter the Asian and European markets. They recommend starting out by licensing your products to a distributor—if you have your own marketing support—or a republisher—if you lack marketing capability. Most developers report that they give up 65–70 percent off the retail price to the distributor, depending on who pays for localization. For publishers or republishers, it is generally 75–80 percent. Developers, however, can receive guarantees and payment for a minimum quantity sold upfront. In Germany, it is anywhere from five thousand to eight thousand units; in the U.K. and France, it is three thousand to five thousand. The licensing agreement might last for two years, which, at that time, the developer can reevaluate and renegotiate, if necessary. If the relationship has worked, developers often consider a partnership with a foreign company that has localization and distribution capabilities.

Most foreign publishers want exclusive arrangements with developers. Developers say that if you opt for this term, make sure you build in safeguards. For instance, the Voyager Company agreed to enter into an exclusive arrangement with Virgin Records for the French market, but for only one title and one platform, *Freak Show* for Windows. Another suggestion is to negotiate for something in return for granting exclusivity, such as doubling the minimum guarantee of units sold.

Hikaru Sasahara, founder and president of Interactive Media Agency, located in Tokyo and Los Angeles, says that a successful relationship emerges if the developer and foreign publisher work closely together to coordinate the release dates of the product in the U.S. and the foreign country. If the product is released in the respective countries simultaneously, there is no incentive for a third party to create a gray or black market, buying the product in one market and illegally distributing it without a license in another.

Counterfeiting and piracy, rampant in the East, are uncontrollable costs that also must be weighed before entering this new market. Unbundling, the process of taking CD-ROMs packaged with another software or hardware product out of the package and selling it at a deep discount, is common in Taiwan, Singapore, and Southeast Asia.[9] Chinese-based companies are well known for their illegal copying and selling of American-made music, movies, and computer software.

SHAREWARE

An increasing number of companies are selling shareware CD-ROM products. One of the best known examples of this approach is the *5-ft. 10-Pak*, a five foot long promotional package of ten CD-ROM games from top publishers distributed by Scottsdale, Arizona based Sirius Publishing Inc. which sells for $29.95 (roughly $3 a game). The product has been extremely successful and was named the number one best selling title in PC Data's "Top 20 CD-ROMS" in August 1994.

In a shareware product, a company like Sirius will select forty games and in some way "cripple" them, or put limited versions of the game on the one CD-ROM disk and sell the product at a reduced price compared to a full CD-ROM game. The consumer ends up with a grab bag of different products for his or her purchase. Some of the titles on the *5-ft. 10-Pak* included: *Doom* from Id Software, *World FactBook* from Wayzata Technology, and *Stellar 7* from Sierra On-Line.

In August 1994, Sirius came out with its second product, *5-ft 10-Pak Volume II*. At Sirius' low prices, "thousands of new users can discover the power of multimedia and can easily collect additional CDs for the home

PC," says Richard Gnant, president of Sirius. In the new title, Sirius included special discount coupons for the titles that appear on the CD-ROM so that consumers can purchase the individual products at a reduced rate.

The developer often receives little or no revenue from the initial sale of the shareware CD-ROM disk, but benefits from the exposure and word-of-mouth selling power. If the consumer who purchased the shareware disk likes the limited or crippled version of the game, he or she may purchase the full game.

Other shareware companies include FormGen, which is based in Phoenix, Arizona and Club KidSoft in Los Gatos, California.

CORPORATE ALLIANCES

Many multimedia software developers and publishers are finding creative ways around the limited shelf space problem and opening up their own unique sales channels. Sanctuary Woods is one of the leaders in crafting innovative relationships with other traditional entertainment companies to find different revenue sources.

In 1993, Sanctuary Wood's president Scott Walchek traveled to a Las Vegas television trade show, where he met a cable TV representative from Comedy Central. About that same time, a Sanctuary Woods business manager happened to be sitting on a plane next to a representative from a well known public TV station, WDBH, which owns the science program, Nova. The chance encounters led to something the companies had ever done before: for Comedy Central and the public TV show, spinning off CD-ROM products, and for Sanctuary Woods, teaming with television and developing new multimedia products. Just as important for Sanctuary Woods, it found a way to advertise and sell its products in a different media: television. After the broadcast of the Comedy Central and the Nova programs, Sanctuary Woods runs a 1-800 number for viewers to receive a CD-ROM.

The serendipity of the meetings and the resulting partnerships illustrate the sort of frontier spirit and competitive zeal that pervades the multimedia business. Sanctuary Woods, in addition to looking for talented developers (just like everyone else out there), wants alliances that provide the company with creative material on an ongoing basis.

Sanctuary Woods agreed to pay for the cost of the programs' development teams, which were brainstorming interactive game ideas. It also agreed to a royalty stream to be paid from resulting products. And the TV producers wanted assurances that the products conformed to their expectations. Sanctuary Woods agreed to give the producers the right to approve each project during various stages of development. In return, the TV shows had between ten and thirty days to approve a particular phase of development, depending on the project. If they disapproved, the shows had to identify specifically what was wrong so Sanctuary Woods' developers could fix it.

To accommodate the long term relationships (both agreements run for five years), Sanctuary Woods developed a master contract to define the overall parameters of the deal. Included in this contract were approval procedures, the appropriate disclaimers, warranties, and the partners' royalty rate. As products are developed in the future, an addendum will be attached, incorporating by reference the master contract. For each product, there are specifications and a list of milestones that trigger approval rights. The addendum outlines the specifics of the title: the development budget, the date of introduction to the market, the type of platform, and any modification to the royalty stream.

THE ONLINE MARKET

Online services are being used by developers in two ways: as a general marketing mechanism for multimedia products and as a way of selling titles. Each online service—America Online, CompuServe, Prodigy, Delphi, and others—has a different culture, some of them allowing businesses to sell more aggressively than others. They also differ in terms of the ratio of female to male users, with most online services populated primarily by male users. According to the Graphics, Visualization and Usability Center at the Georgia Institute of Technology, the demographic profile of the people visiting the World Wide Web, the Internet's fastest growing region, is 90 percent male, with over half of users between twenty-one and thirty years old and 87 percent are white. Eighty-five percent of users on America Online are male. Prodigy does a little better, with women subscribers comprising around 35 percent of total users.[10] If a developer's product appeals primarily to women, this sales channel might not be the best medium. Most online members, however, are in the innovator, early adopter, and early majority consumer categories, and market research shows that as of Fall 1994, 40 percent had CD-ROM players. Presumably, that number has increased.

Some developers and publishers have built their own Home Pages on the World Wide Web, which gives users information about the company and products. CyberFlix is developing a page where users can download new characters to enter into the publisher's new title *Dust*. Electronic Arts' site features audio and video clips, including downloadable product demos for browsers to sample the latest interactive entertainment software.

Other companies include a 1-800 number for the user to call for more information. Because of security concerns, consumers are reluctant to place orders via online. Instead, companies are asking consumers to fax their orders. Some companies are following the lead of Electronic Arts, which has developed a customer identification system that allows Web users to order products without sending their credit card numbers over the Internet.

Other companies have moved to the shareware concept to the online medium. Mike Kulas and Matt Toschlog, founders of Parallax Software Corporation, uploaded a version of their game *Descent* to the Internet to solicit viewers' reactions and generate consumer awareness. The positive reaction that the game received from Internet users helped convince Interplay to sign as Parallax's publisher.

The founders of Id Software Inc. in Mesquite, Texas thought it had developed a great title, with a muscular space marine protagonist who fights off demons and mutant humans on a moon base so abhorrent that it inspired the game's name *Doom*. The creators of the game, however, faced a very common obstacle: how to get its product into the market. Without a big name distributor behind it, Id took a chance: in December 1993, it posted a basic version of the game on the Internet and let people download the game for free. The software maker encouraged anyone to grab *Doom* from any computer hook up to the Internet, so CompuServe, America Online, and Prodigy users received the game for free.

Such a distribution system, known as online shareware, was set up to entice players to send in a $40 check for the full version of *Doom*. Close to five million computers worldwide now have the game on the hard drive.[11] Another one-hundred thousand have paid $40 for the complete *Doom* game, which includes two extra "levels" or episodes, to play.

"The kind of public recognition we've gotten with *Doom*—movie offers, product endorsements—is unheard of," says Id's CEO and business manager Jay Wilbur.[12] "Shareware endears us to the public, especially when we tell people who download the game to play it anyway, even if you don't want to buy it."

Because the ten person, privately held company sold its titles directly over the phone (without giving a percentage of sales to a distributor), their profits soared. Id's 1994 revenues were $6–$10 million.

The company has since authorized Austin Virtual Gaming to license an eight-screen *Doom* arcade setup. An agent is shopping *Doom* movie and literary rights. *Doom 2* was shipped October 1994, with distribution and promotion handled by New York based video distributor, Good Times Entertainment.

Other models of shareware include allowing the consumer to download a product, and based on the honor code, send a fee—$15 or $25—to the developer. Richardson, Texas-based Micrografx, Inc. offers copies of a program for making business presentations. Consumers pay an $8.95 shipping charge for the "free" software program.

The method can work if it attracts consumers who then want to purchase upgrades, another series in a game title, or software support.

"The biggest problem new companies face is building a critical mass of users," says Lisa Thorell, an analyst with San Jose based Dataquest. "With freeware and shareware the product really has to prove itself. It's like a money-back guarantee up front that eliminates the risk for people who try it."

Another online development is Sega's announcement of a Sega Channel that will provide Genesis video games on demand, twenty-four hours a day, over conventional coaxial cable. For $12 a month, the projected two million Sega Channel subscribers will be able to download about fifty already released and somewhat older games from Sega's game catalog as well as teaser versions of new games and soon-to-be released games.

Sega has structured the online service to avoid competing with its distributors: because consumers can only get small bits of new games, users will still have to go to retail stores to buy the full version of the product. Time Warner is offering the Sega Channel to its cable TV subscribers.

An almost certain winner of online distribution is the multiplayer game.

"The computer and video game industry has spent a decade creating sophisticated computer games only to discover we'd rather play against the idiot across the street," says Bill Kunkel, executive editor of *Electronic Game* magazine. "We're talking about the single most popular trend in electronic gaming."[13] Betting on this market's potential are General Electric's GEnie network, which is marketing itself as a gamer's heaven. In November 1994, AT&T jumped into the multiplayer market by spending $40 million to buy The ImagiNation Network in Burlingame, California, which offers multiplayer games for all ages.

Some business experts believe that electronic distribution is the way of the future. It eliminates costs associated with packaging, manufacturing, and pressing. It also does away with the percentage of revenue taken by distributors and potentially broadens the number of consumers who pass through a "store" or storefront to purchase products.

On the other hand, if everyone puts products on the Internet or some other online service, the system will be flooded with titles. Consumers will have to wade through third tier product to find quality products, and at some point, consumers might not choose to devote the time and energy to sorting through this information. It is easier to let someone, like a retailer or a publisher, play the role of gatekeeper and find quality.

In addition, "no one has figured out yet how to make money from the system," says Garry Hare, president of Fathom Pictures.

"I'm skeptical. No one has shown me how companies will make money online," says Hare. "To make money, you need frequent usage by users. You also need to solve the security problem for transactions to occur."

To plan for the future markets, Hare is instead developing interactive titles that he thinks will be appropriate for the interactive TV market. If something like this medium ever develops, he will have a shelf of content ready to go.

Nobody really knows what role electronic distribution will play in the future. But with *Doom* as a proven model of success and the popularity of multiplayer games, many other small developers who cannot find space on the physical retail shelf will try the *Doom* approach. For a while, it might work. But developers recommend devoting time and effort to establishing a relationship with a distributor so that product can be found on the physical retail shelf.

There is a dark side to this form of distribution. Once a product goes online, it is extremely easy for users to copy and download (and infringe the copyright) without paying the developer or publisher. In 1993, Massachusetts Institute of Technology student David LaMacchia, set up a computer bulletin board on the Internet and copied software programs, such as the spreadsheet *Excel* and Maxis' *SimCity 2000*, allowing users to download for free. The government estimated that users copied over $1 million worth of software. The federal government charged LaMacchia with wire fraud, alleging that the transmission of software over a computer network constituted a scheme or artifice to defraud, or for obtaining money or property by false or fraudulent pretenses.

Most likely, the government would have preferred to charge LaMacchia with violating the criminal provision of the Copyright Act. But under that law, LaMacchia must have infringed the copyright willfully and for purpose of commercial advantage or private financial gain.

The case was dismissed because the government lacked evidence that LaMacchia financially benefited from his actions—he allowed users to download the software for free. The judge commented that the software makers could sue for civil copyright violations. Until a pay per game or a monthly subscriber system is set up, developers and publishers are likely to lose money with copy-cat LaMacchia schemes.

DERIVATIVE OR ANCILLARY PRODUCTS

Last year, the Miller brothers, creators of *Myst*, signed a $1 million contract with Hyperion, a publishing subsidary of Disney, which acquired the rights to three novels based on the CD-ROM title. Meanwhile, movie rights are being shopped by Harvey Harrison at the Jim Preminger Agency in West Los Angeles.

"It's almost silly how much attention *Myst* has received," says Robyn Miller. "We knew it was good, but we're the creators. To see everyone else agreeing with us was astonishing."

The popular title *Mortal Kombat* has also resulted in a flurry of spin-offs, including a line of Hasbro Inc. toys, a home video, comic books, a live arena tour, and a $30 million movie from Turner Broadcasting System Inc.'s New Line Cinema.

In the past, the contracts that publishers made with developers included a fairly generous royalty for ancillary products, items such as T-shirts, books, movies, TV cartoon shows, and other consumer products that were created from the original multimedia product. This higher royalty rate seemed to make sense. In the movie and book publishing industry, for instance, sometimes the merchandising generated from a movie or book character results in more revenue than the film itself.

After several years of paying high royalty rates to developers, publishers found that they were losing money on ancillary deals and changed their financing models. Software publishers have concluded that a great deal of initial time should be spent considering different industries' business models and carefully tailoring contracts to cover all possible contingencies.

Publishers no longer view the ability to license a product's character or plot line for an ancillary product as a source of revenue. Instead, it is much more common for publishers to view this opportunity as a partnership, designed to generate advertising and exposure for the underlying CD-ROM product. As a result, publishers are more willing to agree to skinnier deals with traditional media companies and to use their own resources to make the partnership happen. This outlook also means that royalty rates for ancillary products will tend to be much less.

ONE EDUTAINMENT PUBLISHER'S 1993 NUMBERS

Here is one edutainment publisher's financials for 1993. While these numbers are somewhat dated, they illustrate a phenomenon that is still fairly common in 1995: for most edutainment developers, it is critical to secure a bundling arrangement, since retail sales are unlikely to provide enough revenue to break even. In this example, the development costs for the edutainment product amounted to $300,000.

From retail outlets, the edutainment publisher sold, on average, 20,000 units. This publisher was involved in an affiliate label program with another publisher who distributed the edutainment company's titles. As a result, the edutainment publisher gave up 35 percent of the wholesale price to the distributor for distribution as well as some marketing. After deducting development costs, the revenue per title came to $4.48. Consequently, the total amount earned from retail sales was $88,000. The company set up a direct mail system and for each title, it sold, on average 5,000 units at $25 each. Total revenue from direct mail came to $50,000 for each product.

Without bundling deals, this particular title would have put the company deeper in the hole. The company bundled 250,000 units at $1 per unit for a total of $250,000, thus recovering its costs, plus earning a small profit.

---

1. *New York Times*, November 27, 1994.
2. Nicholas Donatiello, president of Odyssey Inc., a market research company in San Francisco.
3. *Time*, December 19, 1994, p. 58.
4. Department of Education.
5. Apple Computer Inc. interview.
6. Apple Computer Inc. interview.
7. See appendix for a list of conferences
8. *Wall Street Journal*, February 27, 1995.
9. *San Francisco Examiner*, August 21, 1994.
10. Fran Maier, director of marketing at Match.Com Online Personals.
11. *Business Week*, August 1, 1994.
12. *San Francisco Examiner*, August 21, 1994, B-6.
13. *The Dallas Morning News*, February 11, 1995.

CHAPTER FIVE

FINDING MONEY: LOVE MONEY, ANGELS, AND VENTURE CAPITALISTS

Unlike floppy-based entertainment software, consumer-oriented CD-ROM multimedia products require so many inputs—video, animation, text, photos, graphics, sound, music, and computer programming—that there are a variety of different ways for an individual to become involved in the industry.

Depending on the level of commitment and entry point, the initial capitalization requirements range from zero to several million dollars. With their skills, artists, animators, video producers, graphic artists, writers, software programmers, and photographers are all in demand and can readily become involved in multimedia as independent contractors or employees in someone else's multimedia company.

The minimum requirements for a multimedia development company are about people—the talent, business skills, and relationships that one can gather to make a compelling product.

WORK FOR AN EXISTING COMPANY

"Money isn't the issue upfront," says Andrew Nelson, co-owner of CyberFlix, the Knoxville based publisher and maker of *Lunicus*, *Jump Raven*, *Skull*, and *Dust*. "More importantly, you need technological know-how, talent, and drive. If you don't have mastery over the technology, you can't show people how talented you are and you can't raise money."

Vortex Media Arts, a developer in Los Angeles with thirty employees, offers its employees stock in the company.

"By giving employees ownership, they see that they can directly benefit from all of their hard work," says Rick Giolito, vice president of business development at Vortex. "There are people here that make more money than the owners. As a founder of the company, you need to keep the long-term vision in mind. You're going to make your money when a larger company invests in you or buys you or you have a hit."

In agreement is Steve Nelson, founder of San Francisco-based Brilliant Media who created *Xploral: Secret World*, an interactive CD-ROM package co-produced with Peter Gabriel's Real World Multimedia. "You need talent, persistence, and a coherent vision," says Nelson.

Steve Nelson started out in 1991 as a one-man production company and brought on board three others as independent contractors to create *Xploral*. In 1994, Nelson formed a core group of six employees, similar to a movie production house. For particular projects, he hires other talent as independent contractors.

"I want a core team of talented people who understand the production process," says Nelson. "Most companies break down because they don't do the planning and production that is needed. They think that in a couple of months, the company can turn out a CD-ROM. If you look at a movie studio, you see specialized people and processes that have been built up over the years. This same sort of structure hasn't been sorted out yet in the interactive industry, but it eventually will have to. It's what we are doing. The sooner you can get really talented people on board, the better."

Because the industry is still new, many people want to get in and learn the business. They are willing to work for a reduced salary in exchange for equity. With this core group of talented people, developers approach an established publisher—a Sanctuary Woods, Electronic Arts, or Brøderbund—and sign a developers' contract to create titles.

"Not long ago, the technical capabilities meant that products couldn't be that deep," says Ruth Kennedy at Electronic Arts. "Now, we need artists who use pen and paper, people with special animation skills, software engineers, and musicians. The range of expertise that is required to make CD-ROM titles is so much broader that it's unusual to find one person or even two who can do it all. Multimedia is a whole new market for a lot of different people with artistic and programming skills."

The San Francisco newspapers and online bulletin boards list advertisements for positions available in multimedia. The going price for a script is anywhere from $20,000 to $30,000 and higher for a completed script. Though that amount is less than a movie script, the prices are increasing each year. Carolyn Miller, a children's TV writer, for instance, wrote the best selling interactive computer geography game for Brøderbund, *Where in the USA is Carmen Sandiego*.

The Bay Area Multimedia Technology Alliance lists openings in multimedia on the Internet at http//mlds-www.arc.nasa.gov/form. Then select BAMTA. Students and others visit the colorful Monster Board on the Internet at http//www.monster.com/.

Another way of becoming involved in the industry is through your preexisting content.

"Two of my clients have developed characters, and they are getting by in the multimedia industry with almost no money tied up in the project," says Carolyn Mead, a San Francisco-based multimedia lawyer. "All they need is a nondisclosure agreement and contacts."

Children's or adult book authors who own the copyright to compelling stories, characters, or drawings are licensing their work to multimedia developers and receiving lump sum payments and/or royalties. Animators, who had been creating animation for corporate clients, are finding a new outlet for their work in multimedia. Musicians are licensing their songs. For content holders, the initial cost to entering the multimedia industry is primarily administrative—finding the right developer or publisher with whom to enter a licensing agreement or the right go-between to create the relationship to the publishing company.

The most common place to meet developers is at the many trade shows, such as MacWorld Expo, Comdex, Electronic Entertainment Expo or the Software Publishers Association conferences. Nonprofit trade organizations have popped up around the country to service the multimedia industry and these groups usually have job listings. The talent agencies such as William Morris and literary agencies such as Lazear Agency in Minneapolis, have been seeking opportunities in the CD-ROM industry. For instance, Jonathon Lazear represented novelist R. D. Zimmerman, who is writing a series of "solve-it-yourself" mysteries to be published both as books and as interactive CD-ROMs. He also represented the author who is writing three books based on the CD-ROM title *Myst*. Lawyers and investment bankers who specialize in this area also are serving as quasi-agents, helping to put together these relationships.

If you are really new to the industry, the advice from developers is to work for an established multimedia publisher before setting up your own company.

"If you have to start in the mailroom at Sanctuary Woods or any company to get in the door, do it," says Steven Rappaport, founder of San Francisco based Digital Trivia, Inc. and developer of *Radio Active*. "Find a company whose philosophy is attuned to where you're at and discover what you have while you're there."

FINANCING FOR A MULTIMEDIA DEVELOPMENT COMPANY

The financial picture dramatically changes when the goal is to form a company to develop multimedia products. For the new developer, the amount of time and energy spent locating and securing pockets of money to keep the company alive is on par with creating a compelling product.

The need for a large amount of funding is partly because of the increasing costs for development of consumer-oriented titles. According to industry experts, in 1993 the median development costs ranged from $100,000 to $400,000 for consumer-oriented entertainment titles. In 1994, that range increased to $250,000 to $750,000. In 1996, $1 million dollar budgets will be much more common, with matching marketing budgets. The development costs for education and edutainment titles are slightly less than the $250,00 to $750,000 range, but are also increasing. (See chapter 2, under Overall Development Budget for more information about the costs of developing multimedia.)

In this chapter, developers talk about the different sources of capital they have found, including friends and family, "angels," venture capital, and strategic alliances.

LOVE MONEY

Substance Interactive Media Inc., a San Francisco company that creates the CD-ROM-based magazine *substance.digizine* represents a fairly common model of developing multimedia by survival, sacrifice, and sheer will power.

Formed in 1992, none of the four partners—who are in their twenties—are "techies." The president of the company, Alex Ragland, is a former English major and earned an MBA from UCLA; Nick Roberts is a former journalism student; Ed Bellinaso is a musician; and Rob Winfield is a graduate student in film.

In 1992, while the riots raged outside their Westwood apartment after the Rodney King verdict, Ragland and Roberts got sick of watching TV sitcoms and listening to the radio and decided to create something new.

They gathered all their computer equipment and crammed it into Roberts' bedroom, leaving Roberts' closet as the only space for his bed. They began to analyze the technology and to piece together what they had conceived of that night during the riots: an electronic magazine for Generation X.

The two wrote a business plan and consulted with Dr. Robert Winter, a music professor at UCLA who helped create titles about Beethoven and Stravinsky for Microsoft, *Multimedia Beethoven: The Ninth Symphony* and *Multimedia Stravinsky: The Rite of Spring*. Roberts and Ragland joined with Ed Bellinaso and Winfield and created a prototype of the magazine. The four partners moved to a San Francisco warehouse, so they could more easily get the technical support they needed from MacroMedia, the company that developed Authorware Professional, the software that Substance hoped to use. With little money, they launched into what would become an overriding theme of their company: hard-headed bargaining.

They convinced their landlord to give them three months of free rent and then converted the second floor of the warehouse into their living space. They built a bathroom and make-shift kitchen, hanging white sheets to serve as walls and separate the space into four bedrooms.

Between the four of them, they scraped together the initial funding for the company, roughly $10,000. It was barely enough to put down the security deposit for the rent—roughly $2,600 a month—put in some phone lines, design and print a press kit, buy a used laser printer for $150, and set up desks for the office. They used two computers that they already owned, two 33 MHz 486 Intel computers with eight MB of RAM and fifteen inch monitors. Bellinaso, the musician, had some of his own equipment to create and record background music for the product.

But they needed a scanner ($1,000), a CD-ROM player ($500), more computers and Authorware Professional software. They also needed to find a way to cover the cost of each issue of the magazine, which was roughly $50,000.

To fill in the gaps in technology, they got on the phone and the fax machine and started soliciting equipment donations. Part of the allure, which turned out to be a selling point at the time, was that they were creating the magazine on a Windows PC platform rather than a Macintosh, the platform that most other developers had chosen. In return for equipment donations, the Substance team promised the companies' names and logos inside the publication. Almost immediately, the large companies stepped up. Epson donated a computer. Logitech chipped in a handheld scanner. Then Epson donated a scanner. Chinon America gave Substance a CD-ROM player. Adobe donated software; so did Microsoft. Ragland called Tele Spectrum, an educational company and was able to purchase Macromedia's Authorware Professional software at a discount, for $1,000 versus $5,000. Eventually, with letter writing, phone calls, begging, and subtle threats, they rounded up thirty donors and $150,000 worth of equipment. The last equipment donation came when Gateway 2000 called and gave them eight computers.

"When people come into our warehouse and see how hard we are working and how we are living, it's amazing how much people want to chip in and help out," says Ragland.

That dedication also led to free professional help, with Copithorne & Bellows providing pro bono PR work, and the law firm Jackson, Tufts, Cole & Black taking on the company's legal work—incorporation papers, distribution agreements, nondisclosure agreements, and licensing—also as a pro bono effort.

To further help the bottom line, Substance bootstrapped their operations by doing multimedia or database work for corporations, such as S3, a chip manufacturer. S3 needed a presentation for the 1993 Comdex convention and called on Substance to put something together. Substance, always on the lookout for an opportunity, developed a demo of their digital magazine for S3's presentation, which created a buzz at Comdex and a couple write-ups in trade magazines. It also drew the interest of possible distributors, including Sony Imagesoft, a division of Sony Electronic Publishing. After nearly two years without paying themselves, Substance Interactive received the adrenaline rush it needed to sustain its operations when—after seven months of negotiations that followed Comdex—it closed a distribution deal with Sony.

Substance gave Sony an exclusive license to distribute and market the magazine for two years in North America. The terms of the deal give Sony 85 percent of the net wholesale price on retail sales, with Substance receiving 85 percent of any revenue generated from selling advertisements for the product. For the demo version, Substance sold $10,000 worth of ads and hopes to sell $100,000 per issue. Ten megabytes of ad space costs $6,000, with a maximum purchase of 15 megabytes for $11,000. The product retails for $29.95. For closing the deal, Sony gave Substance an advance and agreed to devote 10 percent of revenue to promotional efforts. Substance is responsible for soliciting and fulfilling subscriptions, with 15 percent of this revenue going to Sony. "This is not a one shot deal, but a marriage for two years," says Alex Ragland. "It requires more of their manpower to market and distribute four titles a year."

By early 1995, however, a confluence of events led to the dissolution of Substance. Ragland attributes the company's demise primarily to poor sales.

"There's so many products on the shelf and the retailers demand guaranteed margins," says Ragland. "The bottom line was that the market for an electronic magazine wasn't mature enough and we didn't receive the revenue to sustain our operations." In hindsight, Ragland speculates that if the company had hired someone to exclusively sell advertising for the magazine, he would still be in business.

"If we could have brought in $50,000 to $100,000 in ads per issue, we would still be here," says Ragland.

Love money—money from friends, family, and co-owners—is the most common source of initial capitalization for the small developer. The founders bootstrap the company by using their personal resources—mortgaging one's house, tapping into savings, credit cards, or cashing in stock options—to take the company to a stage where it can attract outside financing.

In a 1994 Multimedia Development Group survey, 43 percent of multimedia developers reported using their own funds or private funding sources for support. The founders of Substance Interactive are testimony to what can be accomplished with a little bit of money, a lot of perseverance and survival instincts.

Jim Moore, a retired airline pilot in Pennsylvania, used his home as collateral to help a niece start her multimedia company, Westwind Media. Pop Rocket started by depleting their bank accounts and their relatives' savings.

The developers who have more computer experience tend to supplement their budgets by doing computer-related work for corporate clients. Mondo Media in San Francisco originally developed corporate multimedia projects for companies such as Prodigy, Compaq, Intel, and Microsoft, and used the contract experience and infrastructure as a springboard to develop the CD-ROM titles *Critical Path* and *The Daedalus Encounter* under the developer name, Mechadeus. Both companies remain independent entities serving different needs.

"Providing services on a contract basis is a steady cash flow builder, and the pursuit of an original product concept from a service provider is a common model in many high-technology business," says Timothy McNally, CFO of Mechadeus. "The service business provides a cash flow that supports development of original products, where the product developer must invest well ahead of the time when he receives revenue for that product."

Drew Huffman, founder of Drew Pictures, which developed *Iron Helix* followed the "service work" model by using the $60,000 worth of new equipment that he had accumulated while doing projects for CNN to create his first title. He and three other developers completed $70,000 worth of work for corporations in a two month period to help fund the development of the title. Then in August 1992, Huffman raised nearly $200,000 from five of his best friends from college, his brother, and a Chicago venture capitalist. "There's a lot of different ways to get started," says Huffman. "If you are willing to knock yourself out, and not pay yourself until the end and just pay rent and bills, a couple of hundred thousand dollars goes a long way."

That amount is roughly the start-up funding that Bill Appleton contributed to found the publishing company, CyberFlix in Tennessee and build the company's first title *Lunicus*. With the revenues from this title, the CyberFlix creative team spent hours in Appleton's basement producing the prototype for their second title *Jump Raven*. Founders of San Francisco-based Eden Interactive used their own money, bartering skills and Visa, Mastercard, and American Express to create *Greg LeMond's Bicycle Adventure*, which cost $150,000 in soft and hard dollars in development costs.

"How much does someone need to get started? That's a very difficult question to answer. It's not a set amount. You need a combination of business background, money, credit cards, and the ability to negotiate great deals," says Minoo Saboori, co founder of Eden Interactive. There is as much flexibility in the budget as there are creative ways to save money.

To help their cash flow, for instance, Eden Interactive leases rather than purchases their computers and other equipment.

"We lease all of our equipment because technology becomes obsolete the first day it's issued," says Saboori. "It makes sense to lease rather than buy if you're a small developer who wants to be using the state-of-the-art technology. When you lease, you can turn it in after a while and get the next model."

Overall, Eden pays a premium to lease rather than own, but Saboori justifies the extra cost by the additional control the company gains over cash flow.

"You are not putting out at one time $10,000 to $15,000 to have a computer on your desk," says Saboori. "That's a lot of money for a small developer."

Almost every small developer has a tale to tell about the methods she has found to reduce costs, bargain for a better deal, or pay less rent. Even the well-known creators of the adult adventure game *Myst* started out humbly, in a rural town outside the city of Spokane, Washington.

The Makers of Myst

"I was working at a bank, and Robyn and I were creating children's software in our spare time," says Rand Miller from his Spokane home and headquarters of his company, Cyan, Inc. "We used our own money to get started, and because we worked out of our garage, we didn't need a large investment in the beginning." Money was tight, anyway. Rand, his wife, Debbie, and their three daughters relied on WIC, the government funded food program for Women, Infants, and Children to help pay for meals.

With the success of their children's titles, *Cosmic Osmo and the World Beyond the Mackeral* and *The Manhole*, distributed by Brøderbund Software Inc. (previously distributed by Activision), both brothers were able to work full-time on the development of new software products. They also attracted the attention of a Japanese-based company, Sunsoft Corporation of Aichi, which focuses primarily on consumer cartridge-based games. Sunsoft approached the Miller brothers and negotiated a deal to purchase the rights to localize the Miller's children's software for the Japanese market. After the deal closed, the Miller brothers presented to Sunsoft the idea for a large scale CD-ROM title for adults. Nobody had ever done what they were proposing, and no one was quite sure if adults would buy such a product. Sunsoft, however, was willing to fund the product, which the Miller brothers called *Myst*.

For $350,000 in development money, Sunsoft obtained the rights and royalty stream generated by the cartridge-based version of *Myst*. Sunsoft of America has since given Acclaim Entertainment, Inc. the exclusive

North American rights to publish *Myst* for Sega's forthcoming Saturn system. The Miller brothers retained the rights to the Macintosh and PC version. With the help of independent contractors, Robyn Miller created the art—over 2,500 images produced on the computer—and Rand Miller programmed the adventure game.

Because *Myst* was their first adult adventure title, however, they underestimated the resources it required to finish the project.

"This amount of money turned out to be about half of what we needed," says Rand Miller. "It cost more like $700,000 to complete it because it took two years and it included so many pictures. We thought it would have taken a year and we also miscalculated the size of the product. We thought it would be half as big as it turned out to be."

Rather than give up more rights to Sunsoft, the brothers kicked in $350,000. With a finished product, the Miller brothers went to Brøderbund and entered into a developer/publisher agreement, whereby Brøderbund agreed to distribute and market the title.

"It isn't an affiliate label arrangement because we didn't want to do the marketing," says Rand Miller. "And it isn't a straight development agreement because Cyan, Inc. did not receive development funding from Brøderbund. For that reason, we get a higher royalty rate."

The second critical requirement for a developer is a relationship with a publisher who has or has access to distribution muscle. (See chapter 6, Affiliate Label Program" and "Developer/Publisher Agreement). In this relationship, a developer often finds a funding source for the development of titles.

"A relationship with a significant publisher can bring lots of things to the developer," says Ruth Kennedy of Electronic Arts. "In addition to the distribution component, a relationship can bring development tools, computers, advance money, and artistic talent."

While developers say that a healthy amount of financing is not among the minimum criteria to start a development company, few independent developers would reject it.

"Get everything you can because it makes all the difference in the world," says Steve Nelson. Nelson provided the upfront funding, approximately $100,000, to start his company, Brilliant Media. "Strong financial backing positions the company as a force to be reckoned with. It will decide whether you get to do your own things versus creating projects on a work-for-hire basis, in which you are constantly seeking the next project."

THE PROVIDERS OF DEVELOPMENT AGREEMENTS

After its hit title *Way of the Warrior* for the 3DO Multiplayer, the game developer Naughty Dog Inc. landed a deal with Universal Interactive Studios in which Universal purchased the right to a "first-look" at products produced by the developer. After the developer has gotten off the ground and produced a first title or a working prototype, a demonstration of the product, or—more rarely—a script, the trend has been for a developer to seek a development contract, also called a "work-made-for-hire" arrangement, with an established software publisher or movie studio that has entered the multimedia market. For instance, in addition to its three hundred people who work internally to create products, Virgin Interactive, with offices in Irvine, California, Las Vegas, and the United Kingdom, develops 60 percent of its titles through outside developers.

With a development contract in hand, a small developer with few resources can team with a bigger company and receive development funding and artistic resources. Unfortunately, much of the revenue stream generated from the final product is given to the publisher in a development contract (anywhere from 75 percent to 85 percent of wholesale price). In response, most developers seek to produce several titles so that eventually a royalty stream can be used to self-fund a product.

"There are several ways to succeed in the industry as a developer, one of which is to do multiple titles quickly," says Garry Hare, president of Fathom Pictures in Sausalito. "You can't make money with one title. You can't pay yourself or your overhead. You want three to seven titles to get a royalty stream and save some money so that you will have enough of your own capital to do a title on your own." Hare, whose company now has twelve CD-ROM–based products, says that these dozen titles are generating several hundred thousand dollars a year in royalties. "That money is being used to make a title or so on our own nickel," says Hare. "That's the way we are getting ahead and attracting more financing from outside investors."

Whether you work with a publisher or a movie studio depends on your own strengths because the two financing sources offer different resources. Developers who sign with an established publisher, like an Electronic Arts or Brøderbund, tap into the publishers' established distribution channels, sophisticated technologies, understanding of game theory, and experience delivering interactive entertainment. The developers who sign with a movie studio for funding gain access to sophisticated marketing expertise, and recognizable film and video properties. The movie studios also have access to 3D talent, post production people, special effects artists, and financiers.

For instance, CyberFlix has used some of the properties owned by its distributor, Paramount, to produce new CD-ROM titles based on TV shows. Although this approach of using preexisting content to create titles is a departure from its normal twitch-action games, it is a way to further the relationship and tap into other content that they might like to use for their own future titles.

Whether you are planning to approach a software publishing company or a movie studio, a small developer needs to be fairly far along with her title idea.

"A good script and a well-thought out concept is pretty fundamental if a publisher doesn't yet have a relationship with the developer," says Ruth Kennedy of Electronic Arts. "Ideally, you want a portfolio of your work. If you're an artist, you wouldn't show up without your art, even if it's never been sold out of a gallery. The same holds for multimedia developers. You'd show up with your demo or prototype."

When approaching a publisher about distribution, the 1994 Multimedia Development Group survey found that a developer who only had a written proposal of the product received a much lower royalty rate, often less than 5 percent of wholesale price. If the developer was close to the conclusion of a product, and the request for funding included a prototype that was more than 50 percent completed, the royalties tended to be over 11 percent.

"If you've developed characters, draw them out, name them and do a first draft of the script," says Kennedy. "Show us what you've got."

Hollywood

Hollywood, eager to be a major force in the multimedia industry, is a significant source of development contracts, particularly if the developer brings software programming and game designing skills to the deal, two critical components of multimedia that Hollywood lacks.

In a development agreement, the studio usually is the copyright owner of the final product. Generally a seasoned developer can negotiate and keep the rights to other platforms, and all developers should be able to retain the copyright ownership rights to preexisting intellectual property, such as software engines and interfaces.

In the past, many of these work-for-hire arrangements involved the developer tapping into the studio's preexisting content—its movies or TV shows—and producing titles. Increasingly, studios are using their own intellectual property to create multimedia titles and so there are fewer opportunities for outside developers to license preexisting content held by the studios.

"Compared to 1992 and 1993, there's a lot less licensing going on with the studios," says Mitch Lasky with The Walt Disney Company. "Now that we have our own interactive division, we are not so quick to let our intellectual property slip out."

Nonetheless, licensing arrangements to use the studios' content still occur. In such a situation, commonly called "outbound licenses," the studio licenses its content to a developer in exchange for an advance against royalties. The developer is responsible for funding the development, although the developer might be able to negotiate some funding from the studio.

MCA/Universal, for instance, has tried to create a diverse multimedia product line using its own studio properties. The same is true for other studios.

"We're trolling in Marin County. We're trolling in nooks and crannies in San Francisco. We're trolling L.A., and we're trolling in Manhattan," says Edward D. Horowitz, CEO of Viacom's New Media and Interactive Television Group. "We're being bombarded by ideas. That's good because no one has the right answer. This is still a cottage industry."

The Hollywood Players

According to Lasky of The Walt Disney Company, the following studios are considered "players" in the interactive multimedia industry:

- Time-Warner ranks number one in terms of experience with interactive multimedia and has the broadest title list.
- MCA/Universal has focused its financial resources on developing titles for the 3DO platform. MCA owns a significant interest in The 3DO Company.
- Disney is interested in the industry and is trying to use its movie titles and advanced animation technology to create new multimedia titles.
- Sony's Electronic Publishing division is also looking into its vault of content and producing titles, such as the slow selling *Last Action Hero,* and is preparing for its new PSX or "Sony Playstation" platform.
- Viacom purchased Paramount's interactive unit and has recently formed an interactive division of its MTV cable channel.
- Twentieth Century Fox has a Fox Interactive division with several cartridge games in production.
- MGM made a well publicized deal with Sega to jump-start its involvement in interactive multimedia.

While Time-Warner and Sony have strong internal development programs, most other studios rely on outside developers. In comparison to software publishing companies like Electronic Arts and Mindscape, studios have a much lower percentage of internal development: less than 10 percent versus 25–60 percent in interactive multimedia publishing companies.

Consumer-Oriented Software Publishers

While consumer-oriented software publishers create more titles in-house, there are still opportunities for talented third party developers. The publishers offer years of experience fiddling with interactivity, game theory, and interactive game play, in an attempt to define what makes this medium different from traditional media. In addition, many of these publishers have set up very effective distribution channels to distribute their own titles. However, to make these pipelines cost effective, they need many products flowing through them. Publishers turn to outside developers to increase the flow of product.

Sanctuary Woods, for instance, broke off its affiliate label arrangement with Electronic Arts and has embarked on an ambitious effort to create its own distribution system and expand its list of titles beyond edutainment.

"We've changed our model," says Scott Walchek. "We're concentrating on the core gamer."

In 1994, roughly 70 percent of its titles were in the category of children's education. By paying for the creation of outside developer's titles (see deal structures below) or by contracting with developers to create titles that Sanctuary Woods suggests (see below), the company hopes to reduce the percentage of children's educational titles to 50 percent.

Almost every major publisher has work-made-for-hire arrangements with outside developers. Some of these publishers include: Maxis in Orinda, California, Electronic Arts in San Mateo, Brøderbund in Novato, Spectrum HoloByte in Alameda, Mindscape in Novato (formerly Software Toolworks), IVI Publishing Inc. in Minneapolis, GTE Interactive, and Compton's NewMedia. Other companies with proprietary platforms, such as 3DO, the Sega Saturn, and Sony PSX, are also sources of work-made-for-hire arrangements, hoping to create enough compelling titles for the platforms to convince users to purchase their hardware. Many hardware companies, such as Creative Labs, have started their own software publishing groups and are funding titles to help promote their hardware products.

Companies Involved in the Information Superhighway

Partners who have given financial assistance to new multimedia developers come from all the different industries that are fighting for a place in the new telecommunications world. Large companies—telephone, cable, movie studios, software giants, online providers, and book publishing houses—are hedging their bets through alliances, which often result in funding for the small multimedia developer.

Most of the recent joint ventures and strategic affiliations can be classified into two categories: an alliance between two or more industry leaders in the infrastructure, such as enabling technology and content providing companies; or a union between one of these industry leaders and an entrepreneurial company, such as a multimedia developer, who has artistic talent or creative engineering.

If the joint venture or alliance involves an exchange of equity, multimedia developers usually receive more money for their company from a corporate partner versus a venture capitalist because of the additional, often intangible value for both parties in this relationship.

WORK-MADE-FOR-HIRE DEVELOPMENT CONTRACTS

Two arrangements are commonly used when a movie studio or software publisher decides to fund the external development of a title. Both of these models are considered work-made-for-hire transactions, which means that the studio or publisher owns the copyright in the final product and receives the bulk of the revenues from sales. For more detailed information about development agreements, read chapter 7, under Key Provisions in a Standard Development Agreement.

MODEL ONE: "THE NO PROFIT MODEL." The studio or publisher pays for the direct costs of development, a pre-determined profit—10–12 percent—and an agreed upon allocation for overhead. In return, the studio receives the gold master disk and owns the copyright to the final product, which includes the right to distribute the product, port to different platforms, and create ancillary or derivative products.

"Developers hate this model," says Lasky of Walt Disney. "There's no incentive to produce a great game. They make it, and turn it over to the studio. As long as the studio approves it, then they get paid. But they don't participate in any retail sales revenue." Model two is used more often, because it includes some "pride incentives." If the product does well, the developer receives a royalty payment.

MODEL TWO: "ADVANCE AGAINST ROYALTIES MODEL." The studio gives an advance to the developer for the creation of a title. The advance is recoupable against a future royalty stream. Advances typically cover the cost of development and can go as high as $1.5 million. Royalty rates range from 7.5 percent to 25 percent of net wholesale revenue. When the advance is recouped by the studio, the developer begins to earn quarterly or semi-annual royalty payments.

In both model one and two, the studio or publisher will negotiate for the copyright ownership to the final product so that it has control over all aspects of the title, including the creation of the title, porting to different platforms, and distribution of the final product. Every piece of the title must be approved by the publisher—the script, the technical design document, and the content. To the extent creative differences between the publisher and developer emerge that cannot be sorted out, the publisher generally has the last word.

Developers caution against getting squeezed by the publisher who might pay royalties, not on net wholesale price, but on that figure less some of its own costs, such as overhead, salaries, and marketing expenses. The resulting royalty basis may be so slim that almost no royalties are received.

Hybrid deals have emerged from these two models, and developers with clout and experience have been able to negotiate the copyright ownership to other platforms, the right to find other distributors to service other geographic areas, and higher royalty rates. One well-known developer stabilized its finances by negotiating a royalty rate that increased in conjunction with an increase in the number of units sold. Because Hollywood is in need of programming tools and technology, developers have also been able to license rather than transfer copyright ownership of the developer's tools to the studio.

"We get a little more than the average royalty rate because we guarantee our budgets," says Garry Hare, president of Fathom Pictures. "Because of that, there is less risk for the publisher." Hare says that a 5 percent royalty figure is pretty cheap. Fifteen percent is a high average. Fathom Pictures typically receives 20 percent.

"But there are always exceptions," says Hare. "We just finished a project in which we get 25 percent of net wholesale price."

ADVANCES

Despite the public's excitement about the industry and the flow of creative juices among developers, the financial picture for most developers is bleak. Many developers never see a royalty stream because the advance was so large, and the development agreement required that the advance be recouped based on the royalty rate before royalties are earned.

"As an independent developer without outside financing, the current model of advance against royalties is one that does not work," says Rick Giolito, vice president of business development for Vortex Media Arts in Burbank, California, which formed in 1993 from a merger between Strategic Visions (established in 1991) and Lil' Gangster. "What happens is that the publisher, who has taken the financial risk, is allowed to make back the original investment plus profits before the developer sees a dime. There is no revenue sharing going on."

Giolito says that the advance against royalties model is a natural outcome of the garage developer phenomenon in which publishers deal with developers who work out of houses or basements. Publishers are reluctant to dole out large amounts of money to what appear to be unstable development companies. Over time software publishers have found that they make more money distributing and selling software than developing it, says Giolito. "This is why you have a multitude of entertainment titles done outside the publishing companies," says Giolito. "It's too expensive to do it all in-house."

In a hit driven industry, developers are only as good as their last title. As a developer builds a track record for creating popular titles, she can eventually negotiate a better financial picture by modifying or eliminating the recoupment requirement. "The way a developer makes money in multimedia is to become an indispensable resource to the community of publishers," says Giolito, whose development company creates titles for Time-Warner Interactive, EA/ABC Home Software, Electronic Arts, and Hasbro. "Then they can't help but invest or buy your company to protect their product resource. That's the model for us. We bootstrap it until we become so important to publishers or outside investors that they will want to come in and invest or purchase us."

To make the company irreplaceable to publishers, Strategic Visions, Inc. and Lil' Gangster Entertainment merged in October 1993 to become Vortex Media Arts. Strategic Visions was a game design and programming company and Lil' Gangster was an art and animation company. Together, the two companies thought they would be much stronger and have more to offer publishers.

Giolito's plans for the future are confirmed by big industry players who are hungry for strong, proven development talent. "If someone does a good title, we will try and get the rights of first refusal or a straight exclusivity deal for the next title," says Mitch Lasky with Walt Disney.

Until some investor bites, however, Giolito negotiates "step deals," in which he tries to eliminate or lower the recoupment rate and tie royalty rates to unit sales.

"This structure gives us the incentive to do really great titles," says Giolito.

Unfortunately, the developer will not receive a large advance without a reputation or track record for producing quality work. In the 1994 Multimedia Development Group survey, 40 percent of companies receiving cash advances got less than a $25,000 advance. Only 22 percent received over $100,000 as an advance. About half of the "experienced" developers who have more than two products on the market received $50,000 or more as advances against royalties or for a buyout, while only one-third of the novices received advances of this size. Over half (66 percent) of the novice developers received less than $25,000 as an advance.

When asking for your advance, developers recommend considering all possible costs.

"When calculating its funding needs, the developer should consider the full costs of development. In addition to the direct costs of programmers and artists, the developer needs to have a plan for funding the other costs of running the company, such as rent, management salaries, equipment, insurance, taxes, and legal fees," says Timothy McNally, CFO for

Mechadeus. "Be careful when budgeting for titles that you truly understand the hidden costs. Another important consideration is cash flow; you must plan for the timing of the payments for development in order to avoid strains on the company's cash."

CORPORATE ALLIANCES AND JOINT VENTURES

"None of us wanted to work for 'The Man,'" says Alex Ragland, explaining how the four twenty-somethings who are putting together *substance.digizine* initially decided to forgo luxury, normal food, and a regular living space to form their own company. But two years of bunk bedding gets tiresome and eventually "we found out, we needed help from 'The Man' to get where we wanted to go," says Ragland.

The Multimedia Development Group's 1994 survey found that 48 percent of the funding for product development came from outside or third party sources. Financial participation from corporate partners includes upfront cash advances and back-end royalty payments as a percentage of the wholesale price.

Corporate alliances can provide the financing to help get a company moving to the next stage of growth. But Ragland's view of the "Man" encapsulates a very real tension underlying many of these corporate alliances. The garage multimedia developers often view an affiliation with a large company, especially the movie studios that are new to the multimedia industry and lack experience with the videogame market, as an unpleasant necessity to get to where the small company wants to go. Many of the small creators of multimedia got into the industry because they wanted to dictate their own work schedules, their creativity, and the placement of their final product.

"This is a unique time in history where people who are creative don't need to have some big conglomerate take their product to the box office and share in the proceeds," says Jim Myrick, who founded the San Francisco-based Big Top Productions with his brother John by tapping out their credit cards. The two brothers have created *Felix The Cat's Cartoon Toolbox*, which lets kids create their own animated cartoons and learn how cartoons and movies are constructed.

"It's like a rock band being able to put out their own records, or writing a novel and publishing it yourself. We don't need to wait around. We're the ones doing the magic part. We're the ones making the cool killer titles, and we're going to do it on our own."[1]

In this competitive environment, however, the small developer will increasingly need to turn to larger companies who want a stake in the industry for financing, as well as content and distribution capability.

"There's no way a small company can get to market right now without a big partner," says Julie Schwerin, president of InfoTech, a Woodstock, Vermont firm that tracks the multimedia industry. "Having a big partner also greases the skids for raising more money to keep the company growing."[2]

ANGELS

Angels are wealthy individuals or informal institutions that invest money in private companies on behalf of wealthy individuals. They fund the developer at both the early stages, when the developer only has a demo, as well as later in the process. Often the Angels are not as sophisticated as venture capitalists and therefore might invest in a company that fails some of the tests that a venture capitalist applies. Angels might also provide a higher valuation of the company, and therefore the original owners end up giving up less equity for financing.

Developers have turned to companies like Frost Capital Partners in San Francisco, which has relationships with groups of wealthy individual investors who invest in multimedia companies. Professional financiers have developed networks and know where these pockets of money exist.

DEALS FOR SELF-FUNDED TITLES

From the royalties earned from work-made-for-hire arrangements, developers typically save enough funds to finance part of the development of a title. They next approach a studio with a work-in progress and enter into another development agreement, which has more favorable terms, such as a higher royalty rate. After several years of creating titles, a developer might have enough money to self fund an entire title, which allows the developer to receive a greater percentage of the revenue stream. Garry Hare cautions, however, that a developer should self fund a title and shop it around only if the developer has acquired the skills and experience to create a great title.

"If you aren't any good at multimedia, you shouldn't go this route because you can't get distribution," says Hare. "I know many developers who raised a couple thousand dollars, made a title, and can't get it to market."

Developers who have the talent and the finances to fund their own titles typically find themselves in one of the following deal structures:

STRAIGHT ACQUISITION: The studio/publisher purchases the finished title for a lump sum and receives all rights to the title. Some developers have been able to negotiate for the right to participate in profits from reuses (derivative products) of the intellectual property in ancillary markets.

AFFILIATE LABEL PROGRAM: The most popular arrangement is a publisher's affiliate label program in which one software publisher distributes the products of another publisher for a fee. Under such a set-up, the developer funds the title through the gold master and provides the marketing. (Because the developer is funding the title, the developer would be considered a publisher. But to avoid confusion, the publisher is called a developer here.) The developer gives the affiliate label provider the exclusive right to distribute the product in a defined geographic area. The affiliate label publisher usually provides manufacturing services to stamp the title. The developer's royalty rate varies, from 60–75 percent of net wholesale price, depending on who pays for the cost of goods sold and the expertise of the developer.

The San Francisco-based multimedia publishing company, Luminaria followed this model. They paid the $700,000 for the development of their title *Wrath of the Gods*, the culmination of fifteen months of development work, grappling with a four-hundred page script, thousands of photos of Greece (three hundred of which serve as the game's background), and nonunion actors who appear in the game.

Originally, Joel Skidmore and Jeff Cretcher, the founders of the company, approached Orinda-based Maxis, a publisher with an affiliate label program, seeking a developer's agreement. (See chapter 6, under Key Provisions in a Standard Development Agreement, for more details.)

But Maxis' representatives explained that Luminaria could make more money if they provided their own development funding, and Maxis distributed the title. Moreover, under a developer/publisher distribution deal, any advance given to Luminaria to create the product would be recouped before Luminaria would receive any royalty stream. It could be many months before a $700,000 advance was earned back, and Skidmore doubted that his company could afford such a long wait.

After Skidmore ran the numbers, he agreed with the Maxis business people and opted for an affiliate label arrangement. Under this deal, Luminaria will receive anywhere from 60–75 percent of net wholesale price.

With a reputation for producing quality products, the developer may have a half dozen to a dozen titles to her name, some self-funded, some not. Studios and publishers start approaching the developer to create a title based on one of the studio's or publisher's own concepts or properties. Typically, in such a deal, called an "internal/external hybrid deal," an internal producer at Sanctuary Woods or Paramount guides the development of the title. The in-house producer is more inclined to approve milestones than give day-to-day direction to artists, programmers, and others to create the product. Developers are sought to do the entire title or pieces of it—the art, animation, or programming—with the studio or publisher putting together the finished product.

TRANSITION FROM A DEVELOPER TO A PUBLISHER

Arnowitz Studios in Sausalito, started in 1987 as a developer creating a series of educational titles for publishers such as Holt, Rhinehart & Winston and South Western. They also created a consumer title for Mindscape (formerly Software Toolworks) called, *The San Diego Zoo Presents ... The Animals*.

The Animals product did extremely well, selling over a million copies. Despite the large sales figures, Arnowitz Studio management decided to change course. The company executives examined financial reports and resolved that their best long-run strategy was to self-fund development of titles and become a publisher, with marketing and sales responsibilities.

As a developer, the company was limited to earning only 5 to 20 percent of net wholesale receipts (the amount paid to Arnowitz's publisher by the retailer less a reserve for returns). More importantly, as is typical of most developer/publisher agreements, Arnowitz received an advance to develop a title—anywhere from $300,000 to $500,000—but was required to recoup that amount based on its royalty rate before royalties are paid. While developers with a strong track record for creating successful titles have the leverage to negotiate and eliminate the recoupment requirement (which Arnowitz was ultimately able to do for the updated version of *The Animals*; other developers have negotiated recoupment based on total revenues), it takes a while to achieve that level of success.

Stuck with the recoupment requirement, Arnowitz figured it would take a few centuries to return to the publisher the amount of the advance.

"If you looked at numbers, it was clear that a developer like Arnowitz was trying to live off the wrong end of the pie," says Greg Richey, formerly senior vice president, business and legal affairs at Arnowitz. "While the potential revenue on these products is quite high and definitely worth the investment, it's only if you're on the other side of this arrangement and functioning as a publisher. As a publisher, you own the asset and you generate the revenue from it."

From 1987 to 1994 while functioning as a developer, Arnowitz lost money because of high development costs. To try and narrow the financial gap, the company added the shortfall amount to its next request for an advance to develop a new title.

"You're always behind," says Richey. "It's hard to break the cycle. You hope for a hit so that finally you'll start receiving royalties to get additional revenue and get out of the negative numbers." Richey assessed the investment market and determined that Arnowitz, as a developer of edutainment, rather than the more hyped entertainment games, would find it very difficult to attract private investment in the company.

The management team at Arnowitz felt caught in a Catch 22: Arnowitz needed capital so that the company could grow and become a publisher, but the investment community would only give money to publishers, not developers.

Before considering different ways to structure private financing, Richey recognized that though the revenues are greater as a publisher, so are the costs. Richey reviewed the numbers to make certain that the company could sell enough units to cover the additional expenses.

As a developer, the biggest cost is employees.

"There's a lot of craft that goes into building multimedia titles," says Richey. "Every piece of media that goes into a product needs to be touched, put into context, given an editorial treatment. What makes our products different is that we don't just download content onto a disk; we put more time into editorial treatment. Then every media item must be digitized, logged in, and catalogued. The more content you have, the more staff time it takes to handle it all." A close runner up for the largest cost, at least for the edutainment developer, is content acquisition.

A publisher also has these costs. But there are even larger costs: salaries for a management team, testing, manufacturing, sales, and marketing.

"Before taking the step to becoming a publisher, run the numbers and make sure that the publishing slice of the pie is adequate to cover this additional overhead," adds Greg Weber, former assistant general counsel of Arnowitz.

With this analysis behind him, Richey designed an innovative financial solution to propel Arnowitz from a developer status to a publisher. He developed a financing model similar to the kind of deals used to fund independent film development. It included a two step financing arrangement.

STEP ONE: LIMITED PARTNERSHIP. The first step involved finding eight to twelve private investors who would contribute $1 million or more. This amount of money would allow Arnowitz to develop and fund its own products and distribute them using a publisher or distributor. Because the titles were self funded, they would carry the Arnowitz label.

Richey prepared the financial document. In return for their investment, the private investors received ownership of the titles produced from the investment money, plus a portion of the income until they earned back their initial investment. They also received a specified flat return. The written partnership agreement included an upside potential: if the product did well and sold many units, investors received a stream of revenues based on royalties above and beyond the specified rate of return. After the investors recouped their return, Arnowitz would earn the bulk of the revenues, minus royalty payments to the investors.

On paper, it looked like a straightforward financing arrangement. However, when Richey started discussing the deal with investors, he quickly discovered problems with superimposing onto the multimedia industry a financing model that typically is used to fund films.

"Unlike a film, a multimedia title is not a single thing," says Richey. "It's an ongoing business that needs to be managed. There are operational issues related to porting and upgrades, both of which are expensive. If we want to do a Sega version of a title, for instance, it will cost an additional $100,000. Either the investors have to pony up more money or it comes out of the revenue stream, which reduces the investors' return."

When Richey designed the agreement, he was unable to predict what platforms the title would need to be ported to and when the company would do upgrades. The more operational-type issues that arose, the more difficult it became to structure the partnership. The private investors were not interested in giving Arnowitz, or any company, carte blanche to divert title revenue into upgrades or porting.

The ideal solution would have been to specify in the written financial document the type of platforms that the product would be ported to, how much it would cost, when it would be done, and the possible revenue. In the future, when the industry settles on a particular standard, that might be possible. But given the uncertainties in the market place, it was virtually impossible to include such a provision for either the platforms or the upgrades. Richey finally solved the problem by including in the partnership agreement general provisions for upgrades and platforms: if Arnowitz decided it needed to do an upgrade or port to another platform, it would notify the investors who had a certain amount of time to invest additional money. If they chose not to participate, they were not one of the owners of the upgraded or newly platformed title, and therefore, would not share in any revenues generated from the improved product.

"Investors don't like this arrangement much," says Richey. "They want to know whether the company is overstating its costs, what is the specific rate of return, how will it work, and what are the projections for the revenue stream." Despite these reservations, Richey closed the partnership deal June 1993. A year later, Arnowitz completed two self-funded titles, and on the strength of having own titles, it implemented step two of the plan to become a publisher.

STEP TWO: Arnowitz' second step involved selling equity in the entire company to raise capital for the company itself (as opposed to titles). Arnowitz approached R. R. Donnelly & Sons Company, which manages, reproduces, and distributes print and digital information and 77 Capital

Partners, L.P., Donnelly's venture fund, about doing a private placement. For $2.2 million, Arnowitz gave up roughly 35–40 percent equity in the company.

"In terms of structuring deals, it's definitely the Wild West," says Richey. "There are no standards or rules because it's so new. It's not like Hollywood where the deal structures are well understood. You just negotiate and negotiate until you figure out the deal."

EPILOGUE: Despite their attempts to leap the great gulf between developer and publisher, during Christmas 1994 sales of the company's products were not strong enough to meet their expenses. Management slashed the staff of fifty to fourteen and set out to find new private investors.

The advice from some former Arnowitz employees is for the developer not to become a publisher, unless there is long term financial backing either through self-generated revenue or through a corporate alliance.

"You've got to know you will lose money for awhile as a publisher, whether you are big or small," says Greg Weber. "The big guys can do that for a longer while than the small guys."

The reason a new publisher needs a well-financed operation is because as a publisher, you are financing the development and marketing expenses, both of which are increasing drastically. "Development budgets are going way up and price points are coming down," says Weber. "It's hard to make the numbers work." And at Christmas 1994, the sales were not strong enough for edutainment. Weber says the break even points were roughly 20–30,000 units per title sold. Yet sales for all CD-ROM– based edutainment titles were well under projections. The two titles that Arnowitz was able to self-finance, *Daring to Fly* and *Coral Reef,* sold less than expected. From November 1994 to January 1995, *Daring to Fly* sold 5,300 units of the Mac version and 9,200 for Windows. *Coral Reef* sold 2,900 units of the Mac and 6,900 for Windows.

Rick Giolito at Vortex Media Arts seconds Weber's comments. "Self publishing is a disaster for developers or small publishers. You have to have deep pockets to ride through the bad times. You also need deep pockets to gain shelf space, for a sales staff, to carry inventory and ride out returns and provide quality control."

LIMITED PARTNERSHIPS

At least one company has been formed, Wildwood Interactive, Inc. in Manhattan Beach, by a former Sanctuary Woods executive, Michael Scott, to provide financing for the production of interactive multimedia titles. The company, which was founded in early 1995, will focus on three brands: Wildwood Entertainment, which includes games; Wildwood Lifestyle, which targets groups of consumers with specified interests; and

Wildwood Discovery, which will fund education titles.

The company has already financed three titles: *Operation Quicksilver*, created by two British Columbia developers and a demo version of *The Wizard of Dogs: A CD-ROM on How to Raise and Enjoy your Dog!* developed by Wizard Multimedia. He also has a multimedia title based on the *Rocky Horror Picture Show*. Scott has located distributors in Europe and Japan who have provided one-half the development costs for the *Rocky* title. The other half of the funding will most likely come from Wildwood, which will control the distribution rights everywhere except Japan and Europe.

Scott says he modeled the company after the financing vehicles that support independent film production. Amblin Entertainment, Steven Spielberg's former company, is the most successful example of the independent film production model. Amblin is not a movie studio: it lacks a back lot, sound stages, and a large infrastructure. Instead, it has a small staff of experienced professionals, who identify opportunities, tap into existing production resources, and use the major studios for distribution. For instance, the movie, *Jurassic Park* came from a license obtained on the book written by Michael Crichton. Spielberg put together a production team to make the movie and Amblin contracted with MCA for distribution.

Wildwood, and companies that follow in its wake, operates under the same principles. The money from private investors will be invested in not just one title, like a film, but a bundle of titles to spread out the risk. Scott anticipates reviewing and purchasing titles at the concept or design phase, the partially completed phase, or when the product is done, but still needs financing for marketing or distribution. For instance, the title *The Wizard of Dogs* was presented to Scott in demo form and Wildwood is raising the development funds and locating an appropriate distributor. In exchange for $100,000 to $750,000, which will be given to the developer to produce the product, Wildwood might receive worldwide distribution rights on all platforms in perpetuity and copyright ownership of the product. The developer will receive a certain royalty rate.

Scott says that money to purchase titles will come from several different sources. Products previously purchased will generate sales revenues and revenue from ancillary products. This revenue stream will be used to fund future product acquisitions and development. Private investors have already invested in Wildwood. Wildwood will receive a management fee from the limited partners for developing, marketing, and supporting the title during the product's life; it will also receive a royalty after the limited partnership has recovered its investment.

BANKS

Forget it. Banks give loans based on a company's fixed assets and receivable, neither of which are part of a start-up multimedia.

PRIVATE PLACEMENTS

In early 1995, Garry Hare, president of Fathom Pictures, decided to grow the company even faster by raising $10–12 million. In the past, he had turned to joint ventures and limited partnerships to raise money. But this time, with the assistance of the San Francisco investment bank, Robertson Stephens, which specializes in putting together deals for multimedia companies, the company used a private placement to sell 20–25 percent of the company.

Hare sat down with the investment bankers and went over a list of thirty-eight companies that would be interested in investing in Fathom Pictures, paying attention to particular criteria.

"We wanted investors who could also help us with content or distribution," says Hare. "One or two companies on the list invest money in companies like ours if they can distribute the products." In a private placement, under the Securities and Exchange Commission regulations, the investors must hold on to their equity for two years before selling it to another investor. Because this kind of financing is less liquid than a public offering, investors typically ask for a higher percentage of the company for their investment.

Hare was willing to give up equity but not control of the company.

"Most people realize now if they ask for control of the company, there's nothing to keep me and others from walking out," says Hare. "They invest in you because you know what you are doing. This industry is about human talent and the sophisticated investors understand that they don't want to come in and control you." (See the appendix for other investment banks that specialize in multimedia.)

VENTURE CAPITAL

Very few multimedia developers turn to venture capital, or VC money, for start-up financing, either because it is not available to them (for reasons explained below) or they do not want to give up equity or control of the company. But venture capital is an option for some companies at the early stages, such as Pop Rocket in San Francisco. After three years of development of their title *Total Distortion*, the venture capital firm Hummer Winblad Venture Partners approached the small start-up and asked to see the product. Without a business plan, the venture capital firm invested over a half million dollars in the company, based on the title and co-founder Joe Sparks' track record with an earlier title *Spaceship Warlock* as co-developer.

Many more multimedia developers consider venture capital financing much later in the development process, typically when they have become publishers with several titles to their name. If you are in the market for venture capital, plan to spend six to eight months, at a minimum, closing the deal. With that time frame, it is not possible to start looking for venture capital in January and hope to have the deal closed and a product out the same year for the Christmas season.

Venture capitalists are exclusively interested in high rates of return— around 30 percent on their investment. With that in mind, they are looking for evidence that a multimedia company can deliver that kind of return.

Compared to the computer hardware industry, the interactive multimedia software industry has had difficulty attracting large amounts of VC money because of the type of risk inherent in the industry. Venture capitalists would rather fund a business that faces "development risk" than one with "market risk."

For instance, a company that proposes to develop and market a very fast computer chip would have no problem attracting venture capital funding because if the chip can be designed, the financiers know that there is a quantifiable market for a faster chip. The only risk the VCs are taking is the development risk: can the chip be designed?

With multimedia software, in any of the genres—entertainment, games, edutainment or education—the development risk, for the most part, does not exist anymore. The industry understands how to use the technology and make products. The only unknown variables in the development cycles are whether the developer can get the project done on budget and on time.

The bigger risk, and the one that is difficult to quantify, is the market risk—will consumers buy the product? This risk cannot be assessed until the introduction of the product to the market, after lots of money has been sunk into the title.

While the majority of VC firms are not big investors in multimedia, some companies are heavily involved in multimedia, bringing to the developer not only financing but valuable insights about the industry. Hummer Winblad Venture Partners, falls into that category, investing money exclusively in software companies, and as of 1994, involved with five multimedia companies, or consumer-oriented software companies: Berkeley Systems, Books that Work, T/Maker Company, Humongous Entertainment ($1.2 million), and Pop Rocket (over $500,000).

"We are real estate investors," says Ann Winblad, co-founder of Hummer Winblad. "And the real estate in consumer-oriented software is huge. But this is not like a client server company or a business productivity company, where you can make a judgment about a tight fit to a market need.

You are not really selling these products [multimedia software titles] to meet a need, but [rather] to consumer preferences—and those are very hard to judge. Many TV shows are flops. In fact, there are more flops than hits. The problem in this [multimedia] industry is that you have to figure out what will be a hit before you get there."

To be a company with $10 million in revenue, for instance, a publisher will need to sell a half million CD-ROM titles at the average wholesale price of $20 and the list price at $35 or higher. "A half million is a lot," says Winblad. To grow to a $100 million, you'll need to sell five million units. So, to succeed in this business, concludes Winblad, you need to have hits, like *Myst, Carmen Sandiego, Print Shop, SimCity*, or Berkeley's *After Dark*. And you need evergreen titles, those titles with a very long shelf life.

Though the market risk is high in any entertainment-oriented product, other industries, such as movie or book publishing, have been around awhile and have some indicators of what makes a business successful.

"In the movies, people with pedigrees have emerged," says Dean Frost with San Francisco based Frost Capital Partners, an investment banking firm that specializes in putting together deals in the software multimedia industry. "A lot of people are willing to put their money behind Spielberg's next movie, even though it's a highly creative act with a lot of unknowns. With the movie industry, you know to look for a director with a great resume, stars that people want to see, and a script written by Spielberg. In the software development industry, few people have killer resumes, and people don't know what makes a killer script. Everyone is betting on stuff they don't understand well, but that's part of the problem with any young industry. "

The other risk inherent in the consumer-oriented multimedia industry is limited distribution channels.

"Even if you've built a great title, the risk of getting it to the consumer is still high," says Ann Winblad. "For the venture capitalist, that means the risk extends for a longer period of time."

A venture capitalist will ask to see the company's business plan. Many books already exist that explain how to write a plan, but the next section highlights elements to emphasize in the plan to alleviate VC concerns. Even if your company is not interested in venture capital, a business plan helps to focus the co-owners on what they hope to create and how they are going to get there. Companies such as Coopers & Lybrand, an accounting and management consulting firm, are offering multimedia developers software templates to help prepare their financials.

Key Points in the Business Plan

Venture capitalists do not make their decision based upon how much money you are seeking.

"We are looking for the capabilities of the company," says Ann Winblad. "Most companies don't know how much money they need to raise. Money, to us, is viewed as a way of reducing a company's risk. We ask, how much money will it take to reduce the company's risk so that the developer could get a product in the channel and make some distinguishable movement away from the pack [of other developers]."

1. The first step is to decide where the companies title(s) fits in the multimedia market.

"It's not enough to say you are a multimedia company," says Dan Kaufman, a management executive at DreamWorks Interactive. "You need to ask, 'Are we a game company or a music company? Are you cartridge based or PC? Are you targeting little kids or big kids?'"

By zeroing in on the right market, you can begin to analyze the competition. Some of the answers to this analysis will also help define the company's chances for survival and its sales and marketing strategy. By focusing on the consumer you wish to target, for instance, it will help you decide whether to create for the PC platform or Sega Saturn.

In general, in writing the business plan and discussing investment possibilities with a venture capitalists, you need to ask: who is out there, how are the competitors' products priced (because your products will be priced similarly or lower), and how well is the competition doing?

2. The business plan should discuss how the company will succeed in the long run. Multimedia investors say that one of the biggest failures of new companies is that they do not consider how they will defend their market: If a small start-up company comes up with a great title idea, what will keep a Microsoft, Viacom, or Time Warner Inc. from coming in, tweaking it a bit, and flooding the market with something similar? With a big company's marketing resources, a small company might be blown out of the market, despite its original good idea.

"The question is, "What is your unfair advantage? Why you?'" explains Kaufman. "Your unfair advantage can't be that you are smart or you're hardworking. Everyone in this business is smart and working sixteen hour days," says Kaufman. "You've got to have something more than that."

An "unfair advantage" can be many things.

Berkeley-based Rocket Science, founded in 1993, attracted $16 million in venture capital money because it created proprietary technology, called "Game Science," a high level authoring system that takes a game's artistic content and translates it into a form that can be placed on any game platform—a Sega CD, Saturn, PC, 3DO, Sony CD, whatever comes along.

"A title that was done quick and dirty on Macromind's Director software is not adequate," says Anne Winblad. "Many of the companies we have invested in have proprietary technology to shift platforms, create better animation, or have better compression capabilities."

Knoxville-based publisher CyberFlix has been pursued by venture capitalists because of "The DreamFactory," a set of authoring tools that make it easy for artists and writers to create multimedia titles on CD-ROM. It allows nonprogrammers to design, script, and animate interactive movies on the desktop computer and transfer those titles onto different platforms.

"It can be technology that gives a company's products a lot better graphics or animation," says Ronald Heller with Frost Capital Partners.

Your unfair advantage can be access or a relationship with owners of valuable content. Knowledge Adventure, for instance, has an agreement with Random House to develop and market children's reference multimedia titles based on the book publisher's library of material. Random House will distribute the multimedia firm's software titles to bookstores.

It can be ownership of valuable content. Humongous Entertainment drew an unsolicited offer from Hummer Winblad of $1.2 million because of its hot selling titles that includes the home-made character, Putt Putt, an animated car.

There are "pedigreed" people in multimedia who can draw VC money. Bill Appleton at CyberFlix, for instance, is well known in the software industry for developing authoring tools such as "SuperCard," "HyperDA," "Video Builder," "Course Builder," and "World Builder."

Since multimedia software requires a lot of talent to put the product together, someone with a pedigree can attract and keep that talent.

"The competition in this industry is not for Windows developers, but animators, script writers, and great consumer product managers," says Winblad. "You have to have talented people wanting to work for you. When there is competition for scarce resources, we look to the management team in place and ask: 'Will Suzie, the best artist around, go to you, to an Electronic Arts or Microsoft?'"

If the company has focused on a particular genre and has developed great products in that area, the company may be able to defend its market. For instance, Maxis developed a series of simulation products, based on its popular title, *SimCity*. Though other companies have tried to develop similar products to *SimCity*, Maxis is way ahead in this genre and therefore can continue to defend its niche.

Sometimes the concept for the product is so different from the others that it attracts financing. Pop Rocket Inc. attracted venture capital money from Hummer Winblad because the company's product, *Total Distortion*, a music video adventure game, represented to the VC the next level of interactive media entertainment.

"We are looking for real novelty or a signature on the product so that it stands out from the thousands of titles being introduced into the market," says Ann Winblad. "We are also looking for a product line, a series, that can be built. It's impossible to be a one product company." With a series, like Maxis' *SimCity* and its line of products, the quality of the product becomes predictable to the consumer, who is more willing to buy the next product in the line-up. When that happens, the stream of revenue becomes more certain. Other examples of companies using the series approach include the line of *Carmen Sandiego* products, *Books that Work*, and *Living Books*, the result of a joint venture between Brøderbund and Random House.

Part of the allure of this kind of "unfair advantage" is that the company is able to develop an asset base. VCs are not in the business of funding one title, but a company that acquires assets, builds value, and can eventually be sold or taken public in three to five years.

The Executive Summary

A two to three page executive summary is your calling card. It is the first thing a venture capitalist will ask to see before considering your business plan. It needs to be concise, clear, and to point out your "unfair advantage." Because it is the most important section of the plan, you should write it last to incorporate the essence of the overall business plan. According to Coopers & Lybrand, the summary should include the following: (1) a company overview—what you are developing, the market you are targeting, a brief history, and milestones; (2) the management team, listing members who have pedigrees; (3) products—a brief description of the products, highlighting what makes them different; (4) market analysis—a description of the target market, your competition, distribution channels you intend to use, and growth in the target market; (5) the amount of money requested. You need to state how much you are asking for and how you will use it; and (6) a five year financial projection.

A Good Management Team

Because this industry is so new, venture capitalists resort to investing in people more than relying on product ideas. A well-run, well-managed company has a higher chance of success than one that is not.

VCs are looking for a good management team made up of people they think are highly competent and knowledgeable about the industry. They want to see that someone has a track record of starting a company and succeeding.

"The stakes have gotten very high very quickly," says Bruce Ryon, multimedia analyst at Dataquest, a San Jose, California based consulting firm. "In an emerging market like this, you have people who are very entrepreneurial, creative, loosely structured. But at this point, with the investment levels you're talking about to get out a new title, you need someone who has a good mix of creative and management skills."[3]

Since the CD-ROM market is still relatively new, experience in developing PC floppies ranks high among venture capitalists. To carry out the exit strategy of going public or selling the company, a strong management team and a high powered board of directors early in the game will position the company to take advantage of the public market.

"Because the industry is so new, investors and underwriters are really zeroing in on who is managing the company," says Carolyn Mead, a multimedia lawyer in San Francisco. "Think about this in the beginning, before you become desperately in need of capital and have to scramble to put together such a team."

An Exit Strategy

The business plan needs to identify how the venture capitalists will get their money out of the company. Either the plan should delineate who might be interested in acquiring the company or the steps to take the company public in three to five years.

Timing

Very few companies receive their initial financing from a venture capital firm. Sometimes, however, a company pulls together an stellar team of people and venture capitalists line up at their door, begging to give them money. Jim Clark, the founder of Silicon Graphics Inc., for instance, can get financing anytime, anywhere. But if it is Joe Blow with a computer in a garage, it will take more time. There are stories, however, of developers who have only a prototype and are able to attract a VC. The venture capitalist agrees to help Mr. Blow to take his product to the next level by offering a non-recourse loan, meaning that if the company does well (receives a significant contract or a relationship with a key strategic partner), it will reimburse the VC. If it does not, the VC will not sue to get his money back. Also if the company does well, Mr. VC has the right to invest a significant amount and take a large equity position in the company.

The Advantages and Disadvantages of Venture Capital

The advantage of tapping into VC money is that venture capitalists are often knowledgeable about the workings of start-up businesses. It is their area of expertise: They can be financially savvy, management savvy, and have contacts that could lead to strategic alliances and eventually a buyout of the company.

The downside of VC is that it is very expensive money, probably the most expensive money on the market. VCs take on high risks and require a large reward for doing so, in a high rate of return and sometimes majority control of the company. In exchange for the investment, the VC receives equity in the company and sometimes this leads to a new management team.

Before accepting money from a VC or private financier, investigate what other deals they have been involved in, what happened in those arrangements, and their long term vision for your company.

THE RECOVERY PLAN

If you are receiving money from private investors, venture capitalists, or even friends, and production falls behind schedule, put together a recovery plan so that your investors stay interested. The point of this document is not to highlight how far the company is behind, but the progress that has been made over the months, what needs to happen next, and the expected target date for release of the project.

WHAT DO YOU ABSOLUTELY NEED TO START A MULTIMEDIA DEVELOPMENT COMPANY?

Though there is no "right" formula to creating a multimedia development company, new multimedia developers say that there are some things you need to survive.

Despite the focus on funding in this chapter, the garage developers say it is still early enough in the game that a person trying to break into the industry can use savings, credit cards, and understanding friends who will lend money to build a prototype. Because the cost per disk is less than a dollar (compared to a cartridge which can cost $12-20 per cartridge), and because there are no license fees that need to be paid if a developer is creating for the Mac or PC platform, the barriers to entry are fairly low. Overhead can be kept at a minimum by working out of a home or garage. Because of the off-the-shelf software that exists today, the technological tools are available to start creating consumer oriented software titles.

----

1. *Los Angeles Times*, August 1994.
2. *Wall Street Journal*, August 5, 1994.
3. *Los Angeles Times*, August 1994.

CHAPTER SIX

DEVELOPMENT, AFFILIATE LABEL, AND LICENSE AGREEMENTS

You have depleted your savings account, Visa and Master cards, and IOUs. Your friends and family already chipped in more than their share of financial support. Venture capital is a distant blip on the horizon, and the "angels," or private investors, seem to have found someone else to watch over. The product is nearly finished, but another $125,000 would give you the resources to produce a fantastic video clip, a linear sequence to help set the scene and to introduce the main character.

When funding runs dry, most small developers seek a "development contract" with an established multimedia software publisher or movie studio that is seeking third-party developers to create products and fill its distribution pipeline. In the development agreement, the publisher or studio agrees to provide funding for the development of a title, and the developer creates a finished product, or gold master disk, which she turns over to the publisher.

This section presents in much more detail some of the main provisions you are likely to face when you approach a publisher or studio for funding and negotiate a development contract, some of which run fifty pages. The development agreement is one of the most important contracts that you will sign because it defines the critical relationship between you and the publisher. The developer, who will create the product up to gold master disk, is highly dependent upon the publisher who provides not only the financing, manufacturing, and packaging for the title, but also the "push marketing," to compel retailers to carry the product and "pull marketing" to convince consumers to purchase the product. The publisher is a developer's ticket to the marketplace.

The purpose of this agreement is to cover as many issues early, before production begins, to make the relationship function as smoothly as possible. Among other things, the agreement will present a highly detailed description of the final product, production milestones, payment schedules, and ownership issues. It is wise to have an attorney who specializes in this area review the contract before signing. Courts will enforce the development agreement: if one of the parties does not honor its obligations spelled out in the agreement (in legalese, it is called a breach of the contract), the other party to the contract can sue and receive money damages—enough to put the nonbreaching party in a position he would have enjoyed had the contract been fulfilled. Lawsuits cost money, however, and the more practical approach is for you to discover as much as you need to know about the potential publisher before entering into a relationship.

THE RIGHT PARTNER

Long before you review a development agreement, you should become familiar with the particular publisher's existing product line to see if there is a match between your title and the publisher's in-house resources. This analysis is also a first step in understanding the level of commitment the publisher will have for your product. In addition to providing financing, most well-established publishers allow the developer to use their assets, such as mailing lists of consumers who have purchased particular genres of multimedia products, internal music capabilities, graphic artists, and software programmers. A developer who is creating a sports-oriented title, for instance, should consider Electronic Arts as a possible publisher/distributor because of the company's strong sports products line up—*World Tour Tennis, NHL Hockey,* and *Michael Jordan in Flight.* If the developer is interested in creating an education-oriented title, Brøderbund Software, Inc., with products such as *Carmen Sandiego, Print Shop,* and *Kid Pix* products, might be a more appropriate choice as a publisher. Brøderbund's in-house sales force, which focuses on the school market, could propel a developer with an education-based title into the realm of hundreds of thousands of units sold.

The publisher's existing product line will also reveal what relationships the publisher has developed with retail outlets. A half dozen phone calls to these outlets, asking the retail buyer about the publisher, will help a developer make a decision whether this publisher is the right one.

If the publisher is a publicly-traded company, such as Electronic Arts, Brøderbund, or Spectrum HoloByte, the developer can review the financial statements of the publisher and determine the company's stability in the marketplace. In the latter part of this chapter, the crucial provisions are outlined for an affiliate program agreement and a software licensing agreement.

KEY PROVISIONS IN A STANDARD DEVELOPMENT AGREEMENT

The "development agreement" is used when a publisher or a studio contracts with an outside developer to create a multimedia product. Typically, the publisher provides the funding for the title, and in return receives the copyright ownership to the product. The developer receives money to create the title—an advance against royalties—which range from 5 to 25 percent of net wholesale price, the amount charged to the retailer. Developers say that a 5 percent royalty is on the low side and 25 percent is high.

In this agreement, you need to be as realistic as possible about the kind of product you can deliver and the amount of time it will take to develop it. Whatever time and cost figures you decide, market analysts say to double them, which will give you more realistic estimates. You must identify the platforms that the product will be created for, the graphic resolution, and the programming language. If preexisting material needs to be licensed, you should plot the time and cost required to obtain the rights and licenses so that estimates can be included in the advance amount.

Before you begin work on a title, you should have a valid, signed, written contract to produce the specified product. A proposal or request for proposals (RFPs) that you might have sent to a software publisher or movie studio is not a contract, and therefore, you will not be paid for any development expenses.

Developer's Responsibilities in the Agreement

Since the publisher is funding the project in this particular arrangement, the agreement will most likely specify that every piece of the product must be approved by the publisher before work begins. This section in the agreement covers the "preproduction" work for the product itself—an outline of the work that must be done and deadlines for different phases of the product. Depending on the type of multimedia title that is being created, the publisher will require that some or all of the following specifications be determined and approved in writing before any work is started:

- A detailed description of the product
- The script
- Flowcharts that outline the paths a user can take
- Storyboards that visually depict the product
- A description of the interface
- Content that will be created
- Content that will be licensed
- Time line for different pieces of the product to be completed
- Security procedures to ensure intellectual property is not stolen
- Off-the-shelf software that needs to be purchased
- Testing procedures
- A budget

- Staffing requirements
- Target audience

After presenting the concept for the title or a prototype, you are usually asked to agree to create and give to the publisher three main documents, which incorporate some or all of the above specifications, before starting the actual creation of the product. In the development agreement, you and the publisher should jointly agree on delivery dates for each of these documents.

Software Program Development Plan

First, you might be asked to create a "software program development plan," which outlines the intended users of the product, the skill level of the targeted user, and the composition of the development team that is required to create the product. This exercise helps you and the publisher identify competitive products and decide how to distinguish your product. It will also feed into the marketing plan, which will outline the best way to reach the target audience.

Storyboards

Then, you will create "storyboards," a visual display of the program for the publisher to see how the program will function. The storyboards allow you and the publisher to discuss the product, revising and improving the title before a great deal of money is invested. You will need an artist to draw the computer displays of the anticipated product. Some publishers ask for flowcharts to diagram the interactivity of the product and also the interface designs. At this stage, you and the publisher should talk about whether preexisting content will be used and explore the costs of this material.

If licenses are needed for preexisting content, it is likely to take time and money to locate the copyright holders and negotiate the use of the material. You should build into the delivery schedule more time or condition other important milestones upon the receipt of the preexisting content. Otherwise, the publisher might decide to terminate the agreement under the traditional provision that states that the "publisher/client has grounds for canceling the contract if the developer fails to meet the agreed upon milestones."

Program Design Document

Finally, you will agree in the contract to create a "program design document," which discusses the technical design of the program—the necessary software that will be used to carry out the software program development plan. It will also describe the production path for the different software modules, the testing, and debugging procedures.

For each of these three documents, the publisher will probably insist, in the contract, on veto power over any ideas proposed for the product.

You should negotiate for a stated period of time (thirty days or less) by which the publisher must review and either approve the documents or suggest modifications. If the publisher chooses not to approve the specifications, the development agreement should specify the procedure used to resolve disagreements.

Typically, when creative or technical differences emerge that cannot be resolved, the contract says that the publisher has the last word. But the more seasoned developers retain creative control over the product. Similar to the book publishing industry in which book publishers are combing the manuscript pile for talented writers, software publishers are in tough competition with each other to find and cultivate talented software developers. When they find one, they wisely let that developer create.

After each of these documents is agreed to by both parties, the second stage of the process begins: production. If the developer is relatively new or has not worked with the publisher before, production will occur under the direction of a publisher's producer. In the agreement, the developer and publisher will identify and list the key milestones that need to be accomplished, triggering compensation for the developer.

You should include deadlines for the publisher/client to give approvals or written acceptances for the work that is created so that the staff does not fall behind the production schedule.

Most smart developers also include a clause that requires the publisher to write down his objections and give them to the developer within a certain time frame. This provision protects developers from a situation in which the publisher orally agrees to a part of the product, only to come back later and request changes.

Changes to the Initial Design

During production, deviations from the original preproduction plans and schedule always occur because the hardware and software used to create multimedia are so new. Seasoned developers say that many disputes arise over who is responsible for implementing a change, who pays for the alteration, and the time allotted to fix the product. To avoid conflicts, the agreement should specify how the parties want to handle changes. For instance, one agreement required the developer to immediately inform the publisher in writing when a particular milestone would not be met. The writing had to specify the reason for the delay, the steps to mitigate the delay, and the efforts that the publisher could make to assist.

Include a procedure in the agreement to settle these questions before the problem arises. For instance:

- A deviation occurs from the original plans;
- The party who notices the deviation immediately notifies the other party and provides, in writing, as much information as possible about the problem;
- The developer (or publisher) prepares a document that indicates the reasons for the change, the implications of making the change, both in terms of money and time;
- The publisher reviews the document and accepts/rejects it, and tries to negotiate with the developer to reach a lower cost or a quicker time schedule;
- After an agreement is reached, the developer will at either the publisher's or the developer's expense (negotiable), revise the product within a specified amount of time;
- If the developer fails to fix the problem, the publisher, at his own option, will correct the error and charge the developer (or add it to the overall cost budget). The costs incurred by the publisher will be charged to the developer and may be recouped by an offset to any royalty payments.

If changes need to be made to update the finished program (rather than fix a problem), you should include in the agreement a commercially reasonable price for the additional work. The publisher will probably insist that the changes be made within a specific amount of time. If you do not complete the work, the publisher will demand, in the contract, on maintaining the right to do so, reducing future royalties by the cost.

To lower expenses, you should arrange contingency plans in the agreement if certain preexisting material turns out to be unexpectedly unavailable. In the preproduction phase, the parties should have explored the cost and availability of the photo or film clip. This provision would cover the emergency situation in which the material suddenly becomes unavailable.

What the Developer Must Deliver

After production is concluded, the agreement will specify what the developer has to turn over to the publisher. In addition to the debugged gold master disk, one agreement between a developer and publisher stated that the developer must provide the product's "complete and assembled source code," with sufficient written comment to understand the program. In addition, the developer must say whether any special hardware was used to create the product and provide an overall written description of each module of the code.

Testing

Most agreements specify that the remaining advance money is paid upon successful testing of the finished product. If you produced a consumer-oriented title, most large publishers have testers who test or "debug" the game, adventure, or sports title, playing the game eight hours a day, sometimes four weeks per game, trying to locate errors in the title.

If problems are found, the developer's agreement will typically state the developer must correct the "bugs" within a period of time. This process of testing and debugging can go on for several weeks to months (Spectrum HoloByte's testing of its *Star Trek* title took over five months), especially if the developer did not do much testing throughout the development process. If the testing continues for too long, the publisher typically includes in the "termination" section of the agreement, the right to end the contract for noncompliance. At that point, the publisher would take ownership of the product and try to solve the technical problems without the assistance of the developer.

Ownership: Who Owns What?

Since the publisher provided the funding for the title, the publisher will request copyright ownership of the finished work in the development agreement. If the contract is silent about ownership issues, however, the publisher is not automatically the owner of the copyright. If the publisher does nothing, under the Copyright Act, the developer who worked as an independent contractor and created the work is the copyright owner. In that case, the publisher would have to obtain a license from the developer to copy and distribute the finished product.

Most likely, though, the publisher will ask the developer to sign a form that the finished product is a "work-made-for-hire," which under federal copyright law transfers ownership to the publisher (as long as it fits one of the eight categories listed in the Copyright Act's definition of specially commissioned works, see chapter 9, under Work-Made-For-Hire Agreements). Another way for the publisher to obtain the copyright from an outside developer is through an assignment: an assignment must be in writing and signed by the owner of the copyright, the developer, or the developer's authorized agent. The person who owns the copyright in the multimedia title is generally considered the owner of the product. If the developer signs a written statement assigning the copyright of the final product to the publisher, the publisher as owner can do what it wants with the product within the limitations of the agreement.

For instance, the publisher has the power to sell, license, sublicense, modify, and use the resulting product. It can take parts of the product and use it in other titles, or whatever medium it wants, such as T-shirts, comic books, or consumer goods.

The publisher will also ask the developer to waive all moral rights in the program so that the developer cannot sue the publisher for modifications, distortions, or mutilation to the final product. (See chapter 8, under The Visual Artists Rights Act of 1990.) When the developer has relinquished her copyright to the publisher, she cannot sell copies of the title to anyone else, but she can still use the ideas that were included in the work.

You should be able to negotiate and retain ownership of computer programs developed prior to the developer's agreement. If you do not retain ownership of these parts of the product, you will need a license from the publisher to use them in the future. If you keep the ownership, the publisher will most likely ask for a nonexclusive license to modify, use, and sublicense the code as part of the final product and any derivative products it creates from the original title.

If you plan to use any preexisting material that is owned by the publisher, the agreement for this content should include a provision that allows you to use or modify the material. You also need the right to use the publisher's trademarks or symbols. This section should specify whether you can use the material in a future title.

If you are creating content for the product and working with the publisher who is also developing content, you might turn into a "joint author" if the agreement does not clearly indicate to the contrary. Under the copyright law, a joint work is "a work prepared by two or more authors with the intention that their contribution be merged into inseparable or interdependent parts of a unitary whole." (See chapter 9, Joint Authorship.)

The agreement should also include a nondisclosure provision to protect both parties' trade secrets. Most agreements will list some critical trade secrets that should be protected, such as source code listings and supporting documentation for the program, developer code, and any other software code.

Payment

Money is probably foremost in your mind when entering into a deal with a publisher. In a software publisher/developer situation, typically a developer receives an advance against royalties based on net wholesale price. The amount of the advance is intended to cover the cost of development.

Most new developers underestimate the amount of time (and therefore cost) it takes to produce a multimedia title. Steve Shannon, an associate at Coopers & Lybrand who works with small developers, recommends that for a fixed bid project, budget your development time, then double it. For the hourly rate, added Shannon, a developer should take the average hourly wage paid to an employee and triple it to estimate the billing rate per hour. If subcontractors are used, double their rate.

The advance is spread out over certain milestones, such as the developer and publisher signing the development contract (anywhere from 10 to 25 percent of the entire cost of the product), the creation of a prototype, and delivery of the gold master disk.

These milestones are tied to points in the production phase in which the developer has created something of value: in exchange for payment, the publisher receives another segment of the product. Then, if the developer fails to deliver a gold master disk or files for bankruptcy, the publisher will have something for the cash outlay.

Software publishers prefer to pay an advance against royalties rather than on a "time and materials" basis, which potentially results in larger development costs, with the developer billing the publisher for actual costs and time without a specified cap on these expenses.

Developers who have created their first title quickly learn that the advance needs to include overhead costs, not just the direct costs of production.

"You need to include more than your direct costs because you have no other source of revenue coming in until one of your titles takes off," says Greg Riley, formerly with Arnowitz Studios.

Most of the time, these advances are not refundable and the publisher loses if the developer does not follow through on the project. (The publisher can always sue for breach of contract, though). For the new developer, the publisher normally requires that the advance be recouped before any royalty payments are made. But you should negotiate an arrangement whereby you receive some percentage of the royalty stream immediately so you are not waiting for years to see any cash flow. After a developer has a track record for creating "hit" titles, the developer should be able to negotiate to eliminate the recoupment requirement, or at least have the recoupment rate based on total revenues.

The main "fights" between publishers and developers are over the royalty rate and how much will be deducted from the figure upon which the royalty rate is based. The deals that have been negotiated in the industry are all over the map. The royalty rate in a developer's agreement typically ranges anywhere from 5 percent of sales receipts (see definition below) to 25 percent, with more experienced developers capturing the higher rate. If you are a new developer, you can expect a lower royalty rate, but there might be some bargaining room in terms of what is deducted out of sales receipts. A developer will not receive royalties on products that are sent out for promotional reasons, such as review copies to journalists or copies to retailers to promote the title.

The royalty stream will most likely be based on either of two figures:

sales receipts or *net receipts*. Several publishers define sales receipts as gross revenue received by the publisher from the retailer or leasee (not the price paid by the consumer) minus taxes, reserve for returns (retailers have the right to return the product if it does not sell), and discounts, rebates, or special offers to customers.

Other agreements between developers and publishers deduct shipping insurance, shipping charges, and stock balancing, which involves retailers and distributors returning or exchanging slow-selling titles for more successful products.

Net receipts is typically defined as sales receipts minus cost of goods sold, advances, and costs associated with the creation, manufacture, marketing, and promotion or sale of a product and shipping. Net receipts, which is a lower base to be calculating royalties from, has been used in agreements in which the developer is creating the product in a cartridge-based form, in situations that involve significant licensing royalties (for Sega or 3DO), or in bundling deals. These three situations increase the cost of goods sold and royalties payable (excluding royalties to the developer) as a percentage of sales receipts. One publisher uses net receipts to decide the royalty amount when cost of goods sold and royalties payable equal or are greater than 25 percent of sales receipts.

In direct mail or catalog sales, the royalty is typically based on sales receipts. For ancillary products, such as T-shirts, lunch boxes, and cartoons, royalties are typically based on net receipts. If the product is not selling well, the publisher might try to move the inventory by offering discounted prices. Typically a development agreement will base royalties on net receipts for products sold at a discount.

After the product is completed and in the market, the development agreement will specify that the developer receive royalties on a quarterly or semi-annual basis and within a certain period of time (often forty-five days) after the end of the quarter or semi-annual period. But before royalties are earned, the advance has to be earned back by the publisher. Unfortunately, that could take a long time. Because the installed base of CD-ROM players is still small, few developers have seen a royalty stream.

For instance, you receive a $400,000 advance to develop a consumer-oriented software title and a 10 percent royalty rate based on net sales. The price paid by the retailer to the publisher is $40, so you receive 10 percent of $40, or $4. But first, that advance of $400,000 must be earned back by the publisher. It will require sales of 100,000 units before you receive any royalties, and unit sales of this magnitude are still rare.

To further complicate a developer's financial picture, many developers report that publishers are paying royalties later than the agreed upon time frame, which reduces cash flow and cripples the company. When negotiating a development agreement, instead of receiving a royalty check within forty-five days after the end of a fiscal quarter, you might try for a shorter time period or at least a minimum payment based on the last payment.

If returns of the title are greater than sales receipts, many publishers apply that negative balance to reduce future sales receipts, which will further lower the royalty stream.

Some development agreements are structured so that the publisher can reduce royalties by retaining a small amount of sales receipts for its marketing development fund, or MDF, to be spent on promoting the publisher's entire product line. For instance, if the publisher collects $40 from the retailer for the title, the publisher might deduct a $1 from that amount and put it into a reserve for MDF. Royalties would be based on sales receipts of $39 as opposed to $40. Other publishers require the developer to pay a certain quarterly amount to an MDF fund.

Despite the gloomy financial picture for developers, there are ways for the developer to earn more revenue than provided for in the development agreement. If the publisher's strength lies only in CD-ROM for the PC and Macintosh, for instance, you might consider including in the agreement the right to obtain a non-exclusive license from the publisher to the product, with the right to modify and sublicense the product from the publisher. With this right, you could approach a publisher who has strength in other platforms. The same principle applies if the publisher is most effective in domestic markets, and not international.

The Online Market

To prepare for the online market, you should carefully review your developer-publisher agreement. Under current licensing or assignment deals with publishers, the developer typically receives royalties based on the net or gross sales of units sold to retailers. In addition, these agreements typically include the publisher's right to license and distribute the product in online channels. But most arrangements lack provisions for the valuation of the product in the online channel.

For instance, if your development company created a title for a publisher, the existing developer's agreement probably allocated to you an advance to cover the development costs of the product and a 5–25 percent royalty (after the advance is earned back by the publisher) based on sales to the retailer. If your contract is silent about online valuation, your publisher could make a deal with a new online game channel company, licensing twenty titles—including yours—to the company, which is hooked up to 70 million homes that can download interactive games.

Further, your publisher could agree to license its top titles for a flat fee of $750,000. This fee might be split between the creators of the titles based on the number of units each game has sold over its lifetime. If your title

122 • THE BUSINESS OF MULTiMEDIA

accounted for 10 percent of all titles sold by the publisher, or three hundred thousand copies, you would receive $75,000.

Under the developer's agreement, you normally would receive 15 percent of sales made to the retailer. If your average royalty per disk is $3, you would have received $900,000 from non-on-line sales for the three-hundred thousand copies sold. If the title is still selling well in the retail channel, the $75,000 lump sum seems unfair, especially because online distribution will most likely dry up further retail sales. But if nothing is stated in the agreement, your publisher can value your title for online distribution anyway he wants.

To try and capture some of the revenue from future online distribution, a number of industry experts suggest the following:

- RETAIN ON-LINE RIGHTS: If you are in an affiliate label deal, negotiate to retain these rights. This provision in the contract is the easiest and probably best way to ensure that you receive the right valuation for your product.

  If you are in a developer's agreement, discuss the issue with your publisher. If you are talented, your publisher wants to have a long-standing relationship with you and most likely does not want to create an unfair advantage for himself, thereby potentially damaging the alliance.

- RIGHT OF FIRST REFUSAL: In the agreement, you might try and include a provision that allows you the right to buy back the online licensing rights at the same price offered to the publisher by a third party.

  A publisher, though, might counter that this provision inhibits his ability to negotiate with third parties. But again, if you are talented, the publisher will want to offer favorable contract terms.

- MOST FAVORED LICENSEE: With this contract clause, you would receive the same royalty rate from the publisher that the publisher gives to any other developer. Or, if the publisher receives a certain royalty rate from the online distributor, this clause could require that you also get the same rate.

  If the publisher rejects these clauses, you might try to include a provision that states that if your title is selling equal to or greater than 110 percent (or some other percentage) of the average rate for titles distributed by the publisher using similar marketing strategies, you will receive most favored licensee status. Or, a slight variation on that contract term: if your title is selling more than a certain number of units, you receive a royalty independent of any package deal the publisher enters into with a third party.

- VETO RIGHTS: Another provision that could be included in your developer or affiliated label agreement is the right to veto the inclusion of your product in a package deal. This term will induce the publisher to negotiate with the interactive TV company the best deal possible for the package.

- FAIR MARKET VALUE: A different contract provision might state that your product must be valued at fair market value for any licensing arrangements or deals with third parties. Fair market value could be determined by past royalties received, the likely effect the license deal will have on the historical royalty stream, and economic benefits that are expected from the publisher's deal with a third party.

Warranties and Indemnification

In the agreement, the publisher will ask you to warrant that the product and its components are original, so that later on the publisher will not be sued by a third party for stealing his or her work. This means that for every independent contractor that you hired to work on the project, you need a "work-made-for-hire" or "assignment" on file that transfers copyright ownership. (See chapter 9, under Work-Made-For-Hire Agreements.)

You will also be asked to indemnify and hold the publisher harmless for any breach of warranties, which requires you to pay for the cost of defending the publisher in a lawsuit for infringing on a third party's intellectual property rights as well as any judgment rendered against the publisher.

Most lawyers who represent developers prefer that the warranty state that "to the best of the developer's knowledge, the work does not infringe on anyone's intellectual property rights." That way, the developer is not saying that she "absolutely guarantees" that there are no problems of infringement. This language would protect the developer from a situation in which an independent contractor was hired by the developer to design the graphics for a game but, without the developer's knowledge, reused pieces of work that she had done for another developer. Because of these likely scenarios, you should obtain "absolute warranties" from all independent contractors. In a separate agreement with independent contractors, you might require the hired party to state the following:

- The independent contractor has the right to enter into the agreement and to grant the rights set forth in the agreement;
- The text (or sound, graphics, photos, artwork) is wholly original to the independent contractor and has not previously been published;
- The text (or sound, graphics, photos, artwork) contributed by the independent contractor does not contain any libelous material or any material which would constitute an infringement of trademark, copyright, or any other right.

Especially with the increase in strategic alliances, where one party contributes content and another contributes software, it is important to include warranty clauses. More critical, however, is to engage in a thorough search to be sure that the content or software can be used without risk of liability or an injunction against the entire product.

Marketing

Marketing is another reason many developers opt for a development agreement and function as developers rather than publishers. Under the development agreement, the marketing is the responsibility of the publisher. (But see chapter 3, under Guerrilla Marketing Techniques for some of the low-budget marketing ideas that small developers can do to help push the product.)

In return, the publisher has control over all aspects of the promotion, marketing, and distribution of the product. In the agreement, the publisher will try not to guarantee "successful marketing" or a "minimum level of distribution." Most developers, however, have expressed dissatisfaction with the marketing efforts of their publishers. The more precise the language about the marketing responsibilities of the publisher, the better chance the developer has to obtain a strong marketing commitment by the publisher and potentially higher sales.

For example, you might require that the publisher write a marketing plan and agree to adhere to it. Certain minimum amount of sales or dollars devoted to marketing might be included. Substance Interactive, for instance, included in their agreement with Sony Interactive that 10 percent of sales receipts received by Sony would be devoted to marketing. The developer might include a provision in the agreement that the exclusive arrangement between the parties converts to a nonexclusive relationship if these figures are not met.

"Get everything explicitly spelled out," says Andrew Nelson of CyberFlix. "State who is mailing the betas to the press, and who is contacting which press people. Don't leave any gray areas. Examine the marketing budget, what is being spent, and where. Sign off on the budget."

To reduce the chances of being stuck in a nonproductive relationship with a publisher, many developers agree to only producing one product for a publisher and retain rights over the next titles that may follow in that same line. While that is an effective approach, there is a valid counter argument for a more extended relationship. The publisher will more likely support the product and heavily market it if he knows that a series of similar titles will be produced in the future. Some developers have used the concept of a series of titles not only to raise money, but to create a long-term relationship with a publisher. If the product lends itself to such an approach, you might agree to give the publisher an option to all products created in the series, and in return, obtain a bigger marketing commitment. To trigger that option, the agreement could require the publisher to meet a certain minimum sales performance, such as minimum number of units sold within a specific time period, or minimum revenue earned within a set time.

It might be worthwhile for you to take a tactic from the book publishing world: In many book publishing contracts with authors, the publisher builds in an incentive for the author to market the book, such as increased royalty rates or bonus payments if certain benchmark sales figures are reached. You might build incentives for the publisher to meet certain sales goals.

When planning for your own marketing, you should negotiate the right to show your title, either a demo or the finished product, to other potential publishers so that you can generate more work from other publishers. Moreover, if the developer does contract work for corporate multimedia projects (to earn money to finance its consumer-oriented titles), the developer would probably want to include this title in her portfolio.

Maintenance and Support

You and publisher should agree in the contract which party will provide maintenance and support services when the product is introduced into the retail market.

If you turned over only the object code (machine-readable only), the publisher is beholden to you for future maintenance and repairs of the program. More publishers, and companies in general, are using private entities to hold the source code in escrow in case the developer goes bankrupt or other circumstances require the source code. The agreement might state that the source code be placed in escrow and the conditions upon which the publisher can obtain it.

Termination of the Agreement

Typically, the agreement will include a termination section so that if either party fails to perform its obligations outlined in the contract, the agreement ends. You should make sure the contract includes some specified time frame to rectify a problem before the termination clause can be used.

Not a Partnership

A publisher usually wants to include a paragraph that specifically states that the agreement does not form a general partnership between the developer and the publisher. If a partnership were created, all partners are liable for the debts of every partner.

AFFILIATE LABEL (OR PARTNER) AGREEMENT

If you have enough financing, you might consider entering into an affiliate partner arrangement. An affiliate label agreement is one in which your product, which has been financed by you, is distributed by another publisher who also has distribution capabilities. Under this model, you earn more royalties than in a development agreement, but also have the responsibilities for selling and marketing.

Under an affiliate partner agreement, you are obligated to pay for the product's development and the design and manufacture of the packaging (the cardboard box which holds the jewel box, CD-ROM, and manual), the manual, the CD-ROM, and the construction of the jewel boxes. The developer is also responsible for sales and marketing.

Because you do not receive development funding from the publisher, the royalty rate in an affiliate label agreement can range from 60–75 percent of sales receipts, and you are able to retain the copyright ownership to the software.

The royalty rate fluctuates, however, depending on how the publisher and developer decide to allocate the tasks. Some developers, such as the Miller brothers who created and partly financed *Myst*, decided that they would rather focus on developing product than on marketing or sales. They negotiated with Brøderbund, the company's publisher, to handle the marketing of *Myst*. For this hybrid deal, the developers gave up some royalty percentage points to Brøderbund, even though Brøderbund did not provide development funding.

More deals are turning out to be hybrid arrangements, with both the publisher and the developer determining the strengths and weaknesses of each, and identifying and then spelling out each parties' obligations in the contract.

Ownership Issues

Unlike a development agreement, under an affiliate label program, you retain copyright ownership of the product, artwork, and manuals. You also have the right to set the initial net price for the product.

A publisher will most likely negotiate an "exclusive"—as opposed to the "nonexclusive"—right to distribute your product. You, on the other hand, might benefit from having your product distributed by many distributors, who have strengths in different areas. Developers who have a proven track record are more likely to negotiate an exclusive distribution agreement with a publisher, but confine distribution rights to North America or to a particular platform. The creators of *Myst*, for example, sold the cartridge distribution rights to the Japanese-based company Sunsoft and gave Brøderbund the PC and MAC distribution rights. Eden Interactive signed up with Creative Labs to distribute one of the company's products, but the agreement lasts one year and is confined to retail computer outlets.

Under an exclusive distribution arrangement, many publishers also ask for the right to create and authorize non-software based derivative works, such as pins, T-shirts, posters, and books.

Obligations of the Distributor

SALES AND DISTRIBUTION: The agreement should establish the publisher's obligations to sell and distribute the product. The publisher is responsible for "push" marketing—getting the product on the shelves. The affiliate label is responsible for "pull" marketing—getting the consumer to buy the product.

The publisher will negotiate a provision that states because of the "speculative nature of software" the publisher is not liable for less-than-stellar sales. The developer should consider some of the suggested provisions listed in this chapter in the Development Agreement section on marketing (above).

If the publisher who provides distribution through his affiliate label program negotiated and obtained worldwide distribution rights, the agreement should specify how the publisher intends to distribute internationally. Since other countries have popular platforms that differ from the U.S., the agreement should specify who will port the product to these new platforms. It should also state whether the publisher/distributor has non-exclusive or exclusive rights to distribute the product to the education market.

ORDERS, INVOICING, AND STORAGE: The publisher/distributor is responsible for taking orders from retail stores, other distributors, and direct orders (if that method of distribution is being used), and distributing the product. The publisher is responsible for sending invoices and collecting money owed to the publisher and developer. The agreement should specify how often you should receive inventory printouts, either on a monthly or bi-monthly basis, so that you can maintain sufficient inventory.

The printout should report on sales, the outlets that ordered titles, how many titles, the name of the titles, and returns. You need this information to help formulate your marketing plan and budget.

The distributor also stores your entire stock of products at its warehouses and purchases a bond to insure the inventory.

Developer's Obligations

SOFTWARE RIGHTS AND REGISTRATIONS: You typically are required to file all copyright, trademark, and patent registrations.

FINISHED GOODS: You are also responsible for locating, arranging, and paying for the manufacture of the CD-ROM.

THE PRODUCT: Before the date set to ship to retailers, you are usually required to ship copies—sometimes over one hundred—to the publisher/distributor to be sent to the press, product reviewers, and for other promotional efforts. The developer is responsible for paying the freight to send the product to the distributor's warehouse.

MARKETING AND PROMOTIONS: Under a pure affiliate label deal, you are responsible for all marketing, advertisements, and PR activities, including the creation of press packets, sell sheets, and point-of-purchase displays. Many developers are not interested in doing this part of the business and can relinquish royalty percentage points, delegating this responsibility to the publisher/distributor.

Typically, you will be asked to commit funds to the publisher's own advertising efforts, such as in-house catalogs, special mailings, marketing development fund, or MDF, and cooperative advertisement fund commitments. One publisher in the industry asks for $2,500 per quarter from developers for its MDF.

SALES TRAINING: You are also obligated to train the publisher's sales force and other personnel to use the product. This responsibility is in addition to your obligation to establish customer service and technical support. The contract will also usually require the developer to secure commercial general liability insurance.

PAYMENT: You can negotiate to have monthly payments made directly from the publisher. To offset returns, a publisher will want to establish a reserve fund. One publisher had a reserve fund, the greater of (1) 10 percent of all amounts payable to the developer from the last 12 months, or (2) $150,000.

Most retailers will assume that they have full return rights for products that do not sell. While almost all publishers honor this right, many publishers are trying to import a concept used by the cartridge makers. Instead of having the retailer ship back unsold product, the distributor "price protects" the product: the distributor allows the retailer to reduce the retail price of the product until it starts to sell. In return, the publisher/distributor provides a credit or a reimbursement to the retailer. The discount will be reflected in a reduced sales receipts figure, and hence, a lower amount of royalties to the developer.

In book publishing, the author and publisher often work out an increasing scale of royalty payments according to certain numbers of copies sold. In multimedia, many publishers have taken that concept and applied it to the affiliated label program: if sales receipts exceed a certain amount, the developer might receive 3–5 percent more on top of its normal royalty rate. Sometimes, a contract will include as many as four graduated increases in royalty rates, often going as high as 10 percent above the starting royalty rate.

If the publisher sublicenses distribution to another company to distribute your title outside the publisher's normal territory, you will receive a lower royalty rate, such as 50–60 percent of sales receipts, rather than 75 percent. Typically, you can ask for sole discretion to approve or disapprove the sublicencing arrangement.

If the publisher enters into a bundling deal, you will also receive a lower royalty rate—more like 50–60 percent of sales receipts.

SOFTWARE DEVELOPMENT: Similar to the developer agreement, you will provide the publisher with detailed development schedules, often on a monthly basis. Publishers require this information so that they can plan the release date of the product. The agreement should specify that this information is confidential and protected by a nondisclosure provision.

PACKAGING: You are obligated to design and create, at your expense, all the packaging of the product.

MAINTENANCE: You must debug the program and provide technical support to customers during normal business hours. The phone number is listed in the manual and other materials. If you do not maintain the software, the publisher/distributor will assume that responsibility and charge the cost to you.

WARRANTIES AND INDEMNIFICATION: You will be asked to warrant that the product is created from original works of authorship and that the product does not infringe upon the intellectual property owned by anyone else. You will also be asked to indemnify and hold the publisher harmless for any breach of warranties. You should ask for the same indemnification agreement from the publisher.

Termination

The agreement should include some way to terminate the arrangement. The publisher will probably want to include a provision that allows the publisher to hold onto some inventory to fulfill remaining orders after termination of the agreement.

SOFTWARE LICENSING AGREEMENT

Sometimes the publisher licenses its content or code to a developer to create a new product. In this situation, the developer will be asked to sign a "software licensing agreement." Typically, the developer (licensee) will negotiate for an exclusive rather than a non-exclusive license. With an exclusive license, the developer is guaranteed to be the only company using the publisher's specified intellectual property.

Grant of Rights

The publisher who licenses his intellectual property to a developer will ask that copyright ownership of the final product be "assigned" to the publisher. Without such an assignment, the copyright is owned by the developer for the parts of the final product that she created. If the developer created the source code prior to entering the agreement, the ownership of that code would remain with the developer.

Payments

The developer who is licensing the intellectual property will be required to pay the publisher royalties based on an agreed-upon schedule of payments. Typically, the publisher will negotiate royalties based on sales receipts. Sales receipts are defined as gross revenue from the product and any derivative works less (1) sales commissions paid to independent sales reps; (2) refunds for returns and any reserves for returns; (3) any discounts, rebates, or promotional allowances given to customers; and (4) taxes.

Marketing

The developer typically assumes responsibility for the promotion, marketing, and distribution of the program. The developer should include language that she will use "commercially reasonable efforts" to market the title, but does not guarantee that the title will be successfully marketed.

Distribution

The agreement should include a time frame for the developer to establish distribution for the title. The publisher licensing the material to the developer will probably ask that if that deadline is not met, the agreement will terminate and the publisher will obtain all rights to the product.

If the developer allows other third parties to distribute the product, the publisher will typically ask for the same right to distribute. The developer might include in the agreement that the publisher would be a sublicensee of the licensee and receive the same terms offered to others.

CHAPTER SEVEN

DISTRIBUTION: HOW TO GET YOUR PRODUCT ON TO THE SHELVES

When the five founders of the publishing company, CyberFlix Inc., set out to produce their first title *Lunicus*, they hauled their computers into co-founder Bill Appleton's basement, the very place where ten years earlier, after dropping out of Vanderbilt University, the computer genius settled in to write software code for the Macintosh.

"I quit school, moved into my parents' basement, and didn't come back out into daylight until I had mastered the basics," says Appleton, who describes CyberFlix as an interactive entertainment company. This time, he hoped to create compelling interactive titles and software tools so that nonprogrammers—artists, authors, and musicians—could make their own titles.

In 1993, after thirteen months of development, the CyberFlix team emerged with the title *Lunicus*, a fast paced arcade/adventure game in which the user is a member of a moon-base team whose mission is to free the Earth from aliens. The publishers received tremendous reviews from *MacWorld* and *MacUser*, awarding it "CD-ROM game of the year."

But in a move that they later regretted, CyberFlix turned to a direct mail order outfit to distribute *Lunicus*. According to CyberFlix's in-house lawyer, mail order sales were great, but total sales were not up to the level the company thought they should be.

"There's no way around it: You need to be on the shelf," says Erik S. Quist, CyberFlix's in-house lawyer. So the publisher began looking for a new form of distribution.

At the 1993 MacWorld Expo in Boston, CyberFlix's founders met representatives from Paramount Interactive, the multimedia arm of Paramount Communications, which is owned by Viacom. CyberFlix already had *Lunicus* on the market and was demonstrating a prototype of its title *Jump Raven* at the convention.

Paramount Interactive, along with most of the convention participants, was impressed with the title. Following the trade show, CyberFlix signed a three year affiliate label agreement with Paramount, in which Paramount Interactive agreed to market—both push and pull—and distribute CyberFlix's titles. Paramount also received the right of first refusal on any of CyberFlix's programs produced over the next three years, and CyberFlix agreed to develop a title based on the Paramount TV show "Viper."

"We are responsible for the costs associated with reproducing and building the product, for shrink wrapping it and storing it," says Quist. "We do our own designs for packaging. We contribute a lot to the marketing of the product, all of which makes us more than a developer."

In CyberFlix's deal with Paramount, the publisher is paid a royalty rate of roughly 60–70 percent of net revenues, which is defined in the contract as actual cash received from sales, minus excise and other taxes, shipping, insurance, and similar reimbursements and incentives. For instance, Paramount uses promotional techniques, one of which gives the purchaser of three products another one free. The income from the sale of the three products is spread out among the four, reducing the price of all four, thereby decreasing the royalty stream to CyberFlix.

"We found it's not enough to do mail order alone," says Quist.

Quist speculates that the same holds true for online distribution.

"You need a certain genre of game to succeed with online distribution," says Quist. "A game in which you go around and kill people is ripe for word of mouth."

The final chapter of CyberFlix's relationship with Paramount Interactive was written in 1995: CyberFlix decided to part ways with Paramount for its future titles. It was a mutual decision, say the parties: CyberFlix wanted a distribution partner who knew the retail software industry better; Paramount wanted a publisher who would take the company's preexisting material and create new titles.

THE IMPORTANCE OF DISTRIBUTION

Distribution is the key to becoming a successful development or publishing company. Without it, a developer who has the most compelling title cannot survive. The distributor is the developers' link to the market place, which will provide the revenue stream necessary to make more titles. Few developers, however, actually plan that far in advance when they first sit down at their computers to create their title. Their secret wish, especially the developers who come from the software industry, is that the technology will sell the title, with nothing more required. Whatever truth there was to that business model is now gone.

"Choosing your distribution partner is probably the single most important thing you do," says Drew Huffman of Drew Pictures, which teamed up with Spectrum HoloByte, Inc. to distribute and market its product *Iron Helix*. "You have to get your product out there. It has to be available to be purchased and be in all the right places. It has to be marketed and promoted effectively. You can't hope to sell a half million products without reaching the mass market. And the mass market is not dialed into this. They are not reading the computer magazines to see who's on the cutting edge. They don't care."

Struck by the entrepreneurial spirit, many developers have tried to handle their own distribution. But they have found that retail buyers only have so much time to devote to buying, and they would prefer spending an hour with a distributors' sales representative who has an array of products—everything from adventure games to reference tools—than a developer with only one product to pitch. The sales rep, who has many titles, is also able to help the retailer "stock balance," switching one title that is not selling well for another that might do better.

Before storyboards, before a line of code is written, before the prototype, the developers who have done well have asked and answered the question: "who is the audience for this title?"

The answer determines the proper platform, the most effective marketing, and how best to distribute.

WHAT IS A DISTRIBUTOR?

A distributor warehouses the product, ships it, provides invoicing, and collects the money from the retailers for the publisher's product. Most distributors also have a direct sales force that physically go to the retailers and talk up the distributor's product line. Many publishers are also distributors—Electronic Arts, Maxis, and Mindscape—with direct sales forces that call on a specified number of retailers.

In this chapter, when the term *distributor* is used, unless otherwise noted, it also means a publisher who provides distribution.

WHAT A DISTRIBUTOR CAN DO FOR A DEVELOPER

Developers who carefully select a distributor often find that the relationship yields more than distribution. Publishers who distribute also offer financing, content, and in-house talent. Electronic Arts, for instance, has its own music studio, in-house animators, and software programmers and makes these assets available to developers.

THE DISTRIBUTION SQUEEZE

The multimedia industry is battling the problem of limited shelf space, with the primary retail outlets for CD-ROM titles still the software retail stores, such as CompUSA, Computer City, Egghead Software.

Fortunately, other channels are opening. The discount stores, such as

WalMart, Target, and the Price Club, are making room on their shelves for CD-ROM titles, primarily the top twenty-five best selling products, but not quickly enough to support escalating development and marketing budgets.

Publishers like Voyager in Irvington, New York, known for the product *The Complete Maus*, the CD-ROM version of the book, *Maus*, are helping to educate the bookseller industry about CD-ROM. Voyager is present at every bookstore trade event, including the largest, the American Bookseller's Association annual convention, teaching booksellers about the new technology. Each year, more bookstores decide to carry CD-ROM titles. To move that process along, Voyager supplies bookstores with a special standing circular rack that holds all of the company's forty plus products and offers a quick turnaround for reorders of titles. Random House is also helping bookstores and their customers learn about the new technology by holding "demo days" in bookstores, in which customers can try out CD-ROM titles on computers.

Other distribution channels such as video rental chains and record stores are also opening. Blockbuster Video concluded a test rental program of CD-ROM titles in San Francisco in late 1994. For reasons that have little to do with demand for multimedia and more to do with paying off debt, the company scaled back the test from sixty outlets to fifteen but is adding new cities to the program, according to director of new media Jack Ferry. Based on 1994 results, the product mix in 1995 also changed. Initially Blockbuster emphasized "edutainment" software. Now, Ferry said, 60–65 percent of the titles are games.

New companies have emerged to solve the shelf space problem by putting together shareware CD-ROMs, which include anywhere from one to forty samplings of different CD-ROM titles.

To supplement this narrow channel, multimedia software companies have turned to bundling deals, in which their CD-ROM product is included, or "bundled" with another company's hardware or software. Direct mail and third party catalogs are also pushed by multimedia consultants as an additional way to reach customers. Online distribution is being used primarily as a preview and marketing mechanism. For most developers, the distribution problem requires a myriad of distribution vehicles to sell their products.

EVALUATE THE DISTRIBUTOR BEFORE SIGNING

Thrilled to land a distribution deal, many small developers fail to evaluate the distributor before signing an exclusive distribution contract. Most distributors, however, have special strengths and weaknesses. As the developer gains a reputation for creating great titles, the company moves up the food chain in the developer-distributor relationship and has the leverage to demand more from the arrangement. This extra bargaining power makes evaluation of the distributor even more important.

"Companies that are doing distribution want to hang on to great developers," says Ruth Kennedy of Electronic Arts. "We've done deals where the developer essentially gets to be the publisher [have full creative control over the title as well as receive a higher royalty rate], and we just do the manufacturing. If we've found a top-notch developer, we do a lot to keep that developer in our family." Electronic Arts has also done deals where it advances the purchase price of the title to the developer so the developer has cash flow sooner.

As the industry continues to grow, most multimedia players believe that more companies will step up to provide distribution. While the competition should benefit the developer who should see a decrease in the usual 25 percent distribution fee, it is also likely that some distributors will go out of business because of the new competitive pressures.

Signs of increased competition have already emerged. For instance, Emeryville, California based Publishers Group West, one of the largest book marketing and distribution companies that represents book publishers, has begun to distribute CD-ROM titles to bookstores.

"Distribution fees are going down as distributors compete with others and experience pricing pressures," says Mark Stevens, a multimedia lawyer in Palo Alto. "I am seeing new entrants come into the distribution market and hearing them say that they want to buy market share. To do that, they are being aggressive on pricing to affiliate labels and those developers seeking distribution."

Because of the increased competition, Stevens and others expect a distribution shake out in the near future.

"In my opinion, only a few of the existing software companies/publishers who are also doing distribution will be around," says Stevens.

Signs of some kind of shake out are already present. Media Vision Technology Inc. in Fremont, California which provided distribution and development funding to multimedia developers, filed for bankruptcy in 1994. It reemerged in 1995, a leaner company, without its software publishing division or distribution services. Media Vision had been the publisher and distributor of Mechadeus' titles. Because of possible rough times ahead for distributors, developers should be especially careful in deciding who will be their distributor.

Developers say that one of the most important characteristics to consider when choosing a distributor is the long-term financial stability of the company. This factor is particularly important to consider as competition among distributors increases.

Before they created *Myst*, the Millers created children's titles, which were funded and distributed by Activision. But Activision went bankrupt in 1992, and a dispute arose as to who owned what rights to the products. Activision had given the Millers advance money to develop the children's titles, and when Activision filed for bankruptcy, some of the advance had not been recouped, says Rand Miller.

"We thought we had followed certain steps that brought all the rights back to us," says Rand Miller. "They felt those steps were invalid. We went back and forth on this issue and almost ended up in court."

The Millers recommend including in the distribution agreement such terms that will protect your company if the distributor goes bankrupt. Clearly spell out ownership rights in case of a bankruptcy. If you can, says Rand Miller, request frequent payments from the distributor (monthly would be great) and access to the distributor's financials to determine the health of the company.

Selecting the right distributor is also critical, say developers, because retailers have 100 percent return rights. Like other merchandise, products that are selling slowly (or sometimes if the retailer is low on cash) are returned by the retailer to the distributor. The distributor, in turn, will return the products to the developer and ask for a refund or credit against current or future orders.

Moreover, few distributors are strong at servicing all of the main markets for multimedia: bundling, direct mail, third party catalogs, domestic and foreign retail, and online. There are probably even fewer distributors who can successfully service all the different facets of the domestic retail market, such as bookstores, video rental stores, audio CDs, major discount stores, and department stores.

Eden Interactive, a small developer in San Francisco with three titles, chose to evaluate potential distributors based on their strengths in different retail markets and their marketing capabilities. The company's founders spent all of 1994 looking for strategic partners. Eden Interactive had previously used a company to distribute its products, but severed that relationship when it discovered the distributor lacked the "pull" marketing to move the products off the shelf.

"What we didn't understand before is that you really need tremendous resources to get it [a title] off the shelf," says Minoo Saboori, co-founder of Eden Interactive. "Even without having those resources, we sold a lot of our *Greg LeMond's Bicycle Adventure* title, so we knew we were on the right track."

Saboori and co-founder, Matthew London interviewed nearly forty distributors, in search of a company that had the financial resources to sell their product to both the retailer and the general public.

In July 1994, Eden Interactive became one of the first companies to sign with Creative Labs in Milpitas, California, the makers of Soundblaster cards and recently a multimedia publisher and distributor. The distribution agreement gives Creative Labs worldwide rights, except Japan; is limited to a one year time period; and to one product, *American Visions: 20th Century Art from the Roy R. Neuberger Collection.* In an unusual term for a distribution agreement, Eden Interactive also limited the agreement to only the computer retail channel.

Eden Interactive chose Creative Labs, says Saboori, because the company had the clout to take Eden's product into the existing computer channel, "make it look pretty and stand out on the shelf" and educate the retail sales people about the product so that they recommend it to consumers. Eden is also lining up strategic alliances with publishers to distribute to the book channel, the audio and visual market, the educational market, and the online channel.

Developers recommend talking with other developers and publishers about their distributors. Retailers who deal with distributors also are a great resources in determining which distributors do a good a job servicing their accounts.

Almost all small developers and publishers recommend joining with a distributor that has a direct sales force.

"We signed with Electronic Arts in 1992 because they have a very strong, successful fleet of sales people," says Maura Sparks of Pop Rocket. "And they are one of the largest game distributors in the world and in 1992, when we started negotiations, had a strong vision of the CD-ROM market and where it was going before most other companies." Pop Rocket, however, has several distributors to spread out the risk of selling their title *Total Distortion.* Mindscape is the European publisher and will localize the product for Germany and France. HatNet is the publisher for the Mac version of the product for the Japanese market and NEC will distribute the Windows version in Japan.

When Fathom Pictures in Sausalito put out the word that they were looking for a distributor, nine companies made proposals, five of which were serious, according to Garry Hare, president of Fathom Pictures.

All of the companies had direct sales forces, a prerequisite for Hare.

"Ideally, if you're an aggressive small developer, you want to be with someone who has their own sales force because these people will better represent you and position your product on the shelf," says Hare. "They have a vested interest in selling your product. I didn't want to join up with a distributor who loaded my product on trucks to ship to retailers, only to have the titles shipped back two months later."

Hare narrowed the candidates to three. "We didn't have any criteria to choose from. They all looked good, with good marketing plans. So I picked up the phone and called the vice presidents of marketing and distribution at five major retail stores, such as Babbages and Good Guys and Blockbuster. I explained we had an opportunity to be distributed by these companies and asked for their recommendation. All five VPs recommended Interplay."

To target the North America retail market, developers say to check the distributors' record with retailers. A good distributor will have strong relationships with at least ten major chains, such as Software Etc. or CompUSA, that sell CD-ROM products. The distributor should have a good national account manager who knows the retailers. The distributor's sales force should create "pull" marketing through promotions and targeted ads rather than through discounts on the products. An added bonus would be that your distributor is one of the handful of top distributors who are invited by retailers to make presentations of their product lines at the retailers' national sales meetings.

For the European and Asian market, developers recommend that you find a distributor who can also localize your product.

Developers who are looking for a successful alliance with a publisher to distribute their titles typically consider whether the publisher has:

- A direct sales force;
- Marketing capabilities;
- A presence at major trade shows;
- Similar titles and therefore contact with the retailers who are most likely to carry your title;
- Quality products and relationships with talented developers;
- Strength in the distribution channel in which your product will do well, in terms of territories, platforms, and operating systems;
- In-house talent resources available;
- Strong market share in software or hardware;
- Financial strength to market the title and pay royalties on a timely basis;
- Long term financial viability; and
- Updated direct mail customer lists.

A DEVELOPER'S DISTRIBUTION OPTIONS

Several distribution options exist for the small developer. Though it is fairly common for a small developer to choose a publisher that also provides distribution capabilities, it is also possible for a developer to put together a range of different distribution mechanisms as well as distributors.

Fathom Pictures in Sausalito, has a menu of distributors based on geographic area, genre, and platform. Interplay Productions distributes Fathom's titles in Europe and the United States. E. A. Victor, through a sub-distribution deal via Interplay, distributes the company's products in Japan. For Fathom's nonfiction titles, Voyager handles distribution in the United States. Fathom's CD-i titles are carried by Philips Media and Pony Canyon in Asia.

San Francisco-based publisher Zelos, founded in 1992, did something similar, creating a multi-tiered distribution strategy, which includes bundling, retail software, book publishing, and direct channels. Sony Imagesoft bundles Zelo's *Shoot Video Like a Pro* and *How To Really Start Your Own Business* with its CD-ROM drives. Individual Software, a leading multimedia publisher, distributes Zelos' titles through national distributors such as Ingram and Merisel and to retail computer chains such as Egghead, Fry's Electronics, CompUSA, Sams, and Costco. Publisher's Group West, which distributes books published by independent book publishers, distributes Zelo's titles in the book category. Zelos itself distributes its titles directly to non-traditional outlets such as Tower Records and Blockbuster Video.

Direct Sales

For relatively obscure, niche titles, the developer's only distribution option might be direct sales, through mail, radio, and niche organizations. For titles that appeal to the mass market, direct sales avenues are a recommended way to add revenue to the bottom line.

The benefit of direct sales is that the developer realizes 100 percent of the revenue, less the administrative costs. If you take this approach, you need to hire a marketing person with knowledge of direct mail, or use a company that specializes in direct mail.

A National Distributor

It is extremely rare for a small developer to be distributed directly by a national distributor such as Merisel or Ingram Micro. Merisel focuses on software distribution, whereas Ingram has penetrated all four channels—books, audio, video, and software. Before Ingram decides to distribute your product, you must fill out a nine-page developer profile, detailing your company's revenue for the past three years, your marketing budget, sales figures, and your booth size for upcoming trade shows. Typically, these distributors will distribute only the products of fairly large publishers with titles that sell $75,000 a month. If sales drop below a certain amount, the product is dropped from the distributors' product line and returned to the publisher.

But the developer who is involved in an affiliate label program will, through his publisher, have contact with the national distributors. For instance, a publisher such as Electronic Arts has its own direct sales force that calls on a specific number of retail outlets. But the company also uses the national distributors to service other outlets.

In a typical distribution deal, the distributor receives 20–30 percent of the wholesale price (the price paid by the retailer to the distributor). If the wholesale price is $29, the distributor would receive anywhere from $5.80 to $8.70. If the developer is involved in a development-publisher agreement, the publisher would receive the remaining amount and the developer would receive a percentage of that amount, typically 10 to 25 percent.

If the product does not sell, the distributor has 100 percent return rights. In Europe, on the other hand, distributors do not have return privileges and therefore tend to purchase fewer units, but they represent hard sales. The publisher is responsible for creating the "push" marketing to push the product into the retail channel, and also the "pull" marketing, that pulls customers into the store to purchase the product.

Affiliate Label Program

In affiliate label arrangements, an established company—a publisher or a movie studio with a distribution arm—distributes a smaller publisher's title. In this situation, a developer has financed the development of the title and is considered a publisher. (In this section, however, we will continue to use the term developer.) The developer is responsible for marketing the title and retains copyright ownership of the product. The developer gives the distributor a license to distribute the product. Some distributors offer to manufacture the product with the developer relinquishing another 5–10 percent of royalties for the service.

The distributor takes anywhere from 20–30 percent of net wholesale price, with the developer receiving the largest chunk of revenues.

One of the key provisions to negotiate with the distributor who is offering the affiliate label program is the issue of exclusivity. Most distributors want an exclusive distribution license, arguing that an exclusive arrangement encourages them to promote the product more aggressively. But developers say that if the distributor lacks a presence in a certain territory or retail outlet, the exclusivity should be limited to the areas in which the distributor is strongest. Other limits developers place on affiliate label arrangements include restrictions on the platforms, operating systems, such as Mac, Windows, DOS, or Solaris, or the type of media—cartridge, CD-ROM, floppy disks, and online.

A common complaint among developers involved in an affiliate label program is the perceived favoritism the distributor has for its own titles compared to the developer's products. The distributor makes more money selling his own titles rather than the affiliate label's products. One developer counteracted this problem by building into the agreement an incentive for the distributor to sell his titles: at certain sales units milestones, the distributor would earn a few percentage points more on each sale.

Those offering affiliate label programs include: Electronic Arts, Brøderbund, Maxis, Mindscape, Spectrum HoloByte, Compton's NewMedia, Time Warner Interactive Group, and Paramount Interactive. At the time of this printing, rumors were circulating that IBM was going to start up its own affiliate label program and attract small affiliates by offering a bigger cut of the profits.

Distributors include: Merisel, Ingram-Micro, ABCO Distributors, Josha Distributing, American Software & Hardware Distributors, Inc., and Double Impact Multimedia Inc. (See appendix for phone numbers and more companies).

Developer/Publisher Agreement

Under a developer/publisher agreement, distribution is often handled by the publisher using a two-tier system. The publisher typically has a direct sales force, made up of employees or independent contractors who focus on key retail accounts. To cover more retail outlets, the publisher might also arrange further distribution through national distributors. The downside of this distribution model is that the publisher/distributor receives a large percentage of the revenues. (See chapter 6.)

An Affiliate Label, Twice Removed

Sometimes a developer will rely on a publisher who has an affiliate label relationship with a third party distributor. For instance, Sanctuary Woods has been an affiliate label of Electronic Arts, which provided distribution for Sanctuary Woods' product line in the North American retail channel. Before Sanctuary Woods discontinued this relationship, developers who entered into a relationship to create a title for Sanctuary Woods, ultimately received distribution from Electronic Arts.

This arrangement, however, is financially difficult for the third party developer because she is farther down the revenue food chain. For instance, if Sanctuary Woods agreed to sell a product to Electronic Arts for $30, who in turn paid Sanctuary Woods 50 percent of net wholesale price, the third party developer might receive 15 percent of Sanctuary Wood's 50 percent.

"As a result, if you were negotiating a royalty stream with Sanctuary Woods as a percentage of sales, you would have had to try and bargain for a higher percentage to make any money," advises Mark Stevens, a multimedia lawyer in Palo Alto.

TERMS IN THE DISTRIBUTION AGREEMENT

When developers or publishers draw up the distribution agreement, they pay particularly close attention to specific terms. In this document, the developer or publisher is deciding what rights to give the distributor. With a lawyer versed in multimedia, developers typically review the agreement, bearing in mind the factors listed in the section, "Evaluate the Distributor Before Signing."

1. EXCLUSIVITY: Is the distribution agreement exclusive or nonexclusive? If the developer gives the distributor the exclusive right to distribute the product, should the agreement be limited in any way, such as geographically, by platform, or particular retail channel?

If you grant a distributor exclusive rights, try to include specific marketing requirements such as: a certain number of units sold within a stated time frame; a certain dollar volume in sales; a stated advertising budget; or a certain number of trade shows that the distributor must attend to promote the product. If the distributor fails to meet the performance requirement, a provision in the agreement could state that the contract terminates or becomes a nonexclusive arrangement. Distributors who advanced financing to a developer to create a title have an incentive to aggressively market the title.

An exclusive license to distribute a developer's product has its benefits. The distributor, for instance, is likely to devote more resources to marketing and promoting the title.

2. CHANNELS OF DISTRIBUTION: Limit the agreement to the channels in which the distributor has the most experience, expertise, and presence.

3. PLATFORMS/OPERATING SYSTEMS/MEDIUM: Find out the platforms and operating systems in which the distributor has the most expertise and limit the agreement to those areas. The agreement should also specify whether the distributor has the right to distribute the title in "all media," which would include floppy disk, cartridges, CD-ROM, and newly developed formats.

4. TERRITORY: Restrict the agreement to the geographic areas which the distributor is the most capable of servicing. A distributor most often tries to obtain worldwide distribution rights. Developers caution against granting territory rights to a distributor that exceed and violate the licenses for preexisting content used in the product.

Developers with distributors who have international distribution capabilities should cover in the distribution agreement the issue of localization costs, or the expenses of changing a product to sell it in a foreign market.

5. PRODUCT OR SERIES OF PRODUCTS: The distributor will most likely want to build a long-term relationship with the developer. One way to develop the relationship is to approve in the agreement the distributor's ability to distribute all products created by the developer now and in the future.

Developers typically reject such a far-reaching provision, however. One option might be to sign with a distributor to distribute one product and include specific performance criteria, as listed above. At a certain point in the future, the relationship can be reevaluated to determine whether the distributor should carry other titles.

Another provision that developers use is to give their distributors the "right of first refusal" on future products or a "right of first negotiation," which requires the developer to negotiate with the distributor in good faith.

6. DISTRIBUTOR'S ADVERTISING EFFORTS: In most distribution arrangements, whether with a national distributor, affiliate label, or publisher, the developer is required to contribute a certain amount, either a percentage of sales (typically five percent) or a flat amount, to co-op advertising. The money is used by the distributor to run display ads, participate in catalogs, do mailings, and attend trade shows or other marketing efforts. Many developers are presented with the option of giving the distributor free product instead of cash to meet this requirement. (See chapter 3, under Marketing Development Fund.)

Another 2–3 percent can be contributed to another cooperative fund that is given to retailers to run their advertising efforts. Overall, as much as 7–8 percent of a publisher's marketing dollars might be committed to someone else's marketing programs.

7. BEST EFFORTS: Some developers are able to negotiate in their distribution agreements—be it in the context of an affiliate label agreement, a development agreement, or a national distributor agreement—a provision requiring the distributor to use his "best efforts" to market the title. For example, Steven Rappaport, founder of Digital Trivia, Inc. in San Francisco, negotiated a "best efforts" clause in his agreement with Sanctuary Woods.

It is uncertain whether such a condition is sufficient. Companies in other industries that have included a "best effort" requirement in their distribution agreements have found that some courts will not enforce the provision because the language is too subjective and vague.

Despite the legal uncertainty whether such a clause would be honored by a court, a more specific clause clarifies responsibilities.

"Spell out who is going to mail the betas to the press, which press people the distributor is contacting," says Andrew Nelson of CyberFlix. "The more explicit the agreement, the better, all the way down to approving the distributor's marketing budget. You should determine where the marketing dollars are being spent and approve the plan. You also need to make sure that the marketing people take your title seriously."

A provision stating a minimum amount of units that must be sold in a specific period of time has been used by some developers. Other goals might be a minimum amount of direct calls to retail accounts or a certain amount of dollar sales to be earned within a specific period of time.

8. COMPETING PRODUCTS: Some developers have been able to negotiate noncompete clauses, whereby the distributor agrees not to distribute "competing" products. Developers with leverage have successfully bargained for such a clause, providing that the provision clearly spells out what is considered a competing product.

9. TERMINATION: Most distributors will ask for at least two Christmas seasons and the post-Christmas quarter to distribute the product. But developers who have entered into agreements with newcomers to the distribution of CD-ROM have been able to negotiate a shorter time frame.

If possible, the developer should include performance criteria—revenue goals or a marketing budget amount—that the distributor must meet to avoid termination of the agreement.

10. PAYMENT: The developer might want to include in the agreement a termination clause that ends the relationship if the distributor fails to pay the developer on time, which is a fairly common problem in the industry. That provision is too drastic for some developers, who prefer to trigger a clause that changes the distribution agreement from an exclusive to a nonexclusive license when payment falls behind schedule.

Developers also request a sales report, delineating as much information as possible about sales. Some distribution agreements require the distributor to break down sales by geographic area, type of store, and time frame for the sales.

11. WARRANTIES AND INDEMNIFICATION: The distributor will require the developer to warrant that it owns the work, and that it does not infringe on anyone else's' intellectual property rights.

HOW TO HOOK UP WITH A DISTRIBUTOR

Most developers establish their first contact with a potential distributor by attending one of the many trade shows or multimedia conferences that are held throughout the country.

Substance Interactive linked with Sony Imagesoft at the Fall 1993 Comdex in Las Vegas. Serious negotiations with Sony followed, and for seven months the two companies hammered out an arrangement so that Substance Interactive could be distributed beyond its 1-800 number.

Randy Thier, vice president and general manager, PC Division of Sony Imagesoft said of the arrangement, "We are distributing *substance.digizine* not only because it is innovative, but more importantly because it delivers on the promise that digital magazines should be interactive."

The Los Angeles developer, Vortex Media Arts, formed a relationship with Time-Warner Interactive by turning to the William Morris Agency.

"The talent agencies are a good way to tap into the traditional media companies that want to get into interactive software," says Chris Takami, vice president of creative development at Vortex.

Stories circulate of developers meeting with publishers and distributors at the nonprofit Washington D.C. based Software Publishers Association conferences. For instance, at its 1994 spring symposium held in San Francisco, developers were able to meet one-on-one with venture capitalists, consultants, and international companies.

The more established a developer becomes, the easier it is for the developer to enter a relationship with a publisher who also provides distribution on the basis of a good idea she has for a product.

If you cannot make one of these conferences (some of which are very expensive), then another way to make contact is to call a publisher's Products Development Group, which is the main contact for new developers who are searching for financing.

(OPYRIGHT, TRADE SE(RET, TRADEMARK, AND PATENTS

Although there are four main bodies of law that protect intellectual property, the federal Copyright Act is the one most relevant to the multimedia developers. The other three, trademark, trade secret, and patent law, will also be discussed in this chapter.

BASIC COPYRIGHT LAW

Copyright law is used to protect your multimedia creations from the unauthorized use by other parties. It also protects preexisting content, thereby requiring you to obtain a license from the copyright holder before using the material in your product.

The Copyright Act protects "original works of authorship," including literary, dramatic, musical, and audiovisual—such as multimedia—for the life of the author, plus fifty years. If you file a copyright registration form with the Copyright Office in Washington D.C. to protect your multimedia product and it is approved by the agency, the Copyright Act gives you and those people whom you authorize the exclusive right to do the following:

- To reproduce the copyrighted work;
- To prepare derivative, or new works based on the original copyrighted work;
- To distribute copies of the copyrighted work to the public;
- To perform the copyrighted work publicly; and
- To display the copyrighted work publicly.

If you are the owner of the copyright to your multimedia product, anyone else who reproduces, prepares derivative works, distributes copies, performs or displays the work publicly has infringed on your copyright and is liable for damages. For instance, at the 1995 Intermedia conference in San Francisco, the marketing director for Luminaria spotted twenty-two unauthorized copies of the publisher's title *Wrath of the Gods* and had a police officer arrest the booth manager for selling and profiting from counterfeit computer software, which is a misdemeanor.

If someone takes photos that appear in your CD-ROM and digitally alters them, that person has infringed your copyright because they have created a derivative work without a license. If you take someone's black and white photo and colorize it without a license, you have infringed on someone else's copyright because you have created a derivative work.

You, as copyright owner, can give a license to someone else to exercise the rights that you hold. There are exceptions to this rule, however, that allow another individual to use your work without your permission. These exceptions are listed later in this chapter.

Requirements for Copyright Protection

Several requirements must be met before a developer or any other author can claim a copyright in the work.

1. The work must be fixed in tangible form. If you have an idea for a product, but never write it down or create it in some fixed form, it cannot be copyrighted. For instance, an oral presentation that is not fixed in writing is not copyrightable.

The fixation need not be directly perceptible, as long as it may be communicated with the aid of a machine, such as a computer. A multimedia title on a CD-ROM disk is fixed expression. Once the author puts the idea in fixed form, the author normally becomes the copyright owner, as long as the following conditions are also met.

2. The work must be original. Copyright law requires a minimum amount of originality for the work to be protected: novelty or uniqueness is not a requirement. A work that is not original enough is one that consists entirely of information or facts. For example, height and weight charts, calendars, tape measures, and lists of tables taken from public documents do not meet the originality requirement.

Even if another work exists that is exactly the same, as long as the author created the work on her own, the author can obtain copyright protection for her work under the "independent creation doctrine."

3. The work must fall into one of the categories of copyrightable subject matter outlined by the Copyright Act. Some of the categories include literary works (which include computer programs), musical works, choreography, sound recordings, motion pictures, sculptural and architectural works, and—most important for the developer—audiovisual works.

Some categories that are not listed as copyrightable subject matter include ideas and facts. If the arrangement of those facts is original enough, however, the work could fall into the literary works category and be protected.

4. Notice. For works created after March 1, 1989, you no longer need to attach a copyright notice. However, it would be wise to add notice of a copyright to let others know that you are the owner. It also means that someone infringing your copyright cannot argue "innocent infringement," thereby reducing the amount of damages the infringer must pay.

The notice should contain three elements: (1) The letter C in a circle or the word "copyright" or the abbreviation "copr."; (2) The year of first publication of the work. Publication means that the work has been distributed to the public by sale, rental, lending, or lease. If the work is a derivative work or compilation, the date of first publication of the compilation or derivative work; (3) The name of the owner of the copyright in the work. The notice can be displayed on the computer screen or on the box containing the multimedia product.

The components that make up your multimedia product also affect whether you will own the copyright in the final title. Read in chapter 9, under Copyright Ownership, about the difference between using employees versus independent contractors to create the work. In general, if an employee develops the work—a photo, interface design, code—the employer owns the copyright. If an independent contractor creates it, this hired party owns the copyright, unless the developer obtains an assignment or the work is created as a work-made-for-hire.

If the developer bases her CD-ROM on a preexisting work, such as a novel or children's book, the developer must obtain permission or a license to do so because the multimedia product is a derivative of the book. Only the copyright holder of the book has the right under the copyright law to create derivative works.

Copyright protection is also granted by other countries who are party to the international treaties, the Berne Convention and the Universal Copyright Convention.

REGISTRATION OF THE COPYRIGHT

While you do not have to register with the Copyright Office to gain copyright protection of your work, if you register within three months of first publication or distribution of copies to the public, you gain distinct advantages, such as winning statutory damages anywhere from $500 to $20,000 and attorneys fees in a lawsuit against an infringer. To order a registration form, call the Copyright Office's hotline for forms at (202) 707-9100 or call the public information number at (202) 707-3000. The Copyright Office also provides free publications explaining copyright law and the different forms one must use to register material.

Without registration, you are confined to actual damages suffered and profits lost, which are often difficult to prove.

Registration also gives notice to others that you are the owner of the copyright. To register your work with the Copyright Office, you need to send the following three elements, in the same envelope, to the Register of Copyrights, Copyright Office, Library of Congress, Washington, D.C. 20559-6000:

1. *A completed application form.* For CD-ROM multimedia titles, use Form PA, which stands for performing arts. This form is used for motion pictures and audiovisual works. Though multimedia is not specifically listed, it is most similar to the audiovisual works category. (Form PA is reproduced in the Appendix.) If you only want to register the written script or the manual for your multimedia product, then use Form TX.

2. *A $20 filing fee for each application.*

3. *A nonreturnable copy of the work you created.* For CD-ROM products, you need to submit only one copy of the CD-ROM and all of the materials that are publicly distributed in the CD package, including the manual and printed material in the packaged box. If you have a written copy of the product's script, you need to submit that as well as a copy of the software that operates the CD-ROM, even if it is not embodied on the CD and even if the copyright owner is not the same person as the CD-ROM's. If the Copyright Office does not have the technology to view the product, it will require you to submit a video of the program.

You will need to file only one registration application if: (a) The owner of the copyright is the same person for all components that make up the product; and (b) All elements of the multimedia product were published at the same time (without including preexisting material, which is not subject to a claim of authorship).

If you intend to license some of the components to other people, such as the software engine, then you should file a separate registration form for these parts.

Filling Out Form PA

SPACE 1

Title: Give the title of the work as it appears on advertising and marketing material.

Nature of the Work: For Form PA, state "audiovisual work."

SPACE 2

Name of Author: The author is the person who created the work. If the work was a "work-made-for-hire," the employer is considered the author. Do not put down the names of the employees or the independent contractor.

If you licensed preexisting material, do not list the authors of this content in this section.

Nature of Authorship: Here, you describe the author's copyrightable contribution to the work. For example:

a. If the author created photographic slides, use Form PA and state "photography."

b. If the author wrote the manual, use Form TX and state "text of manual."

SPACE 3

Creation: Give the year in which authorship of the last element of the multimedia title was completed.

Publication: If the multimedia title has been published—that is, distributed to the public by sale, rental, lending or lease—give the date of first publication. If this version of the title is a revised version, give the date and nation of the first publication. If you have not yet "published" your title, then do not fill in this space.

SPACE 4

Copyright Claimant: The copyright claimant is the author or the person or organization that has obtained all the rights in the U.S. copyright. This name is the same one you put in Space 2 under "author."

Transfer: If you are the claimant of the copyright, but not the author, you need to explain how you acquired the copyright. For instance, if you own the copyright through assignment, write "by written assignment" from the author of the work. Other acceptable transfers mechanisms include "by will," or "by written contract."

If the names in Space 2 and 4 are different, but they are the same legal entity, you need to explain the relationship between the names, such as "Mary Johnson doing business as Quick Magic."

SPACE 5

Previous Registration: If you have already registered the work, or part of it, or a previous version, answer "yes." Check the appropriate box indicating why you are seeking a second registration.

SPACE 6

DERIVATIVE WORK OR COMPILATION: Complete this section only if the work being registered incorporates material that (1) was previously published; or (2) was previously registered in the U.S. Copyright Office; or (3) is in the public domain. Essentially, if you used preexisting material, you need to fill out Space 6.

6(a): Describe the preexisting material. For text, "previously published text;" for video "previously published video."

6(b): In this section, you are trying to show that you added enough originality to the preexisting content that you qualify for copyright protection. For instance, you can write, "new text, new photography, and video."

SPACE 7

Deposit Account: Leave this section blank and attach the $20 fee payable to the Register of Copyrights. You can set up a "deposit account" with the Copyright Office if you have twelve or more transactions each year.

SPACES 8 AND 9

Certification: Sign your name.

Mail Certification To: Fill out the mailing label.

THE VISUAL ARTISTS RIGHTS ACT OF 1990

Unlike Europe, the United States historically did not recognize the "moral rights" of an artist. That changed in 1990, when the United States joined Europe in upholding, in a limited form, an artists' moral rights.

Essentially, a moral right gives the author the right to prohibit the intentional distortion, mutilation, or other alterations that would damage the artist's honor or reputation. It also allows the author to prevent the use of his or her name on work not created by the author, or on work so altered that it is damaging to the artist's honor or reputation.

If a developer plans to alter an artist's work, the developer needs to consider whether she might violate the Visual Artists Rights Act, but only if the content is a "work of visual art" created on or after June 1, 1991. If the artist created the work before that date, the Act applies if the copyright to the product was not transferred or given to another person.

Works of visual art include: limited editions of two hundred copies or fewer of paintings, drawings, prints, sculptures, and photographs. The works must be signed and consecutively numbered by the author. The Act does not apply to works-made-for-hire. This right is non-assignable and lasts for the artist's lifetime. If the work was jointly created, the moral rights last for a term consisting of the life of the last surviving author. Even if the author has assigned his copyright to another person, the author still holds the moral right to his work. This right, however, can be waived by the artist.[1]

While the U.S. version of moral rights is narrower than other countries', the developer who plans to distribute her product internationally needs to satisfy the broader international renditions of the law.

WHEN YOU ARE FREE TO COPY PREEXISTING MATERIAL
Fair Use

The law provides a "fair use" exception to copyright infringement for uses that are minimal, contribute to the public dialogue, and do not interfere with the economic benefits of a copyright owner.

Unfortunately, fair use is a fairly ambiguous concept, and it is often difficult to determine without first going to court what is and is not fair use. The Northern California band, Negativeland, for instance, has had a couple run-ins with the fair use doctrine. Like some multimedia developers, Negativeland samples snippets of speech, song, text, and commercial advertising to build its songs of media satire and commentary.

In 1993, the band was sued twice when it released its fifteen minute single on SST Records titled "U2" that parodied the song "I Still Haven't Found What I'm Looking For." The song, "U2," included disc jockey Casey Kasem cursing his underlings while fumbling through an introduction of the U2 song for his "American Top 40" program.

Island Records, U2's label, sued Negativeland and won. SST Records defended Negativeland, then sued the band to recover the $90,000 in legal fees it incurred.

Despite the suits, the members of the band are committed to expanding the interpretation of the fair use doctrine to allow sampling of recorded materials for parody or commentary.

"We've been using bits and pieces of the media as long as we've been around. The bits and pieces that we use are our choices of color, our palette," says Mark Hosler.[2] Obtaining licenses or permissions to use the material is impractical when up to a hundred sources might be used for a single musical piece, adds Hosler.

Fair use is defined by four elements and the courts look at all four rather than relying on one factor to determine whether a use is fair or unfair:

1. Purpose and character of use: If the copying of the copyrighted work is for commercial reasons, this weighs against a finding of fair use. If the newly created work that incorporates a copyrighted work falls into a genre of criticism, commentary, news reporting, teaching, scholarship, or research, then it is probably fair use.

2. Nature of the copyrighted work: If you copied a work that is fiction or unpublished, this factor weighs against a fair use finding. If you copied an underlying idea of the preexisting copyrighted work, then it is likely fair use. Copyright protection is given to original works of authorship that exist in a tangible form of expression. Only when the idea is put down on paper, video, tape, or some other medium is it protected by copyright law.

3. Amount and substantiality of portion used: The more you use of the copyrighted work in your multimedia title, the higher the chance that this factor will weigh against a fair use finding. However, use of even a small part of a work can be considered infringement if it is considered the "signature" portion of the underlying work.

4. *Effect on the potential market for the copyrighted work:* If the challenged use became widespread, would it adversely affect the potential market for the copyrighted work? If so, this finding weighs against fair use. Courts have held this to be the most important of the four fair use factors.

Reverse Engineering of Software

Accolade, Inc., an independent developer, manufacturer, and marketer of computer entertainment software, wanted to make its products compatible for the Genesis console, but first needed to understand the computer code. Accolade reverse engineered—took apart the computer language—Sega's videogame programs. Based on this process, Accolade released the game *Ishido*, which had originally been issued for the Macintosh and PC systems, for use with the Genesis console.

The court held that if reverse engineering is the only means of access to understand the ideas and processes used to make software compatible, then it is a fair use. The court paid particularly close attention to factor number four, the effect on Sega's market. Accolade wanted to be a legitimate competitor of Genesis-compatible games, but the court found that videogame users typically buy more than one game. Therefore, Accolade's *Ishido* has not significantly affected the market for Sega's title, *Altered Beast*.[3]

Parody

Parody is considered a fair use if it meets certain requirements. The underlying copyrighted work that is being parodied must be well-known: if it is not famous, it cannot be poked fun at because no one would recognize the underlying work. The underlying work also must be the target of the humor. Finally, the second work can use only enough of the work to conjure up or recall the object of the satire.

But as noted above, what a court considers to be fair use is hard to determine. For instance, Delrina created a screen saver program that included Opus, a comic strip character, shooting at a "flying toaster," which Delrina claimed was a "fair use" parody of the Berkeley System's *After Dark* screen saver program.[4] The court rejected Delrina's argument and found that the use was not fair use.

Public Domain

Twin Books Corp., a Connecticut-based publishing company, thought it had the rights to the character, Bambi. It had purchased the rights in 1993 from the widower of Anna Wyler, whose father published the original story in 1923. Based on this belief, Twin Books sued The Walt Disney Company in 1994 for infringing its copyright.

But a judge ruled that Bambi had fallen into the public domain because the original author failed to renew the story's copyright until three years after its expiration.[5]

Works in the public domain are not protected by copyright and developers can use this content without obtaining a license. Unfortunately, difficulties still exist when using public domain work.

One way to help navigate the public domain of content is to determine how a piece of material landed in the public domain.

A work can enter the public domain in several ways. A work such as the movie, *It's a Wonderful Life,* can end up in the public domain by mistake. The Copyright Act has been revised several times so there are different sets of laws in operation right now, a situation that can cause confusion resulting in mistakes.

Essentially, there are three Copyright Acts in operation. The first act covers works created within 75 years ago, but before 1978. The second act covers works developed from January 1, 1978 to February, 1989. The third act covers material created after March 1, 1989.

Under the first act, copyright protection lasted twenty-eight years. In that twenty-eighth year, the original author could renew the protection and receive an additional twenty-eight years by filing a "renewal" application at the Copyright Office. If the copyright owner failed to renew, the work went into the public domain.

Under the first act, if the author forgot to place a copyright notice on her work when it was published, it also fell into the public domain.

Under the second act, if the five year period to cure an omitted or incorrect copyright notice has passed, the work would usually go into the public domain.

For works copyrighted and renewed before January 1, 1978, the protection lasts for seventy-five years. So in 1995, works first published before January 1, 1920 are in the public domain in the U.S. Look at the date of the copyright notice: if it is more than seventy-five years ago, the work is likely to be in the public domain.

Newly created products that are based on public domain material, however, might be copyrighted if they meet the requirements of the Copyright Act. Therefore, you can use the public domain content, but not the new products based on the public domain material.

If you are considering distributing your product to international markets, you might need a license even for public domain material because some countries recognize a longer copyright period than the U.S.

Even if you determine that a film has fallen into the public domain, some elements of the film may not have entered the public domain. For instance, the underlying script, music, or voiceovers may still be protected. A work that includes a poem from the public domain may carry a valid copyright in the overall compilation of public domain elements. The underlying work, such as a novel, from which the movie was derived may not be in the public domain. For instance, although the movie, *It's a Wonderful Life*, entered the public domain in 1974, Republic Pictures obtained the copyright in the underlying short story and the soundtrack. As a result, Republic Pictures was able to prevent the distribution of video cassettes and public performance of the movie.[6]

Determining the copyright status of a work is expensive and difficult. A search of the Copyright Office records may help you determine whether a work was renewed or an omitted notice cured. Such a search requires, at a minimum, the name of the author and/or the title of the original work. You can discover what works fell into the public domain this way by ordering a renewal search from the Copyright Office.

Copying Facts

You do not need a license to copy facts from a preexisting copyrighted work. The Copyright Act only protects original works of authorship and facts are not considered original. In 1970, Jay Robert Nash published a book, *Dillinger: Dead or Alive?* about an FBI most wanted criminal, John Dillinger. Nash's book proposed his theory that Dillinger is still alive and the FBI attempt to catch and kill him failed.

In 1984 CBS made a move using Nash's theory. Nash sued, but the court held that the author's copyright lies in the expressions used in the book and the arrangement of facts, but not the facts themselves.[7]

Copying Ideas

Copyright protection applies to original works of authorship fixed in any tangible form of expression. It does not extend to ideas, procedures, processes, systems, concepts, principles, or methods of operations.

Merger Between Idea and Expression

If there are only a limited number of ways to implement an idea, such as the graphic depiction of a spreadsheet, the idea has merged—or is inseparable—from the expression of the idea. In the example, the spreadsheet would not be copyrightable.

TRADE SECRET LAW

The Uniform Trade Secrets Act defines a trade secret as information that "derives independent economic value, actual or potential, from not being generally known to, and not being readily ascertainable by proper means by other persons who can obtain economic from its disclosure." A trade secret is information—a marketing plan, formula, software program, method of research, a technique—that is of value to the employer and that is not known by others. Unlike copyright law, this information does not have to be in tangible form to be protected.

Courts will consider the following factors to determine whether something is protected by trade secret law:

- Is the information known outside the company?
- Do all employees of the company know the information?
- What has the employer done to protect the information from disclosure?
- How valuable is the information to the owner? To competitors?
- How much time, research, and money did the owner invest in developing or gathering the information?
- How easily could others figure out the information?

If a secret is taken by improper means, such as theft or breach of a confidential relationship, then the trade secret owner has a cause of action against the infringer. Traditional software companies have set up elaborate procedures to screen potential employees to avoid using a competitors' trade secrets. When an employee leaves the company, traditional software companies also conduct in-depth exit interviews, pointing out what knowledge the employee has that is considered a trade secret.

If the information is not protected by the employer or loses value, it is no longer a trade secret. But as long as those conditions are met—through nondisclosure agreements with employees, independent contractors, and third parties—the information remains protected, potentially in perpetuity.

TRADEMARK LAW

The design team at a small development company wanted to create a product in which the opening scene included a walk down Main Street and the user passed by companies' signs or billboards, which made fun of the businesses' products. The developer did the storyboards for the product, but the publisher expressed some doubts. The publisher was concerned about a lawsuit based on several causes of action, including trademark infringement.

The developer came back with a different approach: this time, photos of companies' logos or well known products would be merged with photos that connected the corporations with bad PR events. Again, the publisher rejected the idea, concerned about infringing companies' trademarks.

Trademarks are symbols, words, names, or designs used by a merchant or manufacturer to identify and distinguish his goods or services from others'. Tide, Comet, Pepsi, and Pine Sol are trademarks.

The key factor determining whether something will be given trademark status is whether it is a distinguishing mark. A generic term or common descriptive terms, such as "magazine," "decaffeinated coffee," or "light beer," to describe the corresponding product cannot be trademarks.

If the descriptive term acquires a secondary meaning that becomes distinctive of the applicant's goods, it can be a valid trademark. For instance, when the consumers in a particular geographic area hear a descriptive word, the word would have secondary meaning if they thought of a particular product.

A "suggestive" term, such as "Coppertone," that implies rather than describes an ingredient or characteristic of the goods and requires the consumer to use imagination to determine the nature of the goods can be protected under trademark law.

An arbitrary mark, such as Coke, Velveeta, Swatch, and Apple Computer, conveys no information about the product and therefore is the strongest candidate to receive trademark protection.

While it is not necessary to file a trademark application with the Patent and Trademark Office to secure rights to a trademark, you receive stronger protection if you file an application and register the trademark. Protection lasts for ten years and can be renewed, but only if the trademark is still in use. A new aspect of trademark law is that marks not in use can be protected for a limited time by the filing of an "intent to use" form with the Patent and Trademark Office.

To protect your trademark, you need to continuously use it and prevent others from using it in such a way that the consumer is confused. If the trademark becomes a generic terms, such as xerox, aspirin, or yo-yo, you lose trademark protection.

If a developer uses someone else's trademark in such a way that she causes confusion, the developer has infringed the trademark. A court will consider the following in determining whether there is confusion: whether the parties are competitors, the similarity between the trademarks, and the sophistication of the consumers in the particular market.

A highly recognizable character or design should not be used without permission, even if you think the copyright has lapsed, because the mark may still function as a trademark.

As for the developer who wanted to parody companies' trademarks? Courts are not that hospitable to such humor. A T-shirt company, in an attempt to parody Mutual of Omaha, created T-shirts that read "Mutant of Omaha" that included an emaciated human head and the words "Nuclear Holocaust Insurance." The court ruled that the slogan was likely to be confused with plaintiff's "Mutual of Omaha," and therefore infringed on the insurance company's trademark.[8] But there are cases going the other way. A court rejected a "confusion" argument against the study guide, "Spy Notes," parodying "Cliff Notes."

PATENT LAW

In August, 1993, the Patent Office granted Compton's NewMedia a patent on the process and concept of searching databases comprising multiple data types. The patent described the invention as "... a search system [that] uses a multimedia database consisting of text, picture, audio, and animated data. That database is searched through multiple graphical and textual entry paths."

In November, when the patent was announced, multimedia experts cried foul. If upheld, the patent would affect everyone from CD-ROM publishers to authoring tool developers to people putting information on Web servers on the Internet.

In an unusual step, the Patent Office decided to review its own decision, and in October 1994, the PTO rejected all claims in the patent, finding that Compton's technology existed before Compton's patent application and therefore the patent was void.

As a result of the Compton patent problem, the Patent Office changed the rules so that third parties can now participate in re-examination proceedings. The PTO also now publishes patent applications prior to approval.

Patent law can be used by multimedia developers to protect their software. But as the Compton case shows, the processes, inventions, or designs submitted to the Patent Office must be new, a useful improvement, and "nonobvious."

To meet the "new" requirement, you must be the first person to have invented the process or design. Most other countries that offer patent protection require you to be the first to file a patent registration. To receive a patent, you need to file a patent application with the U.S. Patent and Trademark Office, describing how to make and use the invention and defining which aspects of the invention are new, useful, and nonobvious. The invention must be "nonobvious" to someone working in the particular field in which the new creation is used.

The Patent Office will investigate your patent application to determine if the invention was described elsewhere first or if a patent already exists on a similar process or product.

If you are the first to invent an invention or new process (rather than the first to file a patent application), you will receive a utility patent that protects your creation for seventeen years. A design patent is given to the creator if the design is new, original and ornamental. Design patents are granted for fourteen years. Under either type of patent, you are granted the exclusive right to make, use, or sell the invention to the absolute exclusion of others. Patents are infringed when someone, without consent, creates, uses, or sells a patented invention.

Patents are difficult to obtain compared to copyright protection. If you want to patent your software, locate a patent attorney who can advise you.

International Patents

If you will be selling your multimedia title internationally, you should ask your attorney about obtaining separate patent protection in those countries.

U.S. companies that decide to develop an international patent portfolio generally choose to file patent applications in a short list of the key markets for their products. Most common among them are Canada, Japan, Australia, and the European Patent Community (a confederation of Northern European countries with a unified patent examination system).

There are two major international patent conventions, the Patent Cooperation Treaty and the Paris Union Convention for the Protection of Industrial Property, to which the United States is a party. These allow a U.S. company to receive priority based on the date of the U.S. patent application for corresponding applications in the other member countries. In a PCT member country, the application must be filed within thirty months of the U.S. filing. In a Paris Convention member country, the application must be filed within twelve months of the U.S. filing.

Whether they are party to a patent convention or not, most other countries have patent laws that differ significantly from the U.S. scheme. The fundamental difference is that most countries have a "first to file" system, whereas the United States and the Philippines alone have a "first to invent" system.

---

1. See 17 U.S.C. section 106A of the Copyright Act.
2. *Los Angeles Times*, 1993.
3. 92 Daily Journal DAR 24275, 1992 WL 293141, United States Court of Appeals, Ninth Circuit. The court's reasoning is highly disputed by legal scholars. However, this is the law that applies in the 9th Circuit.
4. *Berkeley Systems, Inc.* v. *Delrina Corporation*, Case No. C-93-3345 EFL (N. D. Cal, October 15, 1993).
5. *Twin Books Corp.* v. *The Walt Disney Co.*, 94-00923 CW.
6. *Newsday*, "For Some Viewers, It Won't Be a Wonderful Christmas" (December 5, 1993) at 20.
7. *Nash* v. *CBS, Inc.* 899 F.2d 1537 (1990).
8. *Mutual of Omaha Insurance Company* v. *Novak*, 836 F.2d 397 (8th Cir. 1987).

CHAPTER NINE

EMPLOYEES AND
INDEPENDENT CONTRACTORS

Working out of a San Francisco live/work space, the founders of Eden Interactive know what they will receive in the mail. It is the same thing every day. Eden's commitment to nonviolent, quality edutainment titles attracts twenty to twenty-five new resumes a week, from artists, programmers, and graphic designers, who are interested in becoming part of the Eden creative team.

Minoo Saboori, co-founder of Eden, will open every resume, review it and consider whether the candidate would be appropriate for the next title. The company does not have a war chest of funds to hire forty or fifty employees. If someone looks promising, they will not be brought on board as an employee, but as an independent contractor.

With the help of independent contractors, Eden Interactive has fine-tuned the development process to such an extent that it can accomplish the near impossible: it developed two edutainment products in seven months. Generally, the development time frame for such titles is at least six months. For entertainment titles, the production time is usually eighteen months. During production time, Eden's six core employees and a team of eighteen independent contractors who are hired on a per-project basis, similar to the film industry, work round the clock.

"It's our philosophy to expand by hiring independent contractors for production and contract again when the project is completed," says Saboori. "We don't believe in having infrastructure for infrastructure's sake."

At a minimum, a typical developer's team consists of a handful of critical people: a project manager (also called a producer), a script writer, two programmers, and, if the title is a consumer-oriented one, a marketing director or public relations-type person. In addition to lowering costs, the use of independent contractors and employees to create original material, as opposed to relying primarily on preexisting content, is the simplest way to claim full copyright ownership to the final multimedia title (as long as the developer/employer goes through some hoops to secure the copyright, as explained in this chapter).

"We wanted to create the best possible reputation to draw the best talent in the industry," says Saboori. "We've been able to do that."

While the use of independent contractors is pervasive in the industry and they are often treated as employees, the Copyright Act views employees and independent contractors differently.

INDEPENDENT CONTRACTOR VERSUS EMPLOYEE

Joe Sparks, co-founder of Pop Rocket in San Francisco, used to work at Chicago-based Reactor Inc. and helped create the sci-fi thriller title *Spaceship Warlock*. The product landed on computer store shelves with a splash, but Sparks and his former collaborator Michael Saenz did not feel like celebrating. Instead, Sparks filed a lawsuit claiming that he was a joint author of the product and entitled to the copyright and half the profits of the title. Saenz argued that Sparks was an employee—Reactor's vice president of research and development—and therefore had no copyright ownership in the product because it was produced in the scope of Spark's employment. Saenz said that Sparks was paid in full for his services, $53,000.

The two worked together by phone and fax machine, with Saenz designing the storyboards in Chicago and Sparks creating the music and three-dimensional models in San Francisco, according to Sparks. Between the two of them, Sparks stated that they worked out the overall design, animation, and programming. The lawsuit was finally settled out of court.

Whether someone is an independent contractor or employee is important for determining who owns the copyright to the work. Unfortunately the U.S. Supreme Court developed an unwieldy test, listing thirteen factors to make that determination. While no one single factor settles a worker's status, when a significant number of the thirteen factors point toward independent contractor status, it is likely that person is not an employee.

The safest route is to require all employees and independent contractors to sign an agreement that assigns or transfers the ownership of the copyright of all works created by that hired person, as well as trademarks, trade secrets, and patents to the developer. The assignment should be made on the first day of work.

This gesture may seem overly cautious, but if the developer plans to distribute his product outside the United States, some foreign countries do not recognize the "work-made-for hire" doctrine, and without an assignment, it is more likely that the employee or independent contractor who created the work—and not the employer—will be considered the copyright holder. If that is the case, the developer will have to license the work from the employee to use it in the title.

An assignment also covers the developer if an employee later claims, like Sparks did in his lawsuit, to be something other than an employee. It also ensures that the developer is the owner of patents, trade secrets, and trademarks that are not covered by the work-made-for-hire rule.

Here are the factors to determine whether a person is an independent contractor or an employee. In close cases, an attorney should be consulted.

1. Does the party who is hired have discretion over when and how long to work? If not, the person is most likely an employee.

2. Is the relationship between the developer and the person hired a long or short-term relationship? If it is long term, then that person is most likely an employee.

3. Does the developer provide the instruments and tools for the work to be completed? If yes, then that person is likely an employee.

4. Is the work performed at the developer's office? If yes, then that person is likely an employee.

5. Does the developer provide employee benefits to the hired person? If yes, then that person is likely an employee.

6. Does the developer deduct employee-related taxes for the person hired? If the developer pays a share of the employee's social security tax, withholds the employee's share of social security taxes, pays federal and state unemployment tax and workers' compensation insurance, that person is most likely an employee.

7. Is the work being done by the hired party part of the regular business of the developer? If yes, that person is likely an employee.

8. Can the developer assign additional projects to the person who has been hired? If the agreement with the hired person is not limited to specific project(s), then that person is likely an employee.

9. Does the hired party have a particular skill for which he or she was hired? If not, that person is likely an employee.

10. Does the person who was hired have any responsibility for hiring and paying assistants? If yes, that person is likely an employee.

11. Does the developer have control over the manner and means by which the person hired completes the project? If yes, that person is likely an employee.

12. Is the developer/hiring party in business? If yes, that person that was hired by the developer is likely an employee.

13. How does the developer/hiring party pay the hired person? If payment is through a salary that is paid bi-weekly or monthly, that person is likely an employee.[1]

In practical terms, if the developer/employer deducts social security and other taxes from the hired party's paycheck and controls the conditions of the workplace, the "when," "where," and "how" of the work, it is difficult for the employer to argue that the hired person is an independent contractor.

If most of these factors point to an employee, one more requirement must be met before the employer can claim copyright ownership in the work: the employee must have created the work in the scope of employment. If someone is hired to write interactive multimedia scripts, for instance, that hired party would own the copyright to photographs that were shot by her on the weekends. This activity is outside the scope of her employment.

COPYRIGHT OWNERSHIP

Under the Copyright Act's "work-made-for-hire" rule, work made by employees in the scope of their employment is owned by the employer. The developer (who is considered the employer in this chapter) can sign a written agreement to the contrary, stating that the employee owns the copyright. But if the developer gives away the copyright to an employee, the employee must license it to the developer if it is going to be used in the product.

In most cases, however, when the employee creates the work, the developer will claim ownership of the material under the work-made-for-hire rule. The developer owns the copyright of his employees' work whether the developer is operating as a sole proprietorship, a partnership, or corporation (see chapter 2, under Incorporation). To assure that the employee understands that the developer is the owner of the work, most established developers have their employees and their independent contractors sign a work-made-for-hire agreements on the first day of work. Essentially, the agreement says that the employee agrees to assign and transfer to the company all inventions, creations, designs, software, and improvements made by the employee during the employee's or independent contractor's employment.

Independent contractors, on the other hand, own the copyright to the work that they create—even if the developer specifically ordered it and paid for it. To transfer the copyright from the independent contractor to the employer, one of two things must happen.

1. ASSIGNMENT: The developer obtains an assignment of the copyright from the independent contractor. If it is unclear whether the hired party is an employee or an independent contractor, the developer should assume she is an independent contractor and obtain an assignment.

2. WORK-MADE-FOR-HIRE: If the hired party is an independent contractor, the work created by the freelancer must fall within one of the

legally prescribed categories of "work for hire" set out by the Copyright Act. The developer and the individual must also have a written agreement signed by both parties before the work is started. The agreement should state that the work will be created as a "work-made-for-hire." The categories in the Copyright Act include:[2]

- A contribution to a collective work
- A work that is part of a motion picture or other audiovisual work
- A translation
- A supplementary work—a work prepared as a secondary adjunct to a work created by another author
- A compilation
- An instructional text
- A test
- Answer material for a test
- An atlas

The most likely category in which the work for a multimedia product will fall is—a work that is part of an audiovisual product, or multimedia product. In addition, any smaller work that accompanies a larger work could qualify as a supplementary work. If the work does not fall into one of the above categories, then it is not a work-made-for-hire and the developer should obtain an assignment of the copyright. To bolster an argument that the content is a work-made-for-hire, the agreement should be executed *before* the content is developed.[3]

In most cases, if a developer commissions a freelance or independent contractor programmer to create a software program that will be used in the product, the software will not qualify as a work-made-for-hire because it does not readily fit within one of the nine statutory categories. Even if the programmer agrees to a contract that calls the program a work-made-for-hire, it is safer to obtain an assignment to acquire rights to the software or to enter into a licensing agreement.

ASSIGNMENTS

When *Playboy* magazine paid its freelance writers and artists for articles and artwork designed for the magazine, the publisher thought it had obtained an assignment of the copyrights to the works because the legend on the check endorsement stated that it was an assignment of "all right, title and interest" in the works to *Playboy*. An assignment is a transfer of copyright ownership. But a court found otherwise. The court ruled that *Playboy* also needed to present evidence of an intention on the part of the artist and writer to transfer the copyright to *Playboy*.[4]

In addition to intentions, a valid assignment must be in writing and signed by the holder of the rights or his or her agent. A provision such as the following has been used by developers to obtain an assignment:

"The independent contractor hired for this project assigns to the developer all his or her intellectual property rights in his or her copyrightable works and other creations."

The developer should register the transfer with the Copyright Office so that other developers who might be interested in using the work have notice of the current copyright holder.

This assignment will transfer copyright ownership of the work for thirty-five years. After that, the freelancer can terminate the assignment based on the copyright law, which allows an author of a work other than a work-made-for-hire to terminate an assignment or license granted on or after January 1, 1978 as long as thirty-five years have passed since the assignment was made. For the developers who live in community property states (Arizona, California, Idaho, Louisiana, Nevada, New Mexico, Texas, Washington, and Wisconsin), the developer should have the spouse of the independent contractor sign a "quitclaim" to the copyright, which would relinquish her rights to the property.

WORK-MADE-FOR-HIRE AGREEMENTS

If the work is created by an independent contractor and therefore the freelancer owns the copyright, the other option for the developer to become the copyright owner is to create a work-made-for-hire agreement. The principal limitation on this method of obtaining the copyright is that the work must fit one of the categories listed above. If it does, the developer and independent contractor should sign a written work-made-for-hire agreement before any work is started. In this document, the developer should also include a provision for an assignment, in case the work does not fit one of the categories specified by the Copyright Act. The agreement should also include a warranty and indemnity clause so that the developer has legal recourse against an independent contractor who uses work owned by a third party.

WHEN NOT TO USE A WORK-MADE-FOR-HIRE AGREEMENT

A work-made-for-hire agreement is not as fool-proof as an assignment. For instance, if a developer knows that the product will be sold internationally (and most developers aim for this expansion since the non-U.S. market represents 50 percent of all CD-ROM sales), the developer should obtain an assignment of the copyright from the independent contractor because many foreign countries do not recognize the work-made-for-hire doctrine.

In addition, some court cases have held that the work-made-for-hire agreement must be signed before the independent contractor starts to create the work. If the developer has failed to do so, an assignment is a better method of obtaining ownership of the copyright.

The work-made-for-hire agreement is not effective for works that are unsolicited. It is unlikely a developer would use a work sent through the mail, but if it is done, obtain an assignment.

JOINT AUTHORSHIP

If the developer and independent contractors intended that their contributions become inseparable or interdependent parts of the final product, then each individual is considered to be a joint author of the copyright in the final title.

For instance, when a software programmer who contributes a special software program for a multimedia title teams with an artist, who creates artwork for the project, without an agreement to the contrary, the two are joint authors.

The joint authors will be joint owners of the work, and together they control the work. Any exclusive grants or licenses of the work will require the consent of all joint authors. All profits from the work will have to be distributed equally among the joint authors, regardless of the authors' original contributions. A joint author, however, cannot sue another one of the authors for copyright infringement.

If the hired party is an employee, then the employee does not become a joint author, even if the work created by the employee is intended to become a part of the product.

To avoid a joint authorship situation, the developer should use an assignment or a work-made-for-hire arrangement.

WARRANTIES

When using an independent contractor, a developer faces certain risks, such as a freelancer using work that he or she already created for another developer. If the former developer owns the copyright to the work, the new developer risks infringing the copyright if the work is used in her title. Warranty and indemnity provisions in a contract give you legal recourse if a contractor uses works belonging to someone else. A cheaper way to avoid this issue is to explain the copyright law to new independent contractors and ask if any of the work they are currently using has been used by another developer or in any other capacity.

NONDISCLOSURE AGREEMENT

While the use of nondisclosure agreements is pervasive in the software and hardware industry, not many small multimedia developers require their employees to sign such agreements.

Substance Interactive uses nondisclosure agreements only when a large company that is interested in distributing its titles comes to the warehouse to view the product.

"We basically don't have the resources to sue anyone who might steal what we've created," explains Alex Ragland, co-founder of Substance Interactive. "If we don't want something disclosed, we don't show it to someone."

Part of the reason for the lack of such agreements is the informal environment in which most developers work. The Substance development team has spent nearly two years living and working out of a warehouse in San Francisco.

As development costs and competition increase, however, more developers will likely ask both employees and independent contractors to sign such agreements. Essentially, the document should say that the employee or independent contractor agrees not to disclose now or in the future the employer's confidential information. Such information includes knowledge and "know how" not generally known in the industry and learned by the employee from the employer or the scope of employment. The agreement might list examples of confidential information, such as marketing plans, software codes, development processes, or customer lists, but it should also say that this is not a complete list. It should also note that the nondisclosure requirements apply on a worldwide basis. Both the employee and the employer should sign the agreement. Please refer to the nondisclosure agreement included in the appendix.

Some developers and publishers also have key employees sign noncompete agreements in states in which they are legal to prevent employees from going to work for direct competitors. The limitations must be reasonable and the developer must provide some compensation to the employee for signing the agreement.

---

1. *Community for Creative Non-Violence* v. *Reid,* 490 U.S. 730 (1989). This case lists the factors that the U.S. Supreme Court used to determine whether someone is an employee or an independent contractor.
2. 1976 Copyright Act, U.S.C. section 201(b).
3. *Schiller & Schmidt, Inc.* v. *Nordisco Corp.,* 969 F.2d 410 (7th Cir. 1992).
4. *Playboy Enterprises* v. *Dumas,* No. 91 Ci. 6268 (SDNY September 9, 1993).

LI(ENSING PREEXISTING (ONTENT

For the first issue of their electronic magazine *substance.digizine*, the founders of Substance Interactive slated feature stories about Trent Reznor of Nine Inch Nails and a founder of an independent film company. They also reviewed 130 albums and interactive software product reviews of Win Images Morph and HSC Digital Morph, which allow the viewer (or reader) to change or "morph" images. To deliver the full flavor of the software, the Substance Interactive team wanted viewers to test out the software on well-known images. They decided to try and license a clip from the movie, *Terminator II*.

When the company approached the movie studio, however, the founders say they were told that the minimum fee to license a clip was $19,000. They tried to explain that they needed less than a minute clip of the movie, that they had scant financial resources, and had lived the better part of a year in a warehouse to save money and create their product. None of their arguments budged the studio lawyers from their original stated price.

Substance located other images to use, and did not yet give up hope of possibly licensing preexisting content. The in-house musician, Ed Bellinaso had copied and included in one of his original songs a spoken line from the movie, *Millennium*. Bellinaso had changed the line, by slowing it down and drawing out the spoken words and fit it into the background of his music.

"We didn't want to be sued so we called to try to get the rights to this spoken line," says Bellinaso. "The phrase probably lasted ten seconds out of a ninety minute movie so I thought the licensing agreement would be relatively straight forward."

Bellinaso dialed up the Warner Brothers legal department to explain what he wanted to do and to receive a price and nearly dropped the phone when the company lawyers said the spoken line would cost $5,000. A couple days later, Bellinaso received a letter from the studio, outlining the allowable uses of its intellectual property. But, according to Bellinaso, from the wording of the letter, it was clear that no one had understood how he was going to use the spoken line.

"The letter referred to the rights to the music in the movie," says Bellinaso. "I was talking about one line to put into my own music." Undeterred, Bellinaso called the lawyers again. But the studio stuck to its original quote. Bellinaso removed the line out of his score, never reaching the other licensing issues, such as gaining clearance from the actress who spoke the line so he would not violate her right of publicity. Nor did he get to address the talent union's reuse fees.

"After that, we decided never again to try and license anything," says Bellinaso. "It's not worth it. We'll create samples in-house."

As the entertainment world and the software industry converge, the one guarantee is that there will be confusion about the business practices, particularly when it comes to licensing. Substance Interactive's encounter with licensing preexisting material is repeated almost every day, by both large, established publishers and small "garage band" developers, with even more complicated plot lines.

Sometimes the complexity of the negotiations stems from an anxious content holder concerned about the interactive medium. The publisher, Sanctuary Woods, for instance, spent fourteen months negotiating a license for one character from a children's story book to use in a CD-ROM product. Afraid of losing out on possible revenue generated from the license, the book publisher, author, illustrator, and a couple other parties who held rights in the character sent six lawyers to Sanctuary Woods to negotiate.

The company's standard character licensing agreement, typically five to six pages, started to increase in size. The book publisher's lawyers wanted a clause that if a new character appeared in the same screen image as their character, the book publishing company owned the new character. They also demanded the right to publish any music that accompanied the story line of the CD-ROM.

Sanctuary Woods agreed to these conditions because, from their perspective, the terms were basically throw-away provisions.

"The music that accompanies our products is great for the particular product, but it's not award winning stuff here," says Mike Scott, formerly with Sanctuary Woods. "I talked to the creative guys about giving the rights to any new characters to the publisher, and they had no intention of creating a new character. That was why we wanted to license a known character."

For other deals, the negotiations become complicated because of the size of the project. Parker Brothers chose its all-time, best selling trivia game Trivial Pursuit to convert to a CD-ROM title. The CD-ROM design called for four thousand new questions and answers, enhanced by video and audio. Questions ranged from the name of the song sung by Madonna, accompanied by a clip of the music and a video of the pop star, to which face is missing on Mt. Rushmore, with a photo of the landmark. Although a promising CD-ROM title, for the developers involved, it was a licensing nightmare.

To handle the licensing, Parker Brothers called on Jill Alofs, owner of Total Clearance, a company that negotiates and clears rights for multimedia developers and publishers. Alofs handled the rights to the title's 1,400 digitized photos, an hour of video, and over 500 sound effects, including voices of celebrities. Alofs had to license some 3,000 multimedia bits in video, sound, photo, and art. Says George deGolian, vice president of interactive entertainment for Western Technologies and executive producer of the Trivial Pursuit CD-ROM, "I'[d] already spent ten months on clearance issues, and that's with outside help."[1]

Licensing preexisting film seems to generate the most disheartening scenarios. To license a five-second clip from *Star Wars* for an unspecified product, Alofs pursued permissions from nine sources, including the actors in the clip, the Screen Actors Guild, the stunt performers who appeared in the scene, stunt coordinators, the director, scriptwriters, the music publisher, the musician's union, and the holders of rights to the film as a whole.

If the movie clip had been based on a novel, Alofs says she would also have had to obtain a license from the copyright holder of the novel, either the publisher or author, to avoid liability. (The movie is called a derivative work—it is derived from an underlying work, the novel—and the copyright holder has a right under the Copyright Act to create derivative works. See chapter 9.)

For small developers, who are focusing on product development, running a business, and raising capital to stay afloat, the problems of licensing are often last on the developer's list. This list of priorities, however, can only lead to more complications.

"The earlier you start to think about licensing issues, the better," says Alofs. "It helps you figure out budgetary considerations and puts you in a better negotiation position."

WHY IS IT SO DIFFICULT TO LICENSE PREEXISTING CONTENT?

Whether a developer is creating CD-ROM based education titles or the next great shoot-em-up product, she will eventually find herself at least investigating the market for preexisting content, a thicket of overpriced text, film, still images, music, and computer software, filled with misun-

derstandings of the hyped up multimedia industry and difficulties of identifying who is the copyright holder.

Most of these problems stem from each industry in which a developer
might be seeking content, such as the book publishing, movie, music, and
TV industries, having had a hundred years or more to develop its own
legal customs, business culture, and traditional licensing terms. For instance, the music industry operates under a model in which royalties are
paid every time a song is played, a principle that does not work well in
multimedia because the user of the CD-ROM decides how many times
the music is played.

Unlike any of these existing traditional media industries, multimedia
products are interactive, which makes it impossible to neatly superimpose any one industry model onto the multimedia market. At the same
time, the interactive characteristic of multimedia makes content holders
nervous about losing control over their material and anxious about price
terms. In addition, it might not be clear who holds the interactive rights,
since this type of use might not have been in existence at the time the
movie, book, or photo was created.

The intensity of negotiations is heightened because developers usually
are interested in a popular song or movie clip to create a "marquee" CD-
ROM title. Not only are the studios and networks charging a lot of money
for the right to use this content—and they want the money upfront—
they want a royalty rate based on net wholesale revenues. According to
Becki Walker, founder of Walker & Associates, a consulting company that
offers marketing and production strategies for multimedia companies, a
developer who pays $2 to $3 in royalties per disk to its licensers will have
a difficult time making a profit.[2]

To ease some of their fears, content holders are increasingly asking for
editorial control to make sure the developer creates a quality product. They
also are granting only nonexclusive licenses and limiting the duration of
the license.

"A lot of content holders got burned by licensing their content to a
developer who created a crappy product," says Michael Scott, of Wildwood Interactive. "They are trying to take precautions so it doesn't happen again."

Some of this fear is justified: once one product is created using particular content and it does not sell well, all other products using similar content face an uphill battle for retailers' attention and ultimately shelf space.

When Sanctuary Woods tried to convince retailers to carry its title based
on an Oscar Wilde fairy tale, says Scott, it ran into trouble because another company had already produced a similar title that did not sell well.

"Even though we were a different company and had a different story
line, the buyers already had it in their minds that Oscar Wilde doesn't

sell," says Scott. "Content providers are becoming really scared now of licensing their content with developers. They don't understand how to evaluate what developers are doing or to control what will be done with the content."

DO YOU NEED PREEXISTING CONTENT?

Whether developers of entertainment or games products—as opposed to education, edutainment or reference titles—need preexisting content to create popular products is a hotly debated subject. On the one hand, some industry observers argue that developers must compete for limited shelf space, and the best way to do that is by securing preexisting content to create "hit" or "marquee" value titles. The title *The Lion King* sold extremely well because of the brand awareness generated by the movie.

On the other hand, small development companies that are creating entertainment titles say that they can do without such content. Like Bellinaso at Substance Interactive, they will create their own.

"For the most part, we don't use preexisting material because it's boring," says Garry Hare, president of Fathom Pictures. "If there's already a video tape of the subject or character, we ask 'why does it want to be interactive?' Most of the existing encoded video that we see, we look at it and say, 'So what?'"

Moreover, developers, particularly producers of entertainment, say they are better off creating their own content because whatever the company creates, it will be its own.

If a developer licenses a third party's character, for instance, he will have to pay royalties or a flat fee. If someone wants to make a movie, cartoon show, or consumer product based on the character in the title, some of the money from this ancillary deal will also go back to the third party who originally created the character.

There are several disadvantages, however, to creating original content. More time is spent on the origination of material, with no certainty that the character or plot line will appeal to the mass market. A longer production schedule results and hence a longer period of time before the company receives a revenue stream.

For instance, the publisher, Luminaria Inc., makers of the CD-ROM adventure game, *Wrath of the Gods*, a problem solving adventure, sent co-founder Joel Skidmore to Greece three times to shoot over three thousand photographs of the country, three hundred of which are used to create the game's background of green rolling hills, winding rivers, and lush valleys. Against this backdrop, the hero-in-training (you) has lost his kingdom and crown. The hero makes his way through various puzzles and fights against the mythical monsters Cyclops and Medusa to reclaim his birthright.

Of the fifteen months it took to create the $700,000 CD-ROM title, three of those months were spent creating the background.

Some entertainment and game developers, however, have broken with the trend and are licensing preexisting content. They have found one of the easier routes to approach movie studios for film clips is to form a relationship with a studio and create a title on a work-made-for-hire basis, using preexisting content. The two parties become acquainted and the developer earns enough money to cover overhead (or include overhead in their requested advance amounts) and hopefully save some of the royalty rate which ranges from 10 to 15 percent of wholesale price to eventually license marquee content for their own titles. They are also turning to stock houses, which offer licenses to use music, photos, video clips, text, and clip art.

While the entertainment and games segment of the multimedia market are most capable of relying on original content, the other facets of the market, the reference, informational and educational products, are more likely to succeed if they rely on brand name content and tap into a well-known name, such as *National Geographic, Roget's Thesaurus,* or *Scientific American.* Such popular entities lend credibility to the information provided in the CD-ROM title and make financial sense.

"Top selling CD-ROM games like *Mortal Kombat* have a [rate of] return model that can justify the cost of producing original live video," says Greg Richey, formerly with Arnowitz Studios. "For edutainment products, you can't justify putting $500,000 into a budget for video product on top of $500,000 for general production and still hope to make a good return."

As a result, the developers who are producing edutainment or education products are on the cutting edge of creating novel ways to tap into preexisting content. These developers are resorting to joint ventures, alliances, partnerships, and barter arrangements with content holders as a way of sidestepping exorbitant licensing fees.

When Eden Interactive in San Francisco embarked on its recent title *American Visions: 20th Century Art from the Roy R. Neuberger Collection,* the developers wanted to create the product from the artists' point of view and show that art is not created in a vacuum. That artist Stuart Davis was influenced by Earl Hines and jazz and that the reason Josef Albers paints squares has partly to do with colors.

To create such a title, Eden faced the task of tracking down rights holders of works from 129 artists, only 66 of whom were still alive. Co-founder Minoo Saboori started by calling galleries that had shown a particular artists' work to track down names and phone numbers.

"I next called up the artist, explained the product, our company, and our limited resources and asked how much they wanted for one-time nonexclusive rights to use their artwork," explained Saboori.

With the deceased artists, Saboori followed a complicated web of connections and relationships to locate the artists' estates, which held the rights to the work. Eventually, she was able to secure the necessary rights.

For its first title, *Greg LeMond's Bicycle Adventure*, which includes video footage of LeMond's rides and photos of the cyclist, Eden Interactive traded a certain number of copies of the finished product for video footage. The creators of the footage owned a catalog, *Famous Cycling Videos*, and wanted to financially benefit from the exchange by offering the CD-ROM title in its publication.

For the photos, Eden Interactive bargained with photographers and struck a favorable licensing deal: in exchange for the photographers' names appearing on the CD-ROM screen, the photographers charged a lower licensing fee.

"We can't offer them [the photographers] deep pockets, but we can give them an opportunity to participate in a new medium where they aren't likely to be getting exposure," says Saboori. "Most of the people we've dealt with have been satisfied with that."

Saboori did not have such an easy time putting together the title *The Great Golf CD*. Eden wanted to use video footage in its product and contacted the PGA, which has the rights to the video of all the great golf players.

"The PGA wanted $5,000 for a minute and we said "no thanks,'" says Saboori. "It was upsetting because we really wanted to include video in the product."

HOW TO DETERMINE YOUR LICENSING NEEDS

When you are considering the development of your title and whether you will need to license preexisting material, most developers ask:

1. What materials do you want to incorporate to create your CD-ROM title?
2. Who will provide each of the components—text, still and moving images, sound, and computer software?
   - Can an employee or independent contractor create the content for you at the right price?
   - Can you obtain the content under the work-made-for-hire doctrine, thereby guaranteeing that you will be the copyright owner?
   - Do you have to license the original material from an independent contractor as opposed to a work-made-for-hire arrangement?
   - Do you have to license preexisting content from a third party?
3. If you have to license preexisting content from a third party, what is the best way to locate the copyright owner, given your budget and time constraints?

- Should you do the search yourself?
- Hire a private firm?
- Call the unions or guilds?
- Contact the Copyright Office and have the federal agency conduct the search?
- Find the original artist?

4. What rights do you need? (See section, The Licensing Agreement, in this chapter about possible licensing terms.)
    - Is it possible to get these rights from this third party content holder?

5. Of the preexisting material that you would like to use, which parts need to be cleared?
    - Remember to look for logos or company's slogans in a photo or video clip.

6. Do you plan to use the content holder's name or image in connection with promotion of the product? If so, you need to determine if you can obtain these rights. If the content holder's name is on the product, will that person want to retain any and all necessary approval and other rights over the content and quality of the product?

7. Are there multiple owners of the content?
    - Review the documents stating who owns what.
    - Obtain warranty and indemnity clauses from each licenser.
    - Before signing anything with one of the owners, make sure every owner is committed to licensing the material.

8. If you obtain the material from someone who holds a license to the content, does the licenser have the right to sublicense?
    - Does the licenser have the rights to the work in electronic form?
    - Does the licenser have the rights to use the content in any medium now known or later developed?

9. Did the licenser create the content himself, or through work-made-for-hire agreements and assignments?
    - If the content was created using the help of others, are all the legal requirements met so you will not be sued when you use the content?

10. Has the licenser already licensed the material to another party?
    - What rights were licensed? Electronic rights?
    - How broadly is the first license worded?

11. Has the content holder already signed a distribution agreement?
    - Does the distributor hold the right to distribute the content in interactive multimedia form?

12. If you are not sure whether you need certain rights, can you purchase an option, locking in a rate for specific rights and giving you the ability to buy these rights at a later date?

13. Do you have a back-up plan to use alternative preexisting material?

LOCATING COPYRIGHT OWNERS

After you decide that some content must be licensed, you need to find out who owns the rights to the works. This search is the first step of the licensing process.

If you have to obtain content from a third party, the third party owns the copyright and you must obtain a license—a grant of permission by the copyright owner to use the material in a way that would otherwise be considered copyright infringement.

Remember: If you created the work, you own the copyright to the work and can do whatever you want with it, such as reusing the material in another title, using it on a different platform, or altering it to fit the title. If one of your employees created it in the scope of their employment, you own it under the work-made-for-hire rule (see chapter 9, under Work-Made-For-Hire Agreements). If an independent contractor created the work, you may own it under the work-made-for-hire rule (see chapter 9, under Work-Made-For-Hire Agreements), or she might have to use an assignment to obtain the copyright.

Sometimes it is easy to locate the owner of the copyright, or at least one of the owners of preexisting material. The photo or movie clip might have a copyright notice (notice is optional as of March 1989), and if properly done, lists the name of the copyright owner at the time the work was published.

But this name is not always the creator of the content or the owner of the copyright: the original copyright owner might have assigned the work to someone else. You need to find the current owner of the copyright.

At some point, most developers contact the Copyright Office in Washington D.C. to determine if the work has been registered with this office— that is, if the copyright owner filed a copyright application with the federal agency. Public libraries usually carry the book, the *Catalog of Copyright Entries*, published by the Copyright Office, which lists registered works by title (it also lists copyright renewals for works published before January 1, 1978 that must have been renewed to retain copyright protection). However, it does not list unregistered work.

Another option is to request a search from the Copyright Office, which requires the developer to fill out a "Search Request Form" supplied by the Copyright Office and pay $20 an hour for a search. On the "Search Request Form," mark the "Registration" box. If successful, you will receive the search report with the copyright owner's address.

A more expensive route is to hire a private copyright search firm, such as Thomson & Thomson in Washington D.C., to conduct the search (see appendix for list of possible firms). While the hourly rate might be higher than the Copyright Office's rate, the private firms work faster. In addition, a private company usually handles both the right of publicity releases (see chapter 12, What is the Right of Publicity) for celebrity photos and copyright licensing.

Although time consuming, developers living near Washington D.C., can travel to the Copyright Office and review the automated registration records.

If the copyright owner assigned the copyright to another individual and recorded the transfer with the Copyright Office, the federal agency can do an "assignment search," to locate the new owner.

Use the "Search Request Form" (the same form you used for a registration search), but this time mark the "Assignment" box. Send the form to the Copyright Office's Reference and Bibliography Section. This search, however, is not foolproof. Even though someone has assigned her copyright, the person who received ownership might not have recorded it with the Copyright Office because recording is optional. Unfortunately, this means that the search might not turn up anything, even though the copyright has been assigned.

Or, like the registration search, you can hire private companies to do the search, or physically go to the Copyright Office and check the files.

If the registration search failed to turn up anything, your next step should be to contact the person listed on the photo or the album as the copyright owner and determine whether that person assigned the copyright to someone else. If that person gives misinformation, stating that she did not assign the copyright to anyone else—even though she did—your license will still be valid under the Copyright Act if:

1. You were unaware of the unrecorded assignment at the time you entered into the license agreement;
2. Your license to the material is nonexclusive; and
3. Your license is in writing.

This nonexclusive, written license will take precedence over any later assignments made by the copyright owner. If, however, the copyright owner has granted someone else an *exclusive* license and has also given you a license—either exclusive or nonexclusive—that overlaps with the first licensee's exclusive license, you might infringe the first licensee's copyright (an exclusive licensee is considered under the Copyright Act to be an "owner" in the copyright). Unless the license agreement states otherwise, an exclusive licensee, and not the copyright owner, has the right to grant sublicenses to others and so you would need to obtain the sublicense from this person.

If the preexisting content was jointly created, it is safest to get a license—either exclusive or nonexclusive—from all joint authors.

STOCK HOUSES

Arnowitz Studios licenses a great deal of third party preexisting material for its edutainment titles, like *Daring to Fly: From Icarus to the Red Baron* and *Coral Reef: The Vanishing Undersea World*. *Daring to Fly* contains historical footage from the Smithsonian Air and Space Museum, and hundreds of rare photographs, which let the user go back in time and learn about early visionaries' attempts to fly.

Coral Reef contains six hundred photos of fish, plant, and animal species, allowing the user to explore life in the sea. It also includes sixty minutes of video produced by Peace River Films, the creators of the "Nova" documentaries.

Because such licensing arrangements can be costly, Arnowitz's strategy to stay within budget is to locate a source who has a lot of content, such as an independent video production house, an archive, or stock house, and structure its licensing arrangement so that instead of paying a flat fee for each photo, video segment, or text, it pays a certain royalty rate in exchange for access to the entire library of material.

"That way, our designers can go into their libraries and pick and choose what they need," says Greg Weber, formerly with Arnowitz.

For material that cannot be obtained from this main source of content, the company pays a flat fee, structuring the license arrangement to read that the content can be used "for any platform and all versions hereafter," thereby allowing the company to port the product to the newest hot platform.

Most developers, intent on keeping their costs down, find ways to keep licensing fees within their budget. One of the most important ways that Sanctuary Woods has found to stay within budget is to word its content requests to the stock house or media library as broadly as possible so the search firm can provide a range of different preexisting material with a corresponding variety of prices. For instance, there is not a lot of flexibility or price options if Sanctuary Woods requests a five seconds of the chariot race in the movie *Ben Hur* as opposed to an inquiry for a film or video clip of a chariot race.

If you decide to pursue the stock house route, Jill Alofs of Total Clearance cautions users of this content to carefully read the license agreement.

"The content you get from stock houses may or may not be fully cleared for the uses that a developer needs," says Alofs. "I get calls from stock houses asking for help to clear rights or they refer clients to help clear appropriate rights."

THE LICENSE AGREEMENT

The next step for the developer is to determine what rights she needs and to include them in the licensing agreement. The developer should ensure that the licensing agreement does not limit the use of the content in a multimedia product in such a way that the developer cannot create what she intended. For instance, the developer should hesitate before agreeing to a three year cap on the license agreement: if the product takes off, and the developer decides to upgrade or port it to a different platform and the three year time period has elapsed, the developer would either have to renegotiate the license agreement or remove this piece of media.

Developers frequently forget to negotiate the right to use images and names in promotional materials. Several lawsuits have been filed in the print media arena over the use of celebrities' photos to promote a publication. The magazine *Forum*, for instance, violated Cher's right of publicity when it used a copy line, "So take a tip from Cher and hundreds of thousands of other adventurous people and subscribe to *Forum*." If you know that you would like to use a celebrity's photo or image on your packaging material, marketing videos, or any other materials (such as investor videos or annual reports) make sure you include this right in the licensing agreement.

Because no one can be sure what technology is around the corner, the developer should word the licensing agreement for the preexisting material as broadly as possible, using such phrases as "by any and all means, methods, processes, whether now or hereafter granted," which is likely to allow you to port the material to other platforms that now exist or have yet to be developed. This broad language, however, will most likely result in a higher price for the content.

From the grab bag of rights held by the copyright owner, the developer, at a minimum, needs to include the following in the license agreement:

1. *The right to reproduce the work:* this gives you the license to copy the material.

2. *The right to change/modify/adapt the work or a portion of the work:* most linear content needs to be changed or altered in some way to be smoothly incorporated into a multimedia product. Increasingly, content holders are reserving the right to accept or reject the altered form of their work. If this is the case, make sure you place a time limit by which the content holder must respond.

If you negotiate a license for more than one platform, make sure you include the right to port *and modify* the title to the new platform.

You should also obtain a waiver from the artists and copyright owner of moral rights. Expect a content holder to negotiate a separate paragraph that deals with content being modified to create ancillary products or merchandise.

3. *Distribution right:* even if the title will be used internally by a corpo-

rate client, you will still need this right, especially if there is potential commercial value attached to the title.

4. *Public performance right and public display right:* if your title is geared to the consumer for use in the home, then you do not need to include this right in your license agreement. However, it is safer to include it: if the material is shown in a place open to the public, such as a convention in a demo version of the title, you will need this right.

The above list is an enumeration of the exclusive rights held by the copyright owner (see chapter 8), which the licensee will need to successfully produce, market, and distribute her title. These terms, however, are only the skeleton of the agreement. A well-crafted license agreement will consider and also include terms that go beyond those listed above. If the developer neglects to include a term in the license and uses the content in an unauthorized way, the licenser (content holder) can terminate the license. Other terms that should be considered include:

1. *Geographic distribution:* ideally, if you can get it for the right price, you should negotiate the worldwide rights so that you are not limited in the geographic scope of your distribution. The rights acquired at the front end need to match up with your back end plans.

2. *Term/termination:* After the copyright owner of a work licenses the material, the author of the work (other than a work-made-for-hire) that was made on or after January 1, 1978, has the right to terminate a license or assignment as soon as thirty-five years have passed after the license was granted and only during a five year period. Ideally (and for the right price), you want to get a term that is perpetual.

Expect a content holder to ask for a reversion of all rights if the developer fails to create the product within a specified time frame. He might also ask for specific conditions that trigger the termination of the agreement, such as failure to receive payment, or the developer acting beyond the scope of the license.

For instance, Amuse Interactive Learning Environment in Tiburon, California had licensed some slides from a German company. Amuse's U.S. bank was supposed to wire the fee to the German company. After several months of waiting for the check, the German company sent a letter, threatening to revoke the license, pursuant to the license agreement, for failure to pay on time.

"I was so upset that the bank hadn't wired the money that I almost boarded a plane and personally delivered the money," says Roberto von der Heyde of Amuse. Finally, the check made it to the German company, five and a half months after the date on which it was supposed to be delivered—and $200 short.

3. *Exclusive or nonexclusive:* As content holders become more sophisticated, it is less likely that you will be able to obtain an exclusive license

without paying a great deal for it. A nonexclusive license means that others can also license the same images, sound, or text.

An alternative is to agree to a nonexclusive license but include a noncompete clause so that the content holder cannot license the same material to your competitor. The agreement should specifically define and identify your competition, otherwise the provision might be too vague and unenforceable in a court of law.

If you can only obtain a nonexclusive license, make sure the market has not been destroyed by a poor rendition of the content created by an earlier developer. If it has, increase your marketing budget and prepare to fight a negative image of your product.

If you feel that you must have an exclusive license and yet the content holder prefers a nonexclusive arrangement, try to compromise. You might consider limiting the exclusivity to certain platforms, territories, or specific markets.

If you do negotiate an exclusive license, the agreement must be in writing and signed to be enforced by a court. It is treated by a court as a transfer of copyright ownership. You should record this license with the Copyright Office. If the copyright owner has not registered the work with the Copyright Office, you need to have the owner file a registration notice first before you record your license.

4. Platforms: Because of the variety of platforms on the market, no one is quite sure which ones will dominate. To hedge your bets in what will become the industry standard, it is best to obtain a license for as many platforms "now or hereafter known and later developed" or for all "interactive" mediums. This grant language has been held to include the right to exploit the work through new technologies, even though they are not yet contemplated.

Naturally, a licenser does not want to give up all his rights to all platforms without a financial payoff. One way to counter a large license fee is to have the licenser include in the agreement a "reservation of rights" clause, whereby the licenser spells out the limits to the grant. Or if the developer lacks the financial resources to pay for such a sweeping license, she can ask for a "right of first negotiation" or an "option" to purchase the additional platform rights.

5. Media: Three media exist—the floppy disk, videogame cartridge, and the CD-ROM. Like the platform, the more flexibility you can build into the agreement with the content licenser, the better prepared you will be for future changes in the market.

If you do not address this issue in the agreement, it is generally found that the license covers only those technologies known at the time of the grant.

6. Amount of content: Specify what content and how much of it you intend to use in your product. The content holder will try to limit the amount you use so she is able to license parts to other developers.

7. Uses: What are the number of uses of the work that the content holder is willing to give the developer? Does it include the right to include the content in a movie version of the product, a TV show, a book?

8. Credits: Does the creator of the preexisting material want credit for the licensed work noted in the multimedia product? On the screen? On the packaging? Is there room for all the credits?

9. Localization: Eventually, you will probably want to distribute your product internationally. To prepare for this, you need to include in the license agreement the right to translate the product to fit the international market. You will also need the right to alter the material to fit the new platform that is appropriate for localization.

Several content holders say they have felt burned by the quality of the translation. As a result, it is much more common for copyright owners to insist on retaining the right to approve the translation.

10. Payment: You need to decide whether the content holder will be paid a royalty based on sales, a one time flat fee, or a combination of both.

"Everyone wants an upfront payment plus royalties, or points," says Greg Weber formerly with Arnowitz Studios. At the outset of negotiations, Weber explains to content holders that the company has a limited budget and attempts to negotiate a flat fee. "Otherwise, we'd be giving up all our revenue to content holders," adds Weber.

If you are in a royalty-flat fee combination situation, specify whether the upfront fee is an advance that must be recouped from royalties owed the licenser before the royalty stream kicks in. Try to include provisions that you will at least recoup production costs before any royalties are paid.

11. Updates, future versions: If you think there is a possibility of an updated version of the product, you should specify in the license agreement your right to use the content in this way. If the content holder rejects this term, you can negotiate an option to purchase the right to produce an update.

If you are shooting to produce an "evergreen" title, you will need the right to update so that the product can continue to live out its shelf life.

12. Amount: Typically the price is based on how much of the content you intend to use, the "marquee" value of the product, the extent of rights you have asked for—the farthest-reaching being an exclusive license with worldwide rights, in perpetuity.

When Electronic Arts licensed the worldwide rights to fourteen songs from six different alternative rock bands, including Soundgarden, for its title *Road Rash* for the 3DO system, the company's attorneys considered the following factors to determine price: they weighed the relative strength of the song's composition, the popularity of the recording, the commercial viability of the artists, and the product itself. Electronic Arts also considered the amount of music that *Road Rash* used and the music's importance to the product.

13. Most favored nation clause: When Steven Rappaport set out to create his title *Radio Active*, distributed by Sanctuary Woods, he knew the product needed hit songs from the 1960s, 70s, and 80s. The first music publisher that he approached, EMI, requested a "most favored nation" clause, which would upgrade the publisher's terms if a subsequent publisher received a better licensing deal in the context of *Radio Active*.

"It would be foolish to go to 240 publishers to get rights because that's too much work," says Rappaport. "I found out that EMI is the largest music publisher in the world. I figured if I could cut a deal with them, the terms I worked out here would drive the terms for other deals with other publishers because of the 'most favored nation' clause." With the EMI deal in hand, Rapport approached Polygram International and Sony for other top songs.

14. Warranty and indemnity: Many times a content holder is not sure whether he owns the copyright to all aspects of the content and its possible uses. To protect yourself, you should include a warranty, which is a legal promise that the stated facts are true. If possible, the content holder should warrant that he is the sole and exclusive owner of all rights in the material; that the content holder has the right to grant you a license; and the license does not infringe any outstanding license or intellectual property rights. You should also have a lawyer review any documents that state the licenser owns the content, any previous distribution agreements, or prior licensing agreements.

An indemnity clause should also be included, which would require the copyright owner to pay for all costs due to a breach of the warranties.

INSURANCE

Developers who use preexisting content (and have some extra money) purchase "errors and omissions" insurance policies, which protect the developer from lawsuits based on a violation of the right of privacy or publicity, libel, slander, copyright, or trademark infringement. This type of policy is also necessary to obtain financing from third party investors.

ASSIGNMENT

An alternative to a license is an assignment. However, an assignment is typically more expensive and harder to obtain than a license because it gives you all of the copyright owner's exclusive rights. If you opt for an assignment, it must be in writing and signed by the copyright owner. It is wise to record the assignment with the Copyright Office.

LICENSING ORIGINAL CONTENT FROM AN INDEPENDENT CONTRACTOR

For one of their titles, Arnowitz Studios contacted an independent contractor to compose a song. Though the company loved the music, the independent contractor refused to create the work as a work-made-for-hire, insisting that he retain the copyright ownership of the work and that Arnowitz license the song.

"We had to structure the deal as a nonexclusive license with a noncompete clause," says Greg Weber, formerly with Arnowitz. The noncompete clause stated that the composer would not license the composition to a competing company with a similar product. "It's definitely not our preferred way of doing business."

Most developers and publishers prefer a straight work-made-for-hire arrangement rather than a licensing deal with independent contractors. With a work-made-for-hire deal, the company owns the product and hence can do whatever it wants with it, including using the material again in another title, or porting it to another platform.

While a developer can have all these rights with a well-crafted licensing agreement, the drafting of a license agreement is more time-consuming and likely more costly. Moreover, because no one is quite sure what platform will dominate the market, the license agreement needs to include fairly broad language, such as "the material can be used on any multimedia delivery system now known or hereafter invented" to cover all bases.

A DEVELOPER'S LICENSE AGREEMENT WITH A PUBLISHER

Like the developer seeking content from a third party, the publisher will also seek the broadest rights possible from the developer, so as to avoid having to renegotiate such rights in the future. In most cases, the publisher will insist on an assignment of the copyright. But in some situations, the developer retains the copyright and the publisher must request a license from the developer. One publisher's licensing agreement used the following language:

"The developer grants to the publisher, its licensees, successors and assigns, the nonexclusive and irrevocable right to use the article in any form or medium whether now known or hereafter known throughout the world including, but not limited to, all formats of electronic, magnetic, digital, laser or optical based media, and in connection with any advertising or promotion thereof."

Developers with a strong track record (sometimes it only takes one title), have some leverage to limit the publisher's ownership. If you have this ability, you can use a license agreement and reserve rights, limiting the licensing agreement to those distribution channels and territories in which the publisher has the most experience and expertise.

"Some hardware manufacturers who are interested in promoting their platforms are willing to pay a price—including letting the developer own the copyright—to have a product available on their platform," says Timothy McNally, CFO at Mechadeus.

Similar to a developer licensing content from a third party, a developer should consider the list of issues raised in the section The Licensing Agreement (above), paying close attention to the following:

1. Nonexclusive versus exclusive license. The publisher will argue that the licensing agreement must be exclusive in order to justify his investment in marketing the title. The developer usually agrees, but limits the license by restricting the number of platforms, the term, or the geographic territory.

2. The platform. The publisher will ask for the right to market and distribute the title on all platforms. Developers recommend investigating the publisher, finding out his strengths and limiting the license to those platforms. The developers of *Myst*, for instance, gave Brøderbund the right to publish, distribute, and sell the PC and Macintosh CD-ROM versions of *Myst.* Sunsoft, a Japanese based company, received the cartridge rights.

3. The sales channel and territory. The publisher will ask for the right to distribute the title to all sales channels and geographic areas. Once again, developers recommend finding out the publisher's strengths in these areas. Eden Interactive limited Creative Labs to distributing only to the computer channel.

4. Derivative products. The publisher will request the right to make or license derivative products, such as merchandise, Saturday morning cartoons, movies, or books. Developers usually find out how well the publisher has done in this area for its other developers before handing over this right.

5. Localization. If the publisher has an international presence, like Electronic Arts, it typically requests the right to localize the title or the right to license a third party to localize the title for the international market.

6. The right to create sequels. The publisher will ask for the right of first refusal to sequels to the original title. The developer might request in return that the publisher achieve minimum sales of units or revenue with the first title in order to create an incentive for the publisher to market the developer's first product.

7. Termination. The developer who licensed the title should include some termination provision so that if the publisher fails to do anything with the title, the developer can find another publisher to distribute the product.

You might also phrase this as a reversionary right: the product reverts back to you if the publisher does not follow through on its obligations.

THE MYTHS ABOUT LICENSING

Because of the barriers to obtaining licenses—money, misunderstanding, and time—infringement is believed to be fairly prevalent in the multimedia development community. Copyright infringement is partly due to long-standing misunderstandings about what can and cannot be done under the copyright law. One developer explained that although his development company samples or copies images, they do not violate any copyright or trademark laws because they change the images at least 20 percent.

Once a developer copies a copyrighted work, however, the developer has infringed the copyright (unless there is an exception to the Copyright Act listed in chapter 8 under When You are Free to Copy Preexisting Material).

Even if a developer is unaware that she is copying someone else's' work, she might be infringing. The court ruled, for instance, that George Harrison infringed when he composed the song, "My Sweet Lord" because he had "subconsciously" copied the popular song, "He's So Fine."[3]

Another developer said that they took one line from a song and that the company decided it was such a little amount of preexisting material, that they did not think it could possibly be infringement.

But under the Copyright Act, if what is copied is a "qualitatively substantial portion" of the work, the developer infringed the copyright. The publication, *The Nation* received an early copy of the autobiography of former President Gerald Ford, *A Time to Heal: The Autobiography of Gerald R. Ford*, published by Harper & Row, Publishers, Inc., and decided to run three hundred words of it, without authorization. Under the agreement between Ford and Harper & Row, the publisher had the exclusive right to license prepublication excerpts, or "first serial rights." The court found that *The Nation* had infringed Harper & Row's copyright, despite the small quantity of words used because the publication published the most important parts of the book.[4] Unfortunately, it is difficult to determine when a developer has taken too much (i.e., a qualitatively substantial portion), and a developer will probably have to spend a lot of money litigating to find out.

A publisher who purchased a documentary video on the assassination of John F. Kennedy thought that because he bought the video, he owned it and therefore could copy parts of it for his new CD-ROM.

The creator of the video, however, owns the copyright and under the law, only the copyright holder has the right to make copies. The CD-ROM publisher owns a copy of the work and not the copyright. The only right the publisher holds is the right to resell the video.

Another development company wanted to parody names of companies, restaurants, and institutions in the CD-ROM product. The publisher prevented the developer from doing so because they feared infringement of companies' trademark (See chapter 8, under Trademark Law.)

When Electronic Arts producer Randy Breen created *Road Rash*, he made up names of the motorcycles, rather than use existing ones to avoid having to license the different companies' trademarked names and logos.

---

1. *Windows Sources*, September 1994.

2. *Los Angeles Business Journal*, February 13, 1995.

3. *Bright Tunes Music Corp.* v. *Harrisongs Music, Ltd.*, 420 F. Supp. 177. 1976.

4. *Harper & Row, Publishers, Inc.* v. *Nation Enterprises*, 471 U.S. 539 (1985).

LICENSING CONTENT FROM SPECIFIC MEDIA INDUSTRIES

Operating as a developer in a developer-publisher arrangement with Strategic Simulation, Inc. or SSI (acquired by Mindscape, Inc. in October 1994 for $11.5 million), Don Daglow, president of Stormfront Studios created *Tony La Russa's Ultimate Baseball* and *Tony La Russa Baseball II*. Both products did extremely well, the first one selling nearly one-hundred thousand units and the second breaking that mark.

The revenue generated from the sales of these two products convinced Daglow that Stormfront should become a publisher, at least for the *La Russa* product line, so that *Tony La Russa Baseball III*, scheduled for April 1995, would be under Stormfront Studio's own label, with 70–75 percent of the wholesale price returning to the company's coffers. Daglow, who had founded the company in 1989 with $14,000 of his own savings, had grown Stormfront to $2.5 million in revenues with fifty employees and wanted to take the company to the next level of growth.

Under the developer-publisher agreement, however, Daglow had relinquished to SSI the copyright to the software code and engine of the baseball product line. To complete the transition to a publisher for the third baseball title in the series, Daglow wanted ownership of the code. Otherwise he would have to license the code from SSI, possibly paying an advance and a royalty fee on units sold of new *Tony La Russa* titles. Daglow arranged a meeting with SSI and started to negotiate.

Over the years, Daglow and SSI had worked closely together, and in the negotiations, both parties wanted to ensure that the relationship continued.

"If you don't care about the relationship and can just walk away after negotiations, it sometimes helps you cut through a deal faster," says Daglow. "A party can say, 'these are the terms, take it or leave it.'"

That the baseball product line was so successful intensified the negotiations, contributing to the length of time spent discussing terms, roughly seven months. In the end, Daglow and SSI worked out an arrangement whereby Daglow, for an undisclosed amount of money, received copyright ownership to the software code.

The copyright issue pertaining to the code, however, was only the beginning of the deals that Daglow needed to put together to produce the newest La Russa title. Daglow next addressed the content, putting together a combination of preexisting material with original.

As a diehard baseball fan, Daglow wanted to make *Tony La Russa's Baseball III* as realistic as possible.

"What makes our products special is the attention to detail," Daglow says. "We're fanatics about quality graphics, easy-to-use interfaces, and the accuracy of the content material in our products."

In *Tony La Russa's Ultimate Baseball,* for instance, Daglow built the title using accurate fence distances, wind conditions, and turf surfaces that exist in the major league parks.

Tony La Russa III would have that same level of realism, plus many different kinds of realistic gameplay. A user could play it as a straight videogame, or play baseball games as they would in real life, with players like famous fastball pitcher Nolan Ryan throwing blazing fast balls and San Francisco Giants' third baseman Matt Williams hitting home runs. The user, like a manager, could control some baseball players, mixing and matching strategy and action. When the "manager" thought the pitcher had had enough, she could yank the player and put in a relief pitcher.

Finally, the user can play an entire baseball season in ten to twelve minutes. If a favorite team did not do so well, the user can return to the team a player who was traded last year to see if the team would have done any better in the computer game simulation.

"Former Giant Will Clark doesn't have to leave San Francisco in our game," says Daglow. "Fans who want injury-riddled Mark McGwire to be healthy can make that happen." To achieve that realism, Daglow spent nearly two years securing rights to preexisting text, photos, and stadium architecture and dealing with the baseball union and celebrities.

Daglow relied on stock photography houses to supply photos. He contacted several professional players and obtained their consent to be videotaped against a blue screen to create the animation for the gameplay. He also wanted to give the user a choice of announcers, so three well-known announcers, Mel Allen, Hank Greenwald, and Lon Simmons, were contacted and eventually agreed to participate. A writer wrote an original script, which the three announcers recorded.

"When a baseball player hits a drive to the left, the computer plays an announcer's voice, 'It's a screaming line drive to the left,'" says Daglow. "Once in a blue moon, a shortstop will jump and pull down the line drive and the announcer says, 'He leaps up and makes a great catch.'"

Tony La Russa, who has been associated with Stormfront Studios since the company's inception, was videotaped providing hints for the game play.

To further heighten the realism of the game, Daglow approached the owners of several baseball stadiums to license the right to use the image of the stadiums. The images, in turn, were used to build 3D models for the game.

Daglow, who has been refining his computer simulation model for twenty-five years, needed accurate statistical information to create the simulations. From expert statisticians, he licensed the right to use statistics for every at-bat for each player—whether a particular pitcher gives up more ground balls or fly balls, and whether a hitter pulls the ball, is a spray hitter, or strokes the ball to the opposite field. He acquired information indicating how a ball bounces on artificial turf or natural grass and how Denver's high altitude and the winds at Wrigley Field affect the flight of the baseball.

"If we could have gathered the statistics from multiple sources, then we would have fallen under a journalistic privilege, and we wouldn't have needed a license," says Daglow. "But for the level of detail we were after, we had to turn to specific sources who gathered this kind of in-depth information."

Stormfront Studios hired a composer to create original scores for the game and a specialist in sound effects upped the realism factor with baseball noises—digitized umpire calls like "Stttriiiike Thrrrreeeeee!" and the crack of bat against ball.

He also approached the Major League Baseball Players Association to license the rights to use the images and names of some of the players in the union.

"The MLBPA has a standardized process and agreement for computer game licenses and so there is no negotiation," says Daglow. "The only issue is whether they will accept you as a licensee. If they do, it's a straight forward process, with the union asking for standards to ensure quality."

As a developer makes her way through the maze of content acquisition, the critical question to ask at each step is, "who owns it?" Just as important is "do you know the person who owns it?"

The key to licensing existing content is relationships. Relationships determine whether a licensing deal will be struck, how long it will take to negotiate, and the conditions and terms. It is part of the reason why the bigger publishers and developers who have been in business for awhile have had more success licensing content compared to the relatively new and smaller developer. (The other reason, naturally, is that bigger publishers have more money.)

Relationships can pop up in interesting ways. Electronic Arts negotiated with the alternative rock bands, Soundgarden and Swervedriver, to contribute several of their songs to *Road Rash* for the 3DO. This deal happened, in part, because both bands were fanatic users of *Road Rash* for the Sega Genesis, playing it on road trips to their concerts.

Although it is an uphill battle for a small developer to access preexisting content, it can be done. And once a contact is made, and negotiations are conducted honestly and fairly, the content pipeline is open for future titles.

LICENSING MUSIC

Passionate about music, Steven Rappaport, founder of Digital Trivia, Inc. decided in 1992 to create a CD-ROM–based music trivia product, *Radio Active: The Music Trivia Game Show*. Users would pick a character to represent them in *Radio Active*, whose metaphor was an interactive television show. Clicking on a handle, the user would land on one of several categories of music—top songs from the 1960s, 1970s, or 1980s. A snippet of the song would play, and with a clock ticking, the user would guess the name of the song, earning points for correct answers.

To make the title, Rappaport needed the "multimedia rights"—a combination of synchronization and mechanical rights—to 240 songs, which would give Rappaport the right to use the songs in the product while simultaneously showing visuals, such as photos, animations, and videos. He did not need the "master recording rights" from the record companies because he would not use the original versions of the songs. Instead, he planned to hire unknown singers to create sound-alike versions of the original recordings.

Approaching 240 companies that administered the copyrights to 240 songs was an impossible task, so Rappaport contacted the largest music publisher, EMI.

To help establish credibility with music copyright holders, Rappaport wrote an article for *Billboard* magazine, explaining that although multimedia was still in its infancy, with well-known music in the products, the music industry could help jump-start the multimedia industry that in five or ten years would generate a substantial revenue stream for musicians.

After months of meetings, phone calls, and lunches, EMI opened up its catalog.

"They had 800,000 songs listed in hard copy, not on disk," says Rappaport. Rappaport started leafing through the pages. If he recognized a song's title, he wrote it down. Months later, he had a list of 20,000 songs. EMI owned 100 percent of the multimedia rights to 160 of those songs.

Two years after he had originally conceived of his idea, Rappaport found himself closing a deal with EMI. They agreed on the most important terms of the multimedia agreement: the advance, royalty, territory, term, and platforms. For an agreed upon recoupable advance per song, Rappaport received nonexclusive multimedia rights to the 160 songs for three years, plus a two year window to sell off remaining inventory. He obtained these rights for nine CD-ROM platforms, as well as online multimedia and interactive television with a clause obligating EMI to negotiate in good faith with Rappaport for any new platforms.

"We need not pay any additional royalties to EMI until we sell sixteen thousand units," says Rappaport.

The agreement also included a standard "favored nations" provision, which stated that EMI would receive as good a deal as any other publisher from whom Rappaport licensed songs for *Radio Active*.

With those deal terms, Rappaport approached MCA Music Publishing, Polygram International, and Sony Song Inc. to license the remaining 80 songs. Of the 240 songs he ultimately licensed, 69 had been number one on the charts; the average ranking for all 240 songs was number seven.

With his licensed songs, Rappaport hired talented, unknown singers to perform the songs. He relied on section 114 of the Copyright Act, which allows sound alike recordings to be made without the permission of the original artist. While there are cases that seemingly contradict this section of the Copyright Act, such as Bette Midler's successful suit against Ford Motor Co. for using a sound-alike voice in a TV ad, Rappaport, who is a former lawyer, distinguishes his use from the *Midler* case. In his product, he identifies the actual singer, thereby not misleading the public, and unlike the *Midler* case, Rappaport's singers do not endorse any third party product (like Ford automobiles).

With his prototype, song licenses, and a track record (he had produced two previous titles), Rappaport approached Sanctuary Woods to publish and distribute his title. In an unusual deal struck May 1994, he retained the copyright to the product, even though Sanctuary Woods agreed to serve as publisher, financing the development of the title and providing marketing and distribution. Owning the copyright allowed Rappaport to keep the rights for all platforms not licensed to Sanctuary Woods, as well as all follow-up products in the series. Rappaport is now relying on some of his same contacts established in the music industry to create his next title, which also revolves around music.

Tape an Original Song

Unlike Rappaport, some developers have opted to tape an original version of a song and include that in the product. In Electronic Art's *Road Rash* for the 3DO, for instance, the producer included Soundgarden's song "Superunknown" from the album with the same name. To do this, Electronic Arts' lawyers had to negotiate two licenses: one with the copyright owner of the musical composition, called the synchronization license; the other, called a "master recording license," from the copyright owner of the existing sound recording—the sound recording itself has a separate copyright distinct from the written song. Songs recorded before February 15, 1972 are not protected by the federal Copyright Act, but check with an attorney because they may be protected by state law.

The copyright owner of the sound recording, which is typically a record company, (such as A & M Records for Soundgarden's songs), is usually identified on the CD or tape after the symbol P with a circle around the letter. The copyright for the sound recording protects the original expression added to the composition by the singer. The composer, however, most likely has assigned his or her copyright to a music publishing company, such as EMI or MCA Music Publishing, and in return, the composer receives a percentage of royalties from licenses; if that is the case, you will need a license from the publisher and not the composer.

Create Music from a Preexisting Composition

If you want to create original music from a preexisting composition, like Rappaport did, you need a synchronization license from the copyright owner of the musical composition, typically the music publishing company.

If you are using an independent contractor to sing the song, developers recommend using an assignment or work-made-for-hire agreement with the independent contractor to secure the copyright in the song. Otherwise, the developer has to use a license agreement with the singer to use the song (see chapter 9, under Copyright Ownership).

If you need help obtaining music licenses, many music publishing companies have turned to the Harry Fox Agency in New York to handle licensing matters. The agency has created its own "Multimedia Rights License" agreement.

Price

Common considerations that are being used to determine the advance and royalty rate for music include the following:
1. The relative strength of the musical composition;
2. The popularity of the recording;
3. The commercial viability of the artist;
4. How much music is used in the multimedia product;
5. The music's importance in the multimedia product;
6. Likely sales based on comparable multimedia products;
7. Likely sales based on installed platform base.

Types of Music License

The following is a brief description of the types of licenses used by the music industry. In chapter 10, The License Agreement, talks about the different terms and provisions that you should include in a license. However, music publishers and record companies will usually require that you use their license agreement as the starting point for negotiations.

MECHANICAL LICENSE: When the music will not accompany images in the final product, such as for an audio CD, record, or tape, the music industry issues a mechanical license, which allows the recipient to mechanically reproduce the composition. Some CD-ROM products, for instance, allow the user to watch video with the music, or just listen to music. If your product allows the latter option, and you want to use pre-existing music, most lawyers recommend obtaining a mechanical license to cover this use.

SYNCHRONIZATION LICENSE: This type of license is the most relevant for multimedia developers. It permits a developer to copy the music (not the version sung by an artist) and have it synched or accompanied with visuals, such as film or TV clips, and photos.

MASTER RECORDING LICENSE: This license entitles you to copy and distribute a particular sound recording. If you want to tape an original version of a song, you will need to secure this license. If the record company agrees to such a license, you might also need permission from the recording artist. It is safer to obtain this permission to avoid violating the artists' right of publicity, unless the record company has obtained the artists' signature waiving this right. If the recording artist belongs to the American Federation of Radio and Television Artists, or AFTRA, then you probably will have to pay the union reuse fees.

PUBLIC PERFORMANCE LICENSES: This license allows the multimedia developer to play the music publicly (as opposed to playing music in homes). A public performance license can be obtained from the composer or from organizations such as the American Society of Composers, Authors & Publishers (ASCAP), Broadcast Music Incorporated (BMI), or Society of European Stage Authors & Composers (SESAC). It is unsettled whether music on a CD-ROM is a public performance since an individual is using the product in his or her home. But if you have plans to put the product online, it is likely that this use might constitute a public performance.

VIDEOGRAM LICENSE: Developers also are securing this license, which allows one to copy the sound recording and combine it with an audiovisual work on a CD-ROM and distribute it to the home market.

ADAPTATION LICENSE: Although this is one of the rights listed in chapter 11 "The License Agreement," it is so important to licensing preexisting content that it is listed again. If you know that you will need to make changes to the recording, you need to secure the right to do so in the license. Most copyright holders will demand a quality control provision. If so, be sure to put a date by which the copyright holder must accept or reject the product.

Public Domain or Music Libraries

Another option is to use music that has fallen into the pubic domain. You cannot legally copy an original version of a public domain song, but you can record your own version. BMI and ASCAP in New York have listings of songs that are in the public domain.

The other option is to consult the catalogs of music libraries, which typically have cleared both the synchronization and master use rights to songs.

LICENSING LITERARY WORKS, NONFICTION BOOKS, MAGAZINES, AND NEWSPAPER ARTICLES

Don Daglow at Stormfront Studios had to license baseball statistics and information to create his title. Other developers have licensed particular fiction or nonfiction books' story or plot lines to create their products.

If you need to license something from the publishing world, the parties whom you might be negotiating with include the author, the author's agent (most commonly used for fiction), and the publisher. In the typical arrangement between an author and publisher, the publisher will hold the right of first publication of the hardback and maybe paperback book.

However, an author's agent might have limited the copyright to certain geographic territories, thus allowing the author to assign her copyright to the hardback to international publishers. The author, especially if the book seems promising or the author is well-known, probably holds the copyright to derivative works, such as movies or TV renditions of the book, and audio versions of the book. Other rights that have been spun-off from the publication of a book include the translation rights, first serial rights, and the reprint right.

Older contracts between the author and publisher have not addressed the issue of electronic rights. A developer should review (preferably with the help of an attorney) the publishing agreement to determine who holds this right.

There are two ways to begin negotiating for text. Probably the simplest is to contact the publisher of the book. The second is to work through the author's agent.

If the novel, reference book, or nonfiction book has different elements to it, such as illustrations or charts, then the creators of these different elements might hold the copyright to these components, or at least the electronic rights to the works. You will have to approach these other parties to license this material. If the material you would like to use is in an anthology—a group of printed works gathered together under one title— you will first need to obtain a license from the original publisher or author of the work.

The amount you will pay for the use of text or plot line usually depends on the quantity of text you intend to use and the popularity of the book. You will want to secure the story rights, character rights, book title rights, and adaptation rights so you can change the material to fit your unique product and distribution rights. You should also consider purchasing the sequel rights so that a competing product using the same characters does not enter the marketplace. If you intend to write a manual that accompanies the product and want to use some of the book's text, include the reprint rights in the licensing agreement.

Most newspaper articles are written by a paper's employee, called a "staff writer," and thus the newspaper company would own the copyright in the article under the work-made-for-hire doctrine (see chapter 9, under Copyright Ownership). Magazines, however, typically rely on freelancers to write their articles with the magazine only purchasing one-time publication rights. The contract between the magazine may or may not specify who holds the multimedia or electronic rights to the article. You will need to read the contract.

If the developer wants to use only facts cited in the article, she does not need a license because facts are not copyrightable.

LICENSING PHOTOS AND ARTWORK

Amuse Interactive Learning Environments missed their Christmas 1994 deadline partly because of licensing problems. Out of approximately one thousand pieces of content, roughly 10 percent consisted of a famous Italian artist's artwork that the company wanted to license. Unfortunately, the art was at the Vatican, which claimed it held the electronic rights to the work.

Typical of the self-starter developer, Roberto von der Heyde at Amuse wrote to the Vatican, in both English and Italian, explaining the multimedia title and the desired content. Six months later, he received a postcard from the Vatican, not directly rejecting his request, but at the same time, not giving the go-ahead. Von der Heyde wrote again, addressing the letter this time to a friend of a friend that worked at the Vatican.

While waiting for a response, the programmers and designers continued to work on other parts of the product. Another six months went by and finally, von der Heyde received a letter rejecting his request. But there was no explanation for the denial.

"Once you get a 'no,' you want to know why," says von der Heyde. "If you know the reason why, you might be able to address that concern. The Vatican might have been too busy and just rejected outright because he had a stack of five hundred letters to respond to. Or maybe they thought there was no money in the project. Or they might not have guidelines for electronic licensing, so rather than develop them, they just reject our request."

Von der Heyde wrote again. He heard nothing, until six months later, when he received a fax. This time, the letter stated the reason for the rejection: "It said that when it comes to electronic rights, the Vatican is the owner of these rights. They are too afraid to give away these rights for fear that everyone will copy the artwork," says von der Heyde.

He tried to explain to the Vatican representative that Amuse planned to include coding so that consumers could not copy the artwork. But von der Heyde also knew that to cover all possible ways of copying would have added anywhere from $150,000 to $200,000 to the project's budget. About this time, von der Heyde resorted to the company's back-up plan and used other versions of the artwork.

"We will try again with the Vatican for the second edition," says von der Heyde. During his next trip to Europe, he plans to go to the Vatican and meet the people in charge of electronic rights. "I think it's going to come down to relationships."

Copyright ownership of still photos or other art works is separate from the physical ownership of the work. The right to reproduce a work must be obtained from the copyright owner or his licensee, not merely from the owner of the physical copy of the work. The magazine or book publisher who published the photo might have used an independent photographer to shoot it, and the publisher may have received only a limited grant of rights. Even if the publisher has the right to license the photo, there may be restrictions on this licensing right, such as size, color resolution of the photo, or alterations to the photo. A developer needs to review the contract between the publisher and the photographer to determine who owns what rights.

A developer also has to pay attention to the content of the photo.

"Just because you have licensed a photo doesn't mean you've necessarily cleared all rights associated with it," says Jill Alofs, founder of Total Clearance. "You still have to find out who holds the copyright—is it the magazine, the book publisher, the photographer? You need to get clearance from Adidas, for instance, for the guy in the photo who is wearing a shirt with their logo on it. Or there might be a billboard in the picture and a company trademark in the ad. You can't just black it out because that's altering the content and you need permission to do that. If the photo has a well-known building in it, perhaps Rockefeller Center, that's a trademarked image and you need permission to use it."

If you use a photo of a sculpture or artwork, you need to obtain a license not only from the photographer, but also the creator of the artwork. If a person or celebrity appears in the photo, you need to clear the right of privacy or publicity issues.

Another alternative is to approach stock houses, which have large collections of photos and are in the business of granting rights to photos taken by individual artists. For instance, The Image Bank, the largest international stock photography agency, recently put many of its photos on a Photo CD Catalog. The Library of Congress has an online service that will soon offer photos. And Picture Network International also has images, with prices based on the use, including how prominently the image is portrayed in the overall product.

Some stock houses own the copyright outright; other houses act as licensing agents and the photographer retains the copyright. Make sure that the stock house has cleared all the rights you need for your product, including the right of publicity and privacy laws (see chapter 12, under What is the Right of Publicity and What is the Right of Privacy).

Prices usually depend on the type of product you are creating, the term of the license, and territory in which the product will be distributed. A stock house will often give you a discount if you license a certain volume of its work.

LICENSING SOFTWARE

If a third party owns the authoring system software you are using, you need to obtain a license. Off-the-shelf shrink-wrapped software includes a license agreement in the package, and the act of opening the package or envelope is intended to indicate that you accept the terms of the license. Though no court has ruled on this, you should read the license agreement to determine what rights the copyright owners of the software grant to you as a licensee.

If you have in-house software created by a programmer who is an independent contractor, determine whether you want to use a work-made-for-hire agreement or an assignment to secure the copyright ownership in your name.

LICENSING VIDEO, TELEVISION, AND FILM CLIPS

Small developers' attempts to license video or film clips seem to generate stories that have the most characters, plot twists, and drawn-out time lines. As Greg Weber, formerly with Arnowitz Studios put it, video is the hardest to get and the most expensive to produce independently.

While at Arnowitz, Weber relied on video production houses, entities that own a lot of video, to license video for the company's edutainment titles and paid a certain royalty rate, instead of a flat fee per second, to gain access to the entire library.

More than any other preexisting content, licensing film or video clips can require clearance from a dozen or so parties:

1. The scriptwriter, who may not have created the work as a work-made-for-hire for the producer (see chapter 9, under Work-Made-For-Hire Agreements) and therefore would still hold the copyright;
2. The director, who might have directed the movie as a work-made-for-hire for the producer, but retained the right to refuse alteration of the work. You should also obtain a waiver of the director's moral rights;
3. The unions, which typically bargain with the studios and require the payment of a reuse fee if the film is used in a different medium;
4. The talent, who created the music, voice-overs, or choreography in the movie who may not have operated under a work-made-for-hire agreement;
5. The creator of an animated or real character from a popular TV show. You will need to use a "merchandise license," which authorizes you to use the character;
6. The stars who appear in the movie or TV show. You will need to clear the right of publicity and reuse rights;
7. The owner of the copyright in the film or video itself;
8. The author if the movie or TV series was based on a book. You also need to obtain a waiver of the author's moral rights;
9. The creators of any material incorporated into the video, such as film or video clips, still photos, sound, and animation; and
10. The composers if the clip contains music.

While the video production house might have cleared all the rights issues, Arnowitz Studios has found that the licensing terms quoted to multimedia developers often do not work for multimedia products. The problem is that the video houses try to superimpose business models used for TV onto multimedia.

Arnowitz argues that multimedia created for the CD-ROM is similar to the videotape industry, which receives eight to ten year licenses for material. But the video production houses prefer to price it more like a TV show, limiting the use of the video clip to one to three years.

"For us, we need the longer term to reflect the time span for a CD-ROM product that will be upgraded and ported to other platforms," says Greg Richey, formerly with Arnowitz.

Another term that Arnowitz has had problems with is the minimum amount of seconds per cut of video that it can purchase. Arnowitz is frequently quoted that the minimum amount of video that can be purchased is ten seconds. But Arnowitz often only needs three or four seconds.

"If you don't negotiate, you end up paying for ten seconds and video license fees add up quickly," says Weber, who says it is common to pay $30 a second. For a Warner Brother film, on the other hand, expect to be asked to pay $4,000 per minute.

To locate copyright owners of films or video, developers have turned to the American Film Institute (with offices in New York City and Los Angeles) which catalogs films by genre and subgenre and maintains all credit information. For film, the list of credits may identify names or studios that you can contact for permission. The University of California at Los Angeles is a great resource for locating rights holders of films.

PERFORMING ARTS GUILDS AND UNIONS' REUSE FEES

If the multimedia developer wants to use a preexisting film or video clip developed under a guild/union contract, she must contact the Screen Actors Guild (SAG), or the American Federation of Television and Radio Artists (AFTRA), for clearance rights to the performers who appear in the scenes. These two unions then contact the agents of the performers or the executors of the deceased performers' estate, and the developer must negotiate with these parties about a reuse fee. The reuse fee is required when content is taken from an existing product and put into—or reused in—another product. The minimum price you will pay is the minimum amount required for use of the talent. For instance, if you were to hire an on camera performer for a day, it would cost $504. In your budget, you should note that to reuse material from a film, it will cost at least that much, perhaps more because the performer decides the final price.

This fee is separate from the amount the performer can charge to license her right of publicity. While you might pay a reuse fee for a video clip, that transaction does not require you in the future to use only union talent in your original creation of video. If you sign SAG's or AFTRA's interactive media agreement, you will be required to pay union wages. Both unions offer one-time only agreements, limiting the use of union talent to the particular project. (See Using Union Talent in chapter 2, for more information.)

CHAPTER TWELVE

RIGHT OF PUBLICITY

In the raging battle to determine the dominant multimedia platform, Philips Interactive Media in Los Angeles created an enviable, star-quality advertising campaign for its video recorder called the CD-i, or compact disc interactive. In a series of TV advertisements, Philips used movie clips that included Tom Cruise.

The industry hummed with rumors about what kind of deal Philips had put together to sign up Cruise, who had never before appeared in a TV commercial. Not long after the first ad ran, however, the speculation stopped because those who had followed the campaign had their answer.

In a lawsuit filed early in 1995 against Philips, Cruise alleged that he never agreed to the use of his image to endorse the CD-i video recorder and that the company had violated his right of publicity. Cruise sought $10 million in damages, an amount he claimed represented a reasonable license fee to use his image, and to compensate for harm done to the actor's career. Cruise maintained that the commercials created the impression that his career was on the skids and, as a result, he had resorted to commercials. Cruise also demanded an injunction against the use of the ads.

Philips' lawyers countered that the company obtained a license from Paramount Video to use all of the studio's images from its film library, including the image of Cruise.

Even with a team of inside and outside lawyers, Philips still found itself in the middle of a lawsuit involving a license agreement for preexisting content. If such a suit happens to big companies in this industry, where does that leave the little developer?

Unfortunately, the creation of interactive CD-ROM based products requires an understanding of many aspects of the law, or at least when to consult a multimedia lawyer. After copyright law, the right of publicity is the most important area of law to understand so as not to violate it. It is one of the areas of law frequently neglected by multimedia developers. The other area is its companion, the right of privacy.

The right of publicity is one of the reasons that Steven Rappaport, founder of Digital Trivia, Inc., did not use the voices of famous singers in his title *Radio Active* that includes 240 hit songs.

"I didn't want to have to go to every person who sang the song and get their permission to use that version," says Rappaport. Instead, he limited his licensing efforts to music publishers who held all the rights to a song and used talented, unknown singers.

Garry Hare, president of Fathom Pictures rarely uses preexisting material. But on one the few occasions he did, he ran into problems, many of which included the right of publicity. In a joint venture with ABC Sports, the TV network gave Hare twenty seconds of existing footage from a real baseball game to use in an interactive multimedia title. In the product, at one point a center fielder runs out on to the field and catches the ball. Hare thought the clip would work well for this segment.

"After we'd done the title, ABC pointed out that they only had rights to the footage and had not cleared anything with the players themselves," says Hare. "We either had to go back in and change the designation of the numbers on the uniforms so that the players were not recognizable to anyone. Or to shoot it ourselves."

"Going through the trouble to clear the rights was not an option. The Major League Baseball Players Association only owns its name," says Hare. "The association also represents the players, except those players who represent themselves."

"Even dead players—Babe Ruth, Lou Gerig—are represented by their estates," says Hare. "The teams own the team's own logo and designation. The teams insist that the local broadcast contractor owns the video rights to the footage."

"By the time we would have gone through everyone, we would have been broke," says Hare. "They all ask for royalties, about 5 percent, on the sales of the product."

In the end, Hare clothed some famous baseball players in blue hats and uniforms and against a blue background, videotaped them playing ball.

WHAT IS THE RIGHT OF PUBLICITY AND THE RIGHT OF PRIVACY?

Actors and other performers have the right to control the commercial use of their names, voices, signatures, or likenesses. The right has been applied to movie stars, sports stars, and civil rights leaders, such as Martin Luther King Jr., and extends to materials that are preexisting, newly created—even content in the public domain. Typically, lawsuits filed alleging a violation of the right of publicity arise when an image or voice-sound-alike is used to endorse a product without first obtaining permission from the celebrity.

For a celebrity to win a right of publicity lawsuit, that person needs to establish: (1) celebrity status; if the person is not known, then the only possible recourse is a lawsuit based on the right of privacy; (2) that the developer used his or her recognized name, likeness, image, or voice or sound-alike voice of the celebrity without consent; (3) the developer's use is not protected by copyright law, statute, contract, or the First Amendment, such as in a news or factually-based story; (4) it is a commercial use because the image is used to sell, promote, or advertise a product; and (5) in some states, the celebrity needs to establish commercial loss. If you can show that one or more of these elements are not met, then you have not violated the right of publicity.

For preexisting material, in addition to the right of publicity, a developer needs to attend to the "reuse rights." The actors' unions, the Screen Actors Guild and the American Federation of Television and Radio Artists, have established something called the Rule of Reuse. If a developer includes a clip with a recognizable image of an actor or famous stunt person, she needs to clear the reuse rights *and* the right of publicity with the actor's agent. Although there is crossover between the unions, in general, if it is a film, contact the Screen Actors Guild; if it is a videotape, contact the American Federation of Television and Radio Artists.

Private individuals possess a similar right, called the right of privacy, which gives someone who does not rise to the status of a "celebrity" the right to sue the party for several intrusions: (1) an invasion into a person's seclusion; (2) public disclosure of private facts; (3) portraying a person in a false light; and (4) commercial appropriation of a person's image.

In the first instance, the interest protected is the person's right to physical solitude or her private affairs and concerns. For instance, if a developer photographed a person standing in his or her living room, that would be an invasion into a person's private affairs. The intrusion must be highly objectionable or offensive to a reasonable person, and the harm suffered must be mental anguish, rather than loss of financial gain (as in the right of publicity).

A violation of the right of privacy also occurs if another party publicly discloses to a third party private, embarrassing facts about a private citizen—even if the facts are true. If a developer photographed someone in the privacy of his or her own home and used that photo in the product, it might be a violation of privacy. The standard, again, is whether the disclosure would be offensive to a reasonable person. If the developer can argue that the disclosure is in the public interest, or is "newsworthy," the developer might win such a suit.

A violation of the right of privacy might also be found if the facts used by the developer are distorted in such a way as to place a private individual in a false light. A false light means attributing to the person views that she does not hold or actions that she did not take. For instance, a developer considered using a video clip of a well-known participant in Mothers Against Drunk Drivers and dubbing in another person's voice expounding the virtues of drinking and driving. It is likely this juxtaposition of image and sound would present the person in a false light. Again, the false light must be such that a reasonable person would find it highly offensive. A developer accused of violating this aspect of the right of privacy could argue that the statement is true or the person consented to the message.

With these rights given to a private citizen, it seems nearly impossible to use a photo of someone who might have accidentally been included in a photo of something else. Typically, a developer can use this kind of a photo, especially if the person was in a public setting, because there is a lessened expectation of privacy when a private person appears in public. If the photo of a private individual was taken through a telephoto lens, with the individual in his home and unaware of the photographer, the private citizen has a much stronger case for a violation of his right of privacy.

Since there have been no court cases on this issue for a multimedia product, it is safer to obtain a release from the private individual who appears in the photo.

A developer can avoid a "false light" situation if she carefully checks the text or audio that accompanies photos or images of people. Distortions and exaggerations can lead to a cause of action.

THE DECEASED'S RIGHT OF PUBLICITY

A multimedia developer traveled to Hollywood to snap a picture of an Elvis Presley look-alike, the perfect opening for his CD-ROM title. The developer paid a flat fee and obtained a license from the Elvis look-alike. Production of the product moved ahead, until the company received a threatening letter from the Elvis Presley estate, stating that the use of the image violated the real, deceased Elvis Presley's right of publicity.

"I'd never heard of such a thing," says the developer. "A dead person has a right to control his image? This is bizarre."

The developer immediately contacted a lawyer who advised that if the company wanted to use the look-alike images, the developer also needed a license or release from the Elvis Presley estate. Without it, the estate could obtain an injunction, stopping the shipment of the product, and receive damages based on the reasonable price for a license to use the look-alike image.

In some states even if the celebrity is deceased, the right of publicity passes on to the star's heirs and is controlled by the estate. In California, for instance, if the heirs can show that the celebrity exploited his publicity rights while he or she was alive, they have a valid lawsuit against someone who uses the deceased celebrity's image without permission. The courts view the publicity right as similar to property, which can be inherited by heirs.

BROADENING OF THE RIGHT OF PUBLICITY

Over the last two decades, the right of publicity has been greatly expanded. Courts have adopted a liberal view of whether a person's "image" or "persona" has been appropriated. They have also used an expansive interpretation of a "commercial use."

A violation of the right of publicity was found, for instance, when Samsung Electronics developed a series of futuristic TV advertisements, one of which used a female-looking robot turning a "Wheel of Fortune" type device. A statement accompanying the ad read, "the longest running game show, 2012 A.D." Vanna White, who appears on the actual TV game show, "Wheel of Fortune," sued Samsung, arguing that the use of the robot violated her right of publicity. The court agreed.[1]

The decision has been roundly criticized for confusing Vanna White, the person or image, with her occupation as a person who spins a wheel on a game show. Despite the attacks, the law still stands.

Though courts did not recognize a violation to the right of publicity, they did find that Ford Motor Co. misappropriated Bette Midler's voice when it used a voice in a TV ad that sounded like Midler's without identifying that it was another singer's. The same situation occurred with Frito Lay using a voice that sounded like Tom Waits in a TV ad.[2]

The courts have also broadened the meaning of commercial use, a factor used to determine whether there is a violation of the right of publicity. A commercial use is one in which an image, likeness, or voice promotes or is included in the advertisement for actual goods or services. Like the Cruise lawsuit, it is often associated with advertisements that use the image of the celebrity or use of a celebrity's image in a commercial product.

Media use, on the other hand, does not violate the right to publicity and is a use that relates to news, commentary, or entertainment. Though no court has ruled on it, a "news" or documentary style CD-ROM product is arguably a media use and exempt from the right of publicity.

If a developer is using a news clip in an entertainment-oriented multimedia product, however, it most likely will not be considered a "media use." For example, when the Rodney King video was broadcast on TV in news reports, it was considered news: television broadcast networks paid nothing or very little to the original cameraman to air the video clip on the evening news. But when director Spike Lee wanted to use it in his film *Malcolm X*, the cameraman sued him for copyright infringement.

The problem for multimedia developers is whether consumer-oriented software products is "entertainment" in the same vein as a movie, or solely "informational."

Since this area is new, little guidance exists for developers. The only answers come from court decisions pertaining to traditional media. Print publishers have been sued for using celebrity images to promote their magazines.

At the same time, there is no violation if the celebrity's image or voice is used to illustrate a point in the context of a film documentary or an article on a subject of general public interest. Magazines have also been able to use celebrity photos to advertise their publication, as long as an endorsement is not implied. For instance, *Sports Illustrated* did not violate football player Joe Namath's right of publicity when it used the quarterback's photo in an ad under the caption, "How to Get Close to Joe Namath."[3] Magazines have been able to use photos of celebrities to accompany a news article, even though the subjects in the photo have minimal connection to the issues discussed.[4] If the publication's details of a celebrity are accurate, then the right of publicity cannot be used to stifle discussion or commentary. This rule has also been applied to nonprint media, docu-dramas, and documentaries.

The print media has also been allowed to use photos of nonfamous people involuntarily drawn into the public limelight because of an event, or association with famous or infamous people. One critical aspect in all these cases, involving both celebrities and private citizens, is that the use of the photo or likeness is in conjunction with editorial, educational, or similar applications that do not rely on the value of the individual's personal image as the source of value for the product. Another important thread is that the use of a name or likeness in advertising does not violate the right of publicity where the individual involved is the author of or a performer in the work being advertised.

HOW TO AVOID VIOLATING THE RIGHT OF PUBLICITY

If an image of someone will appear in the multimedia product, that person should sign a release of all publicity or privacy rights. If the developer intends to use the image or video in the work, advertising for the title, or ancillary products, the release should specify each use to avoid confusion and possible lawsuits.

For preexisting material, if a celebrity's image or persona (voice or lookalike) appears in the content, the developer should obtain a release. If the celebrity will not sign a release, the developer should pull the image from the multimedia title. Or, consult an attorney and find out if there is a way to use the image under a First Amendment argument or fair use analysis.

If a lawsuit has been filed against you, alleging violation of the right of privacy or publicity, consult an attorney and consider any First Amendment defenses. The reporting of news, for instance a fictionalized documentary about an individual, is protected by the First Amendment.

Parody, based on the Copyright Act or the First Amendment, is also a defense (see chapter 8, under Parody).

DEFAMATION

On Prodigy's "Money Talk" bulletin board, a subscriber posted a claim that investment bank Stratton Oakland Inc. had committed fraud while handling a company's initial public stock offering. Stratton Oakland filed suit against Prodigy for $200 million, claiming that the company had been defamed, or libeled. In a 1995 decision, a New York judge upheld the bank's suit, reasoning that Prodigy's efforts to market itself as a computer network for the family, with editorial control, opened the online service up to libel suits. Prodigy says it will appeal the decision.

Defamation is written or spoken words that harm the reputation of a person (or corporation) or subject that person to hatred, contempt, or ridicule. Even a message that evokes sympathy for the person will be considered defamatory if it causes a third person to stay away from the person. A statement is defamatory to an organization if customers stop doing business, making charitable contributions, or drop their memberships at the establishment.

Defamation includes two subsets: *libel*, which is in some permanent form, such as a writing, film, videotape, or CD-ROM, and *slander*, which is spoken. Only assertion of facts can be defamatory, not opinions. In both cases, the words must be written or spoken to a third person to be the basis of a lawsuit.

A person (or corporation) who claims libel must prove the following: (1) the statement was false; (2) it was communicated to others; (3) it was reasonably understood to be referring to the injured person; (4) and it did injure the person, by tarnishing the person's reputation or subjecting that person to ridicule and hatred.

Our laws have been established to encourage free speech. Therefore, a public figure who believes she has been libeled by the media has a higher standard of proof before winning a lawsuit for defamation. She must show that the statements were made by the speaker or writer who knew they were false or who exhibited reckless disregard for the truth. A public figure is an elected official or an individual who has created the public perception that he has substantial government responsibility and power. It also applies to anyone who voluntarily put herself into the public arena or to a private person who is has been thrust into the public eye.

A lower standard of proof is allowed if it is a private individual, who only has to show that the developer acted negligently or carelessly. If the person succeeds, she can win monetary damages plus punitives, designed to punish the offending party.

If a developer is sued for defamation, the best defense is that the defamatory message is true. If the developer found the information in a public record, hearing, or proceeding, the fact that it is printed in such a form, available to the public, is also a defense. The other defense that developers might rely on is parody.

---

1. *White* v. *Samsung Electronics America Inc.*, 971 F.2d 1395 (9th Cir. 1992), cert. denied 113 S. Ct. 2443 (1993).
2. *Midler* v. *Ford Motor Co.*, 849 F.2d 460 (9th Cir. 1988); Waits v. Frito-Lay Inc. 978 F.2d 1093 (9th Cir. 1992).
3. *Namath* v. *Sports Illustrated*, 371 N.Y.S. 2d 10 (1975) aff'd mem 39 N.Y. 2d 897 (1976).
4. *Arrington* v. *New York Times, Co.*, 434 N.E. 2d 1319 (N.Y. 1982).

CHAPTER THIRTEEN

A FINAL WORD FROM THE DEVELOPERS: WHAT I WOULD HAVE DONE DIFFERENTLY

The multimedia developers and publishers who entered the market early have endured the industry's bruises, set-backs, and hard knocks created by a business with few deal parameters and scant rules. They have a wealth of war stories about what they have learned and how they have made it in an industry that is defining itself every day. With 20/20 hindsight, the seasoned developers discuss what they would have done differently if they had a chance to do it all over again.

FRITZ BRONNER, president of Vortex Media Arts in Burbank, California, developer of *Buzz Aldrin's Race into Space* and *Madeline and the Magnificent Puppet Show*.

"You're going to go through expansion phases and you need to be careful during these times. Don't overspend and don't count on future revenues and payments coming in on time, because they won't. If your margin is close between success and failure, chances are, you are going to fail because you can't get by the delays in payment."

GARRY HARE, president of Fathom Pictures, Inc. and The Griffin Fathom Company, a joint venture between Merv Griffin's The Griffin Group and Fathom Pictures, Inc. in Sausalito, California. Developer of *Return to CyberCity*, *The Riddle of the Maze*, *Escape from CyberCity*, *The Palm Springs Open*, *ABC Sports presents Power Hitter*, *CD Coach*, *ABC Sports presents The Palm Springs Open*, and *The Skins Game at Bighorn*.

"I would have raised money sooner, gotten bigger faster. You need a critical mass to have people around to do things. You can't do everything yourself."

MAURA SPARKS, co-founder of Pop Rocket in San Francisco, California, publisher of *Total Distortion*.

"We underestimated the time and money that it would take to create *Total Distortion*," says Sparks. "But we tried our best to make a really cool title that could become an evergreen hit. *Total Distortion* is the first cornerstone in our company. It's going to launch Pop Rocket, as well. For our first title, it was important to get demo versions out in the market. In the future, I think we will be more reluctant to show early versions of our titles. But at the time, it was important to demonstrate it because the whole industry was exploding around us in San Francisco, and it helped place our company on the map and attract good people to the company, including investors and distributors."

TIMOTHY MCNALLY, chief financial officer for Mechadeus in San Francisco, California, developer of *Critical Path* and *The Daedalus Encounter*.

"Build a plan with more flexibility. This business changes so fast that, when you start a title, you don't even know all of the technologies, platforms, or partners that will be involved by the end of the title. I would focus more on managing the marketing of the product—being proactive with the publisher, getting the best counsel for structuring agreements for intellectual property and promotion with the star talent, and driving business development opportunities. There are tremendous opportunities for very special products, but they need to be nurtured by someone focused on the product.

"And recognize that every member of the team is learning and growing over the course of the project. Watch for and nurture individual staff members' developing skills as contributors and managers, making sure that administrative and technical issues do not get in the way of creating great works. Put the team's existing and new found skills to best use so that the process and the resulting products are special."

STEVE NELSON, founder of Brilliant Media in San Francisco, California, producer of *Xplora 1: Peter Gabriel's Secret World*.

"I didn't have enough capital when I started out—only $100,000. I would have worked harder to get additional funding upfront. But by creating successful products, we're in a good position and can get a better valuation. There's a big break between a little company doing little projects and a bigger capitalized company, able to create new products.

"My advice? Get all the money you can because it makes all the difference in the world. It puts the company in a position of being a force to reckon with. You can do your own things versus someone else's in a work-for-hire situation, which, when it ends, you're constantly seeking the next project. Ask yourself, 'are you a post production house or do you create your own things?'"

ANDREW NELSON, co-founder of Cyberflix in Knoxville, Tennessee, publisher of *Lunicus, Jump Raven, Dust,* and *Skull.*
"I wish we'd been more organized, but that's hard to do with a start-up. We should have had more structure, paid more attention to deadlines. I don't know, it may not have solved anything. Call back in a year."

ERIK S. QUIST, co-founder of Cyberflix in Knoxville, Tennessee.
"*Lunicus* didn't take off as fast as it could because it was with a distributor that was a mail order operation. You need a distributor with the muscle to get you off the shelf. And just because your distributor is a company with a big name doesn't mean it knows anything about this industry."

BRUCE GOEDDE, co-founder of Modern Media Ventures in San Francisco, California, developer of *Gus Goes to Cybertown, Gus Goes to Cyberopolis.*
"We might have planned to raise more money upfront. We have fourteen investors, mostly family and friends. If we had had more money, it would have minimized everyone's anxiety and moved the business further, faster. But practically, I'm not sure we could have done that and still have met our start date."

RAND MILLER, co-founder of Cyan, Inc. in Spokane, Washington, developer of *Myst.*
"We had legal trouble with some companies when we started out. What we thought were contracts, weren't. We also learned that contracts don't mean anything when you don't have money to enforce them. We learned that you shouldn't do business by contracts, but by relationships with people you can trust and who will work hard with you."

ED BELLINASO, co-founder of Substance Interactive Media in San Francisco, California, creator of the electronic magazine, *substance.digizine.*
"We had no money. I would have started out with more money rather than no money. But then again, it made us work hard. We had to do stuff to pay the rent. We did a presentation for S3, a chip manufacturer that got us to Comdex. For that project, we had to come up with animation, so we paid someone, Goose, $500 to put together the animation. But then the music wasn't synching. The video card didn't work. We had to figure it out. So having no money made us learn stuff."

ALEX RAGLAND, co-founder of Substance Interactive Media in San Francisco, California.

"I wouldn't have set up the company so that everyone's stock vested right away. You never know what's going to happen, and someone who seems really committed in the beginning might decide to leave in six months.

"We tried to run the company democratically—everyone had an equal say. But at some point, someone has to lay down the bottom line. I would also have all co-founders read and sign the business plan so that everyone is on the same page, with the same vision for the company. You will run into problems if one founder wants a five person company that produces six titles a year and another founder envisions a business with 500 employees and 100 titles a year. I say 'sign the plan' because people are more likely to read it.

"So many products are out there that I think it's real important to bring in-house some sales and marketing people. Especially for us, we were trying to create titles and at the same time sell advertising.

DREW HUFFMAN, founder of Drew Pictures in San Francisco, California, developer of *Iron Helix*.

"Get a PR agency as soon as you've launched your product. I wish we had had more of a developed plan, where we were going, how we'd get there. But that would have been impossible. No one had a plan. Now we know where we are going. We didn't have any serious financial projections when we first started out. There were lots of times that all the money ran out and we needed to borrow. I'd get on the phone and borrow $10,000 from a friend of family member. It was a nightmare. It's hard to make product that way.

"I spent most of 1993 on business issues. I wish I delegated that responsibility to someone else because I want to work on product. That's what I like. It's what I'm good at."

MINOO SABOORI, co-founder of Eden Interactive in San Francisco, California, developer of *Greg LeMond's Bicycle Adventure, The Great Golf CD, American Visions: 20th Century Art from the Roy R. Neuberger Collection.*

"Make sure that you understand products don't sell themselves. You need to have merchandising and marketing, whether you do it yourself, which I don't recommend, or a strategic partner who does it. It's not an uncomplicated exercise. I recommend signing up with established firms in particular channels. These partners can create a presence for us in the market.

"Understand the importance of what you are providing and make sure you are providing the best and highest quality product possible.

"If don't believe you have perseverance and tenacity, don't get into this market. This is not a lifestyle that's easy. We don't do anything but work. I love it, though. We live, breathe, and eat this stuff. Rejection is constant but you only need one."

MIKE FAKE, president of Orbital Studios, Inc. in Emeryville, California, developer of high-end PC CD-ROM entertainment products as well as children's entertainment products like *Dinonauts.*

"The most common mistake I've seen among developers is that they are unrealistic about the time it takes to develop a product. They have an idea for a game and project it will take twelve to fourteen months to produce. But in reality it could take eighteen to twenty.

"The ramifications of this affects all negotiations and expense models. Advances are negotiated by developers based on incorrect expectations. Therefore, they underestimate the amount of money they need and put financial strain on the project. This could directly affect the quality of the product."

OBSERVATIONS FROM INDUSTRY EXPERTS

ANN WINBLAD, co-founder of Hummer Winblad Venture Partners, venture capitalists based in Emeryville, California who invest in multimedia companies.

"Are you a studio or a full blown company? Can you launch multiple titles, a line of products, or one or two titles that someone else should publish. Too few companies ask themselves who they are, what they want to be. Companies also should be aware of not just the development issues, but the distribution and sales channel issues. That's the next thing they will face after they get their product out. Too many people don't look that far down the road and think how hard that will be. So many people think they can launch a full-fledged company without realizing how difficult it can be.

"The industry has evolved from one programming person, who is largely responsible for the product to a team of people. Now, there's programmers, artists, musicians, graphic specialists, designers, all working under a producer. It's important to have good producers who are skilled in product management. This person helps your group work together to make sure the product is being completed in a timely manner. Each component needs to progress. This can be a big problem for a small company with limited products; if one big product is late and there's no other titles being sold, you are incurring expenses with no revenue coming in. You have to make sure products are introduced to the market in a timely fashion, otherwise developers face big cash flow problems."

RONALD J. HELLER, managing director at Frost Capital Partners, Inc. in San Francisco, California, an investment bank that specializes in multimedia software deals.

"The most realistic thing to do is become a developer and then segue into an affiliate label. We don't encourage people to become full-fledged publishers right away because the ante is going up dramatically. The marketing dollars will soon be in excess of development dollars. In our mind, Acclaim, which spent $10 million in marketing for a recent title, is the right model. So to be a publisher in the mainstream, it takes a lot of money, more than ever before."

RUTH KENNEDY, general counsel of Electronic Arts in San Mateo, California.

"Sometimes developers undersell themselves because they are so happy to get a deal with a publisher. If they are really good and have a good concept, publishers will fight over them. From my perspective, good developers are few and far between. They've got a lot of leverage and should be asking for higher royalty rates. Or, if they don't think the publisher has the right marketing sense, the right creativity and resources, these talented developers should go to someone else or make sure their deal with the publisher is limited in some way."

CONCLUSION

The multimedia developers are the ones who are defining this industry, creating a new form of story telling, and a new way of using technology. They are caught in the center of the storm. Gripped by their vision, living mostly on the excitement of a new industry, they are struggling to get by, to produce the one multimedia product that makes a name for the company. As Minoo Saboori says, "rejection is constant but you only need one."

For the developers, the passion for what they do has nothing to do with the hype that has propelled "multimedia" into nearly everyone's conversations. It has everything to do with moving far away from the dreary sameness of predictable movies and TV sitcoms.

Fortune magazine ran an article not long ago lambasting the industry for its shoddy titles. While linear video is still being slapped onto CD-ROMs, most developers who are in for the long haul handle each piece of content with extreme care, thought, and creativity. As a result, each year, the titles are getting better, with the really interesting stuff coming from the fringes, from the garage band developers, hunkered down, scrapping by, living on their passion for their work.

Most developers would agree with Maura Sparks, "There is always room for really good titles, and that will never change."

APPENDIX

1. LICENSING SEARCH FIRMS

Thomson & Thomson
500 E. Street #970
Washington D.C. 20024-2710
1-800-356-8630
Search service for trademarks, copyrights, titles, designs, characters, film, and TV.

Total Clearance
Jill Alofs
P.O. Box 836
Mill Valley, CA 94942
415-389-1531
Clearance service for all media, including television, film, photographs, video.

The Clearing House Ltd.
849 Broadway, 7th Floor
Los Angeles, CA 90014
213-624-3947
Music clearances for television and multimedia producers.

U.S. Copyright Office
Library of Congress
Washington, D.C. 20559
202-287-8700
The Copyright Office hotline number for ordering forms is 202-707-9100, and the number for public information is 202-707-3000. Free publications are also available upon request.

BZ/Rights & Permissions, Inc.
125 W. 72nd St.

New York, NY 10023
212-580-0615
Provides clearance services for music, film, literature, and television. Publishes The Mini-Encyclopedia of Public Domain Songs, *which lists over six hundred songs that are in the public domain in the U.S.*

Public Domain Report
P.O. Box 3102
Margate, NJ 08402
1-800-827-9401
The PDR *assists in determining the public domain status of works.*

Harry Fox Agency, Inc.
205 East 42nd Street, 18th Floor
New York, NY 10017
1-212-370-5330
Provides clearance for synchronization rights.

Copyright Management Inc.
1102 17th Ave S. #400
Nashville, TN 37212

2. STOCK HOUSES

UCLA Film & Television Archive
   Commercial Division
1015 N. Cahuenga Blvd.
Hollywood, CA 90038
213-466-8559
Maintains the largest university-based collection of motion pictures and broadcasting

programming. The archive's services include a newsreel collection that is available to media producers.

The American Film Institute
2021 N. Western Avenue
Los Angeles, CA 90027
213-856-7600
A nonprofit organization that preserves film, television, and video. Open to the public.

Budget Films
4590 Santa Monica Blvd.
Los Angeles, CA 90029
213-660-0187
For film and video.

The Image Bank
4526 Wilshire Blvd.
Los Angeles, CA 90010
213-930-0797
For photos.

Archive Photos
530 W. 25th Street
New York, NY 10001
1-800-688-5656
For photos.

Archive Films
530 W. 25th St.
New York, NY 10001
1-800-875-5115
Fourteen thousand hours of historical and entertainment footage. Twenty thousand historical photographs. Computer catalogued, copyright cleared, priced in volume.

American Society of Composers,
   Authors & Publishers
1 Lincoln Plaza
New York, NY 10023
For music.

Broadcast Music, Inc.
320 W. 57th Street
New York, NY 10019
212-586-2000
Blanket licenses for music.

Society of European Stage
   Authors & Composers
156 W. 56th Street, 24th Floor
New York, NY 10019

212-586-3450
For music.

3. VENTURE CAPITAL & INVESTMENT BANKING FIRMS

Accel Partners
San Francisco, CA
415-989-5655
Investments: Books That Work, Spectrum HoloByte, and Macromedia.

Alex Brown & Sons
New York, NY
212-237-2000
Investment banking firm.

AT&T Ventures
East Hanover, NJ
Investments: Knowledge Adventure, Spectrum HoloByte, and Enter Television.

Draper Associates
Redwood City, CA
415-599-9000
Investments: Accolade, Medior, and T/Maker/Deluxe.

E.M. Warburg, Pincus & Co.
New York, NY
212-878-0600
Investments: Maxis.

Frost Capital Partners, Inc.
San Francisco, CA
415-274-8899
Investment banking services.

Gabelli Multimedia Partners
Rye, NY
914-921-5395

Hummer Winblad Venture Partners
Emeryville, CA
510-652-8061
Investments: Berkeley Systems, Books That Work, Pop Rocket, and Humongous Entertainment.

Institutional Venture Partners
Menlo Park, CA
415-854-0132
Investments: LookingGlass Technologies.

Kleiner Perkins Caufield & Byers
Menlo Park, CA
415-233-2750
Investments: 3DO, Crystal Dynamics, Edmark, Electronic Arts, Enter Television, Macromedia, and Spectrum HoloByte.

Merril, Pickard, Anderson & Eyre
Menlo Park, CA
415-854-8600
Investments: Rocket Science Games, and Enter Television.

Mohr, Davidow Ventures
Menlo Park, CA
415-854-7236
Investments: Books That Work, Enter Television, Knowledge Adventure, Media 3, and Rocket Science Games.

New Enterprise Associates
Baltimore, MD
Investments: Cottage Software, Enter Television, The Learning Company, and Star-Press Multimedia.

Robertson Stephens & Company
San Francisco, CA
415-781-9700
Investment banking firm.

Technology Partners
Belvedere, CA
415-435-1935
Investments: 3DO, Crystal Dynamics, Silicon Gaming, and Spectrum HoloByte.

4. MULTIMEDIA CONSULTING SERVICES

Interactive Media Resources
email: inrcybergate.com,
JIMWTHOMAS@aol.com
209-658-8020
A Multimedia consulting firm.

Becki Walker
Walker & Associates
2306 Pisani Place
Venice, CA 90291
310-821-5898
Provides individualized analysis of the multimedia market, a company's competition, and profiles of potential partners.

S.O.S., Inc.
Joanna Tamer (Joie)
100 Driftwood #1
Marina Del Rey, CA 90292
310-306-1814

Fairfield Research Inc.
Lincoln, NE
402-441-3370
Provides financial and market analysis information.

PC Data
Reston, VA
703-435-1025
Market research firm that tracks retail software sales on a monthly basis.

Dataquest
San Jose CA
408-437-8000
Market research firm.

5. TRADE ASSOCIATIONS

Software Publishers Association
1730 M St. N.W. #700
Washington, D.C. 20036
202-452-1600

Optical Publishers Association
P.O. Box 21268
Columbus, OH
614-442-8805

San Francisco Multimedia
  Development Group
2601 Mariposa Street
San Francisco, CA 94110
415-553-2300

International Interactive
  Communications Society
P.O. Box 1862
Lake Oswego, OR 97035
503-579-4427

6. NATIONAL DISTRIBUTORS

Double Impact Multimedia Inc.
9855 Stevens Creek Blvd.
Cupertino, CA 95014
408-366-1838
email: D.Impact@applelink. apple. com.

A distributor to bookstores, video, music, computer, education and mail order, and original equipment manufacturers.

Ingram Micro
1600 E. St. Andrews Place
Santa Ana, CA 93705
714-566-1000

Merisel
200 N. Continental Blvd.
El Segundo, CA 90245
310-615-3080

Josha Distributing
9246 Trinity Dr.
Lake in the Hills, IL 60102
708-854-5600

American Software & Hardware
  Distributors Inc.
502 E. Anthony Dr.
Urbana, IL 61801
1-800-225-7941

ABCO
400 Route 59
Monsey, NY 10952
914-368-1930

7. PUBLISHERS & STUDIOS WITH DISTRIBUTION CAPABILITIES

Compton's NewMedia
2320 Camino Vida Roble
Carlsbad, CA 92009
619-929-2500

The Discovery Channel Multimedia
7700 Wisconson Ave.
Bethesda, MD 20814
301-986-0444

Electronic Arts
1450 Fashion Island Blvd.
San Mateo, CA 94409
415-571-7171

Mindscape
60 Leveroni Ct.
Novato, CA 94949
415-883-3000

Virgin Interactive
15127 Califa St.
Van Nuys, CA 91411
818-908-9663

Time Warner Interactive
2210 W. Olive Ave.
Burbank, CA 92506
818-295-6600

Spectrum HoloByte, Inc.
2490 Mariner Square Loop
Alameda, CA 94501
510-522-3584

Maxis
Two Theatre Square, Ste. 230
Orinda, CA 94563
510-254-9700

Brøderbund
500 Redwood Blvd.
Novato, CA 94948
415-382-4449

8. EDUCATIONAL ASSOCIATIONS & EVENTS

American Association of State
  Colleges & Universities
202-293-7070

Association for the Advancement
  of Computing in Education
804-973-3987

Association of American Colleges
202-387-3760

American Association of
  School Administrators
703-528-0700

EDUCOM
703-683-8500

Computer Using Educators
510-814-6630

9. PUBLICATIONS
Multimedia Daily
Pasha Publications

1616 N. Fort Myer Drive
Arlington, VA 22209
800-424-2908
A daily newsletter that comes across your fax machine every business morning, tracking multimedia deals and dealmakers. $495/year.

Multimedia Strategist
Leader Publications
345 Park Avenue South
New York, NY 10010
800-888-8300 ext. 6170
A monthly newsletter covering the legal, financial, and business issues of multimedia. $155/year.

DV Finance Report
Title Connections
600 Townsend St., Suite 170E
San Francisco, CA 94103
415-252-7400
e-mail: titles@netcom.com.
Focus on multimedia title financing. Charter subscription rates: $350/year.

The Multimedia Directory
The Carronade Group
P.O. Box 36157
Los Angeles, CA 90036
213-935-7600
A list of developers, publishers, and other players in the multimedia software and hardware industry.

The Interactive Multimedia Sourcebook
Templin Bogen Associates
507 Howard St., Ste. 200
San Francisco, CA 94105
415-281-3666
Over 2,000 company profiles on disk.

Multimedia Law and Practice
by Michael D. Scott. Published by Prentice Hall Law & Business. *The bible for legal issues affecting the multimedia industry.*

Multimedia Law Handbook
by Dianne Brinson and Mark E. Radcliffe. *A legal guidebook to the multimedia industry.*
213-935-7600

Multimedia Law Contracts on Disk
213-935-7600

10. UNIONS

American Federation of
  Television and Radio Artists
6922 Hollywood Blvd.
Hollywood, CA 90028
213-461-8111 or 415-391-7510
Call and ask for a copy of the 1994 Interactive Media Agreement.

Screen Actors Guild
1515 Broadway 44th Floor
New York, NY 10019
212-827-1474
Call and ask for a copy of the 1994 Interactive Media Agreement.

Writers Guild of America
8955 Beverly Blvd.
West Hollywood, CA 90048
310-550-1000

11. BREAKDOWN OF A PUBLISHER'S COSTS

In the following example, the cost breakdowns are for a relatively mature multimedia publisher of consumer-oriented software who is responsible for manufacturing the CD-ROM, for packaging, purchasing the jewel box and the cardboard box in which the jewel box is placed, as well as marketing and sales. Most of these items make up the cost of goods sold (except the sales and marketing) in the model shown below.

Even if the developer has no desire to ever become a publisher, most likely the developer will be pairing up with a publisher who provides distribution capabilities or financing. In negotiating an affiliate label agreement or a developer's agreement, the developer stands on firmer ground if he or she understands the breakeven points of the publisher.

In this model, it is assumed that the publisher does not license material. The publisher is making one stock keeping unit, or SKU. The percentages are based on net revenues, which is gross revenue less a reserve for returns. On average, publishing companies are experiencing a 20 percent return rate.

1. COST OF GOODS SOLD: *30 to 40 percent of net revenue, or anywhere from $3.00–3.75 per unit produced for the Mac or PC CD-ROM.*

The cost of goods sold includes any costs incurred in putting together the entire shrink-wrapped box which is purchased by consumers off the retail shelf. That includes the (1) cost of manufacturing and stamping the CD-ROM; (2) the CD-ROM itself; (3) the plastic box around the CD-ROM called the jewel case; (4) the plastic shrinkwrap paper around the jewel case (if used); (5) the printed manual; (6) the cardboard box that holds the jewel case and the manual; (7) the shrinkwrap around the cardboard box; (8) a registration, system, and a license agreement card; (9) the costs associated with shipping the product to the store; (10) the royalties paid to outside developers; and (11) capitalization of software development costs (some publishers do this, some do not).

The cost of goods sold fluctuate the most: a developer or publisher can select different styles for the manual and reduce or increase his costs. One publisher inserts the license agreement card into the manual instead of using a more expensive separate sheet of paper. Another publisher reduced cost of goods sold a small percentage by not placing the CD-ROMs in plastic baggies.

The more CD-ROMs that are stamped, the less the cost of goods sold because typically, third party manufacturers offer a better rate for higher volumes.

Though the cost of goods sold can be reduced, most publishers agree that it is difficult to get the cost of goods sold under 20 percent of the gross revenues. And as prices for multimedia products decrease, and revenue declines, cost of goods sold as a percentage of net revenues will increase.

The accounting literature states that software should be capitalized—just like any other asset—and therefore, it must be amortized or depreciated over time and included in the cost of goods sold. This proposition is fairly controversial, however: some consumer-oriented software publishers follow this principle. Some do not. Those that do not argue that what is being capitalized are the development costs that go into making the software—the developer's labor, programmer's labor, outside consultants, and sound studio work.

For those companies that do not capitalize their software, the expense is put into product development as an operating expense.

Most publishers use third party manufacturers to press their CD-ROM products. These publishers' cost of goods sold include the overhead and labor associated with managing the third party manufacturer. For instance, Maxis uses a third party manufacturer, but has a manufacturing person that coordinates—does scheduling, production, negotiations—with the outside manufacturer.

For those publishers who do their own manufacturing, the cost of goods sold includes not only the overhead, but the direct labor associated with the manufacturing of the product. If the publisher also manufacturers cartridge based products, like Electronic Arts does, cost of goods sold rises dramatically, sometimes to 60 percent of net revenue because of the $12 to $20 cost of the cartridge itself.

2. OPERATING EXPENSES: *Sales and marketing make up 15–30 percent of net revenues.*

Most industry consultants are recommending that the development costs for a product equal the marketing budget. That one-to-one ratio, however, is rarely met. In fact, the marketing budget is often the one cost element that causes the most friction in the relationship between developer and publisher. Almost every developer and publisher involved in a development agreement or an affiliated label program expresses frustration at their publisher for the lack of adequate marketing.

The tension surrounding marketing budgets will only increase. As more titles are produced and the market becomes more competitive, marketing and sales efforts assume even greater importance. As Robert Derber at Maxis says, "These numbers equate to sales, so if you change them, you know that you will be reducing your sales estimates and this means the fixed costs (development, box design for instance) are spread over a smaller number of units and become a higher percentage of gross revenues."

Some of the costs that go into sales and marketing include the following: in addition to the magazine advertisements and TV ads, sales and marketing costs include the actual design of the cardboard box, the manual (the writing of the manual would be a development cost), and the registration, system, and licensing agreement cards.

3. PRODUCT DEVELOPMENT: *15 percent of net revenue.*
This operating expense is the amount of money devoted to in-house development of products and payment to outside developers. As technology changes and companies develop new platforms, this figure increases.

4. GENERAL ADMINISTRATIVE & OVERHEAD; *5–15 percent of net revenue.*
General administrative and overhead refer to the corporate infrastructure—the finance department, the accounting function, human resources, legal services, rent, and any management information system personnel.
This percentage increases if the company is brand new and has recently hired a president, a chief financial officer, and other executives to form a management team. It will also increase if the company is involved in a financing deal.

5. NET INCOME BEFORE TAX; *20–25 percent of net revenue.*

6. NET INCOME AFTER TAX: *10–15 percent of net revenue.*
For a publisher involved an affiliated label program, the numbers are nearly the same, unless the publisher delegates the manufacturing functions to the party providing the program. Under those circumstances, the affiliated label would have less cost of goods sold, but it would also receive less net revenues because the publisher providing the program would demand a higher percentage of sales.

12. SAMPLE NONDISCLOSURE AGREEMENT

This agreement was provided by Carolyn Mead, a partner at Graham & James, who specializes in providing legal assistance to multimedia companies. This is only a sample to give you some ideas of what should be included in your agreement. The "receiving party" identified in the agreement could be another company that you are working with or an employee of your own company.

Confidentiality Agreement

This Confidentiality Agreement (this "Agreement") is entered into on _____ , 1995, by and between Multimedia Co., a [insert the type of legal entity] ("Disclosing Party") and _____, a _____ [insert the type of legal entity] ("Receiving Party").

INTRODUCTION

WHEREAS, Disclosing Party possesses certain confidential proprietary information; and

WHEREAS, in connection with the pursuit, evaluation and/or feasibility of a business relationship, and/or the consummation of a transaction between Receiving Party and Disclosing Party (collectively the "Business Purposes"), confidential proprietary information of Disclosing Party may become available to Receiving Party.

WHEREAS, Disclosing Party desires to prevent the unauthorized use and disclosure of its confidential proprietary information.

NOW THEREFORE, in consideration of these premises and for other good and valuable consideration, the receipt of which is hereby acknowledged, the parties agree as follows:

I. "CONFIDENTIAL INFORMATION." For purposes of this Agreement, Confidential Information shall mean all strategic and development plans, financial condition, business plans, co-developer identities, data, business records, customer lists, project records, market reports, employee lists and business manuals, policies and procedures, information related to processes, technologies or theory and all other information which may be disclosed by Disclosing Party or to which Receiving Party may be provided access by Disclosing Party or others in accordance with this Agreement, or which is generated as a result of or in connection with the Business Purposes, which is not generally available to the public.

II. NONDISCLOSURE OBLIGATIONS. Receiving Party promises and agrees to receive and hold the Confidential Information in confidence. Without limiting the generality of the foregoing, Receiving Party further promises and agrees:

   A. to protect and safeguard the Confidential Information against unauthorized use, publication or disclosure;

   B. not to use any of the Confidential Information except for the Business Purposes.

   C. not to, directly or indirectly, in any way, reveal, report, publish,
disclose, transfer or otherwise use any of the Confidential Information except as specifically authorized by Disclosing Party in accordance with this Confidentiality Agreement.

   D. not to use any Confidential Information to unfairly compete or obtain unfair advantage vis a vis Disclosing Party in any commercial
activity which may be comparable to the commercial activity contemplated by the parties in connection with the Business Purposes.

   E. to restrict access to the Confidential Information to those of its of-
ficers, directors, and employees who clearly need such access to
carry out the Business Purposes.

   F. to advise each of the persons to whom it provides access to any of
the Confidential Information, that such persons are strictly prohib-
ited from making any use, publishing or otherwise disclosing to others, or permitting others to use for their benefit or to the detriment
of Disclosing Party, any of the Confidential Information, and, upon
the request of Disclosing Party, to provide Disclosing Party with a
copy of a written agreement to the effect signed by such persons.

   G. to comply with any other reasonable security measures requested
in writing by Disclosing Party.

   III. EXCEPTIONS. The confidentiality obligations hereunder shall not
apply to Confidential Information which:

   A. is, or later becomes, public knowledge other than by breach of the
provisions of this Agreement; or

   B. is in the possession of Receiving Party with the full right to disclose
prior to its receipt from Disclosing Party, as evidenced by written
records; or

   C. is independently received by Receiving Party from a third party, with
no restrictions on disclosure.

   IV. RETURN OF CONFIDENTIAL INFORMATION. Receiving Party agrees,
upon termination of the Business Purpose or upon the written request of
Disclosing Party, whichever is earlier, to promptly deliver to Disclosing
Party all records, notes, and other written, printed, or tangible materials
in the possession of Receiving Party, embodying or pertaining to the Confidential Information.

V. NO RIGHT TO CONFIDENTIAL INFORMATION

A. Receiving Party hereby agrees and acknowledges that no license, either express or implied, is hereby granted to Receiving Party by Disclosing Party to use any of the Confidential Information.

B. Receiving Party further agrees that all inventions, improvements, copyrightable works and designs relating to machines, methods, compositions, or products of Disclosing Party directly resulting from or relating to the Confidential Information and the right to market, use, license, and franchise the Confidential Information or the ideas, concepts, methods, or practices embodied therein shall be the exclusive property of Disclosing Party and Receiving Party has no right or title thereto.

VI. NO SOLICITATION OF EMPLOYEES. Receiving Party agrees that it will not, for a period of five (5) years from the date of this Agreement, initiate contact with Disclosing Party's employees in order to solicit, entice, or induce any employee of Disclosing Party to terminate an employment relationship with Disclosing Party to accept employment with Receiving Party.

VII. LOSSES. Receiving Party agrees to indemnify Disclosing Party against any and all losses, damages, claims, or expenses incurred or suffered by Disclosing Party as a result of Receiving Party's breach of this Agreement.

VIII. TERM AND TERMINATION. This Agreement shall commence on the date first written above. Receiving Party's right to use Confidential Information in connection with the Business Purpose shall continue in effect until _____, 19____, or until Disclosing Party provides Receiving Party with written notice of termination of such right, whichever is earlier. Notwithstanding the foregoing, Receiving Party's obligations with respect to the Confidential Information hereunder shall continue in full force and effect until further notice from Disclosing Party.

IX. REMEDIES. Receiving Party understands and acknowledges that any disclosure or misappropriation of any of the Confidential Information in violation of this Agreement may cause Disclosing Party irreparable harm, the amount of which may be difficult to ascertain and, therefore, agrees that Disclosing Party shall have the right to apply to a court of competent jurisdiction for an order restraining any such further disclosure or misappropriation and for such relief as Disclosing Party shall deem appropriate. Such right of Disclosing Party shall be in addition to the remedies otherwise available to the Disclosing Party at law or in equity.

X. SUCCESSORS AND ASSIGNS. Receiving Party shall have no right to assign its rights under this Agreement, whether expressly or by operation of law, without the written consent of Disclosing Party. This Agreement and Receiving Party's obligations hereunder shall be binding on the representatives, permitted assigns, and successors of Receiving Party and shall inure to the benefit of the representatives, assigns, and successors of Disclosing Party.

XI. GOVERNING LAW. This Agreement shall be governed by and construed in accordance with the laws of the State of _____.

XII. ATTORNEYS' FEES. If any action at law or in equity is brought to enforce or interpret provisions of this Agreement, the prevailing party in such action shall be entitled to reasonable attorneys' fees.

XIII. ENTIRE AGREEMENT. This Agreement constitutes the sole understanding of the parties about this subject matter and may not be amended or modified except in writing signed by each of the parties to the Agreement.

RECEIVING PARTY'S NAME	DISCLOSING PARTY'S NAME
TITLE	TITLE

13. SAMPLE COPYRIGHT ASSIGNMENT

WHEREAS, _____, ("Assignor") is owner of the copyright on the work called _____ [insert name if it has one] ("Work");

WHEREAS, _____, Multimedia Company, a [type of legal entity] ("Company"), seeks to obtain all rights, title, and interest in the Work;

NOW, THEREFORE, in consideration of these premises and for other good and valuable consideration, the receipt of which is hereby acknowledged, the parties agree as follows:

1. Assignor irrevocably assigns to Company all rights, interests in, title to the copyrights of Work, and all rights, interests in, copyrights with material created in connection and for Work.

2. At the request of Company, Assignor will execute in other documents of assignment to establish ownership of record of all copyrights transferred by this Assignment.

Assignor has executed this Assignment on ____ [day] of _____ [month], 199___.

ASSIGNOR	COMPANY
TITLE	TITLE

FORM PA

For a Work of the Performing Arts
UNITED STATES COPYRIGHT OFFICE

REGISTRATION NUMBER

PA   PAU

EFFECTIVE DATE OF REGISTRATION

_____ Month   _____ Day   _____ Year

DO NOT WRITE ABOVE THIS LINE. IF YOU NEED MORE SPACE, USE A SEPARATE CONTINUATION SHEET.

1

TITLE OF THIS WORK ▼

PREVIOUS OR ALTERNATIVE TITLES ▼

NATURE OF THIS WORK ▼ See instructions

2 a

NAME OF AUTHOR ▼

DATES OF BIRTH AND DEATH
Year Born ▼   Year Died ▼

Was this contribution to the work a "work made for hire"?
☐ Yes
☐ No

AUTHOR'S NATIONALITY OR DOMICILE
Name of Country
OR { Citizen of ▶ _____
Domiciled in ▶ _____

WAS THIS AUTHOR'S CONTRIBUTION TO THE WORK
Anonymous?   ☐ Yes ☐ No
Pseudonymous?   ☐ Yes ☐ No

If the answer to either of these questions is "Yes," see detailed instructions.

NATURE OF AUTHORSHIP   Briefly describe nature of material created by this author in which copyright is claimed. ▼

NOTE

Under the law, the "author" of a "work made for hire" is generally the employer, not the employee (see instructions). For any part of this work that was "made for hire" check "Yes" in the space provided, give the employer (or other person for whom the work was prepared) as "Author" of that part, and leave the space for dates of birth and death blank.

b

NAME OF AUTHOR ▼

DATES OF BIRTH AND DEATH
Year Born ▼   Year Died ▼

Was this contribution to the work a "work made for hire"?
☐ Yes
☐ No

AUTHOR'S NATIONALITY OR DOMICILE
Name of Country
OR { Citizen of ▶ _____
Domiciled in ▶ _____

WAS THIS AUTHOR'S CONTRIBUTION TO THE WORK
Anonymous?   ☐ Yes ☐ No
Pseudonymous?   ☐ Yes ☐ No

If the answer to either of these questions is "Yes," see detailed instructions.

NATURE OF AUTHORSHIP   Briefly describe nature of material created by this author in which copyright is claimed. ▼

c

NAME OF AUTHOR ▼

DATES OF BIRTH AND DEATH
Year Born ▼   Year Died ▼

Was this contribution to the work a "work made for hire"?
☐ Yes
☐ No

AUTHOR'S NATIONALITY OR DOMICILE
Name of Country
OR { Citizen of ▶ _____
Domiciled in ▶ _____

WAS THIS AUTHOR'S CONTRIBUTION TO THE WORK
Anonymous?   ☐ Yes ☐ No
Pseudonymous?   ☐ Yes ☐ No

If the answer to either of these questions is "Yes," see detailed instructions.

NATURE OF AUTHORSHIP   Briefly describe nature of material created by this author in which copyright is claimed. ▼

3 a

YEAR IN WHICH CREATION OF THIS WORK WAS COMPLETED   This information must be given ◀ Year in all cases.

b DATE AND NATION OF FIRST PUBLICATION OF THIS PARTICULAR WORK
Complete this information ONLY if this work has been published.
Month ▶ _____ Day ▶ _____ Year ▶ _____
◀ Nation

4

COPYRIGHT CLAIMANT(S) Name and address must be given even if the claimant is the same as the author given in space 2. ▼

See instructions before completing this space.

TRANSFER If the claimant(s) named here in space 4 is (are) different from the author(s) named in space 2, give a brief statement of how the claimant(s) obtained ownership of the copyright. ▼

APPLICATION RECEIVED

ONE DEPOSIT RECEIVED

TWO DEPOSITS RECEIVED

FUNDS RECEIVED

DO NOT WRITE HERE
OFFICE USE ONLY

MORE ON BACK ▶   • Complete all applicable spaces (numbers 5-9) on the reverse side of this page.
• See detailed instructions.   • Sign the form at line 8.

DO NOT WRITE HERE
Page 1 of _____ pages

EXAMINED BY	FORM PA
CHECKED BY	

CORRESPONDENCE ☐ Yes	FOR COPYRIGHT OFFICE USE ONLY

DO NOT WRITE ABOVE THIS LINE. IF YOU NEED MORE SPACE, USE A SEPARATE CONTINUATION SHEET.

PREVIOUS REGISTRATION Has registration for this work, or for an earlier version of this work, already been made in the Copyright Office?

☐ Yes ☐ No If your answer is "Yes," why is another registration being sought? (Check appropriate box) ▼

a. ☐ This is the first published edition of a work previously registered in unpublished form.

b. ☐ This is the first application submitted by this author as copyright claimant.

c. ☐ This is a changed version of the work, as shown by space 6 on this application.

If your answer is "Yes," give: **Previous Registration Number** ▼   **Year of Registration** ▼

5

DERIVATIVE WORK OR COMPILATION Complete both space 6a and 6b for a derivative work; complete only 6b for a compilation.

a. **Preexisting Material** Identify any preexisting work or works that this work is based on or incorporates. ▼

b. **Material Added to This Work** Give a brief, general statement of the material that has been added to this work and in which copyright is claimed. ▼

6

See instructions before completing this space.

DEPOSIT ACCOUNT If the registration fee is to be charged to a Deposit Account established in the Copyright Office, give name and number of Account.

Name ▼   **Account Number** ▼

7

CORRESPONDENCE Give name and address to which correspondence about this application should be sent.   Name/Address/Apt/City/State/ZIP ▼

Area Code and Telephone Number ▶

Be sure to give your daytime phone ◀ number

CERTIFICATION* I, the undersigned, hereby certify that I am the

Check only one ▼

☐ author

☐ other copyright claimant

☐ owner of exclusive right(s)

☐ authorized agent of _____

Name of author or other copyright claimant, or owner of exclusive right(s) ▲

of the work identified in this application and that the statements made
by me in this application are correct to the best of my knowledge.

Typed or printed name and date ▼ If this application gives a date of publication in space 3, do not sign and submit it before that date.

date ▶

Handwritten signature (X) ▼

8

MAIL CERTIFI-CATE TO

Name ▼

Number/Street/Apartment Number ▼

City/State/ZIP ▼

Certificate will be mailed in window envelope

YOU MUST:
· Complete all necessary spaces
· Sign your application in space 8

SEND ALL 3 ELEMENTS IN THE SAME PACKAGE:
1. Application form
2. Nonrefundable $20 filing fee in check or money order payable to *Register of Copyrights*
3. Deposit material

MAIL TO:
Register of Copyrights
Library of Congress
Washington, D.C. 20559-6000

9

*17 U.S.C. § 506(e): Any person who knowingly makes a false representation of a material fact in the application for copyright registration provided for by section 409, or in any written statement filed in connection with the application, shall be fined not more than $2,500.

January 1995—400,000 ♻ PRINTED ON RECYCLED PAPER   ☆U.S. GOVERNMENT PRINTING OFFICE: 1995-387-237/33

INDEX

ABOUT THE AUTHOR

Nina Schuyler covers technology issues for *California Lawyer* magazine. She has focused on the legal aspects of multimedia, the online market, and the changing telecommunications industry.

ALLWORTH BOOKS

Allworth Press publishes quality books to help individuals and small businesses. Titles include:

Electronic Design and Publishing: Business Practices, Second Edition
by Liane Sebastian. (softcover, 6¾ × 10, 200 pages, $19.95)

Licensing Art & Design, Revised Edition
by Caryn R. Leland (softcover, 6 × 9, 128 pages, $16.95)

Legal Guide for the Visual Artist, Third Edition
by Tad Crawford (softcover, 8½ × 11, 256 pages, $19.95)

The Law (in Plain English)® for Photographers
by Leonard DuBoff (softcover, 6 × 9, 208 pages, $18.95)

Careers by Design: A Headhunter's Secrets for Success and Survival in Graphic Design by Roz Goldfarb (softcover, 6¾ × 10, 224 pages, $16.95)

Looking Closer: Critical Writings on Graphic Design
edited by Michael Bierut, William Drenttel, Steven Heller, DK Holland (softcover, 6¾ × 10, 256 pages, $18.95)

Business and Legal Forms for Graphic Designers, Revised Edition
by Tad Crawford (softcover, 8½ × 11, 208 pages, $22.95)

Business and Legal Forms for Illustrators
by Tad Crawford (softcover, 8⅞ × 11, 160 pages, $15.95)

Business and Legal Forms for Fine Artists, Revised Edition
by Tad Crawford (softcover, 8½ × 11, 144 pages, $16.95)

Business and Legal Forms for Photographers
by Tad Crawford (softcover, 8½ × 11, 192 pages, $18.95)

Business and Legal Forms for Authors and Self-Publishers
by Tad Crawford (softcover, 8⅞ × 11, 176 pages, $15.95)

Writing Scripts Hollywood Will Love
by Kateherine Atwell Herbert (softcover, 6 × 9, 160 pages, $12.95)

Please write to request our free catalog. If you wish to order a book, send your check or money order to Allworth Press, 10 East 23rd Street, Suite 400, New York, NY 10010. Include $5 for shipping and handling for the first book ordered and $1 for each additional book. Ten dollars plus $1 for each additional book if ordering from Canada. New York State residents must add sales tax.

If you wish to see our catalog on the World Wide Web, you can find us at Millennium Production's Art and Technology Web site:
http://www.arts-online.com/allworth/home.html
or at
http://interport.net/~allworth